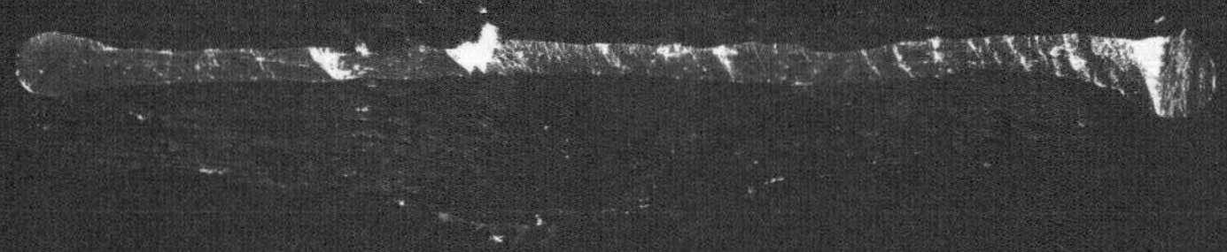

A COMING - OF - RAGE STORY

IMAGE COMICS, INC.
Robert Kirkman - chief operating officer
Erik Larsen - chief financial officer
Todd McFarlane - president
Marc Silvestri - chief executive officer
Jim Valentino - vice-president

Eric Stephenson - publisher
Ron Richards - director of business development
Jennifer de Guzman - pr & marketing director
Branwyn Bigglestone - accounts manager
Emily Miller - accounting assistant
Jamie Parreno - marketing assistant
Emilio Bautista - sales assistant
Jaemie Dudas - administrative assistant
Kevin Yuen - digital rights coordinator
Tyler Shainline - events coordinator
David Brothers - content manager
Jonathan Chan - production manager
Drew Gill - art director
Monica Garcia - senior production artist
Vincent Kukua - production artist
Jenna Savage - production artist
Addison Duke - production artist
www.imagecomics.com

RA

writer
BRIAN WOOD

artist
MING DOYLE

colors
JORDIE BELLAIRE

letters
CLAYTON COWLES

CHAPTER ONE

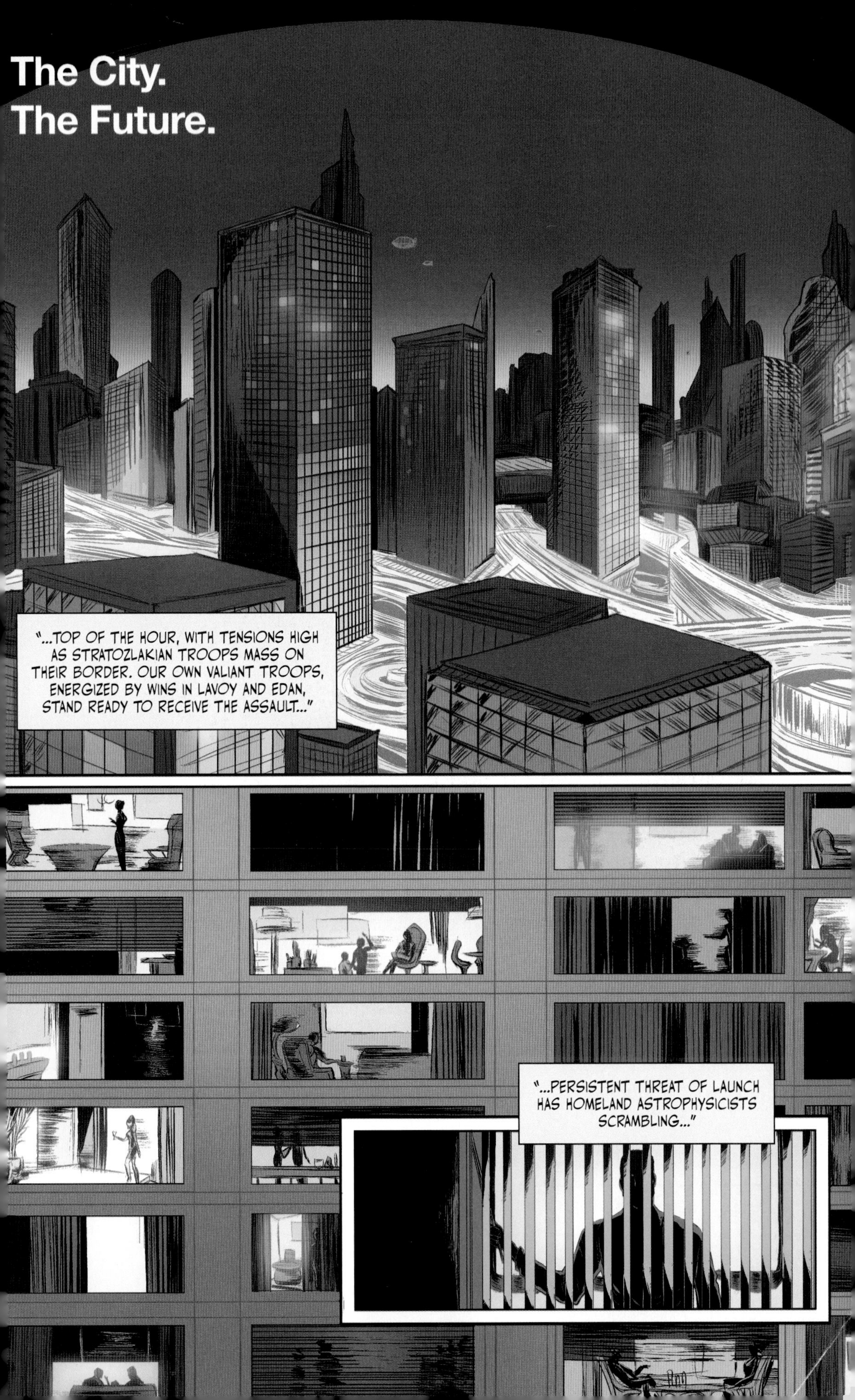
The City.
The Future.
"...TOP OF THE HOUR, WITH TENSIONS HIGH AS STRATOZLAKIAN TROOPS MASS ON THEIR BORDER. OUR OWN VALIANT TROOPS, ENERGIZED BY WINS IN LAVOY AND EDAN, STAND READY TO RECEIVE THE ASSAULT..."
"...PERSISTENT THREAT OF LAUNCH HAS HOMELAND ASTROPHYSICISTS SCRAMBLING..."

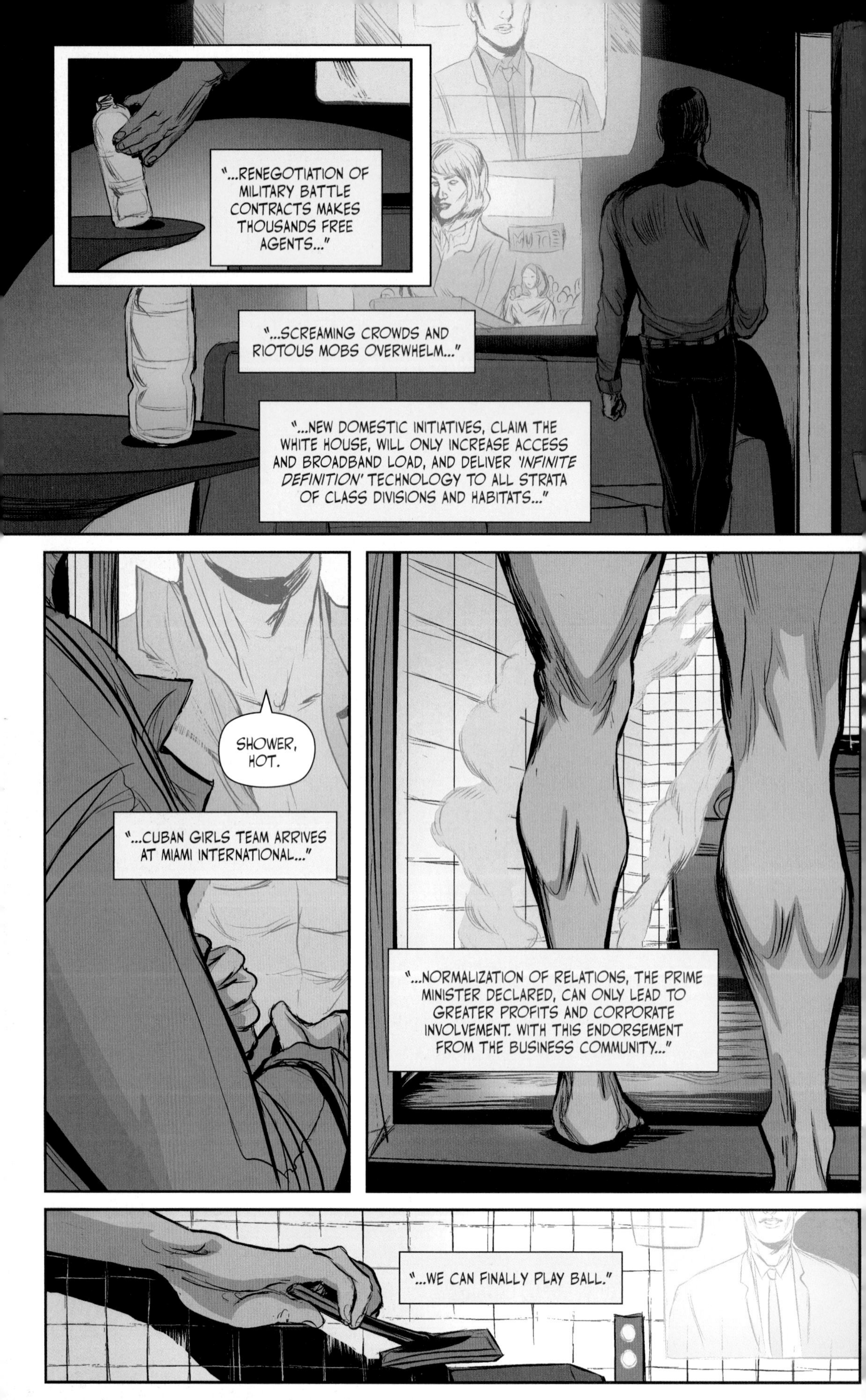
"...RENEGOTIATION OF MILITARY BATTLE CONTRACTS MAKES THOUSANDS FREE AGENTS..."
MUTE
"...SCREAMING CROWDS AND RIOTOUS MOBS OVERWHELM..."
"...NEW DOMESTIC INITIATIVES, CLAIM THE WHITE HOUSE, WILL ONLY INCREASE ACCESS AND BROADBAND LOAD, AND DELIVER *'INFINITE DEFINITION'* TECHNOLOGY TO ALL STRATA OF CLASS DIVISIONS AND HABITATS..."
SHOWER, HOT.
"...CUBAN GIRLS TEAM ARRIVES AT MIAMI INTERNATIONAL..."
"...NORMALIZATION OF RELATIONS, THE PRIME MINISTER DECLARED, CAN ONLY LEAD TO GREATER PROFITS AND CORPORATE INVOLVEMENT. WITH THIS ENDORSEMENT FROM THE BUSINESS COMMUNITY..."
"...WE CAN FINALLY PLAY BALL."

LADIES AND GENTLEMEN, THE *PAN-CONTINENTAL SPORTS LEAGUE* IS PLEASED TO PRESENT...

...IN ASSOCIATION WITH *UNINATIONAL OIL AND GAS*, AND THE *ARMY*-- 'MOVE MOUNTAINS AND PART OCEANS, IN THE ARMY'...

...AND WITH PLATINUM SPONSORSHIP BY THE *GRAND COLONIAL HERITAGE FUND*, AND THE *PAX ORGANIZATION* FOR EXCELLENCE IN PHYSICAL FITNESS...

...TONIGHT'S *PREMIERE* EVENT...

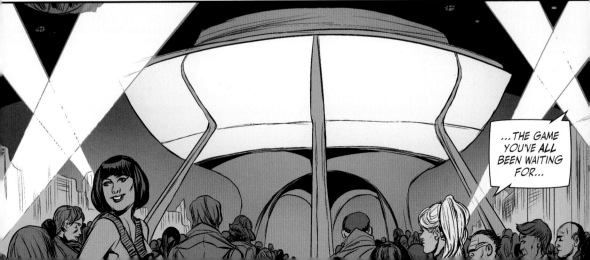

...THE GAME YOU'VE *ALL* BEEN WAITING FOR...

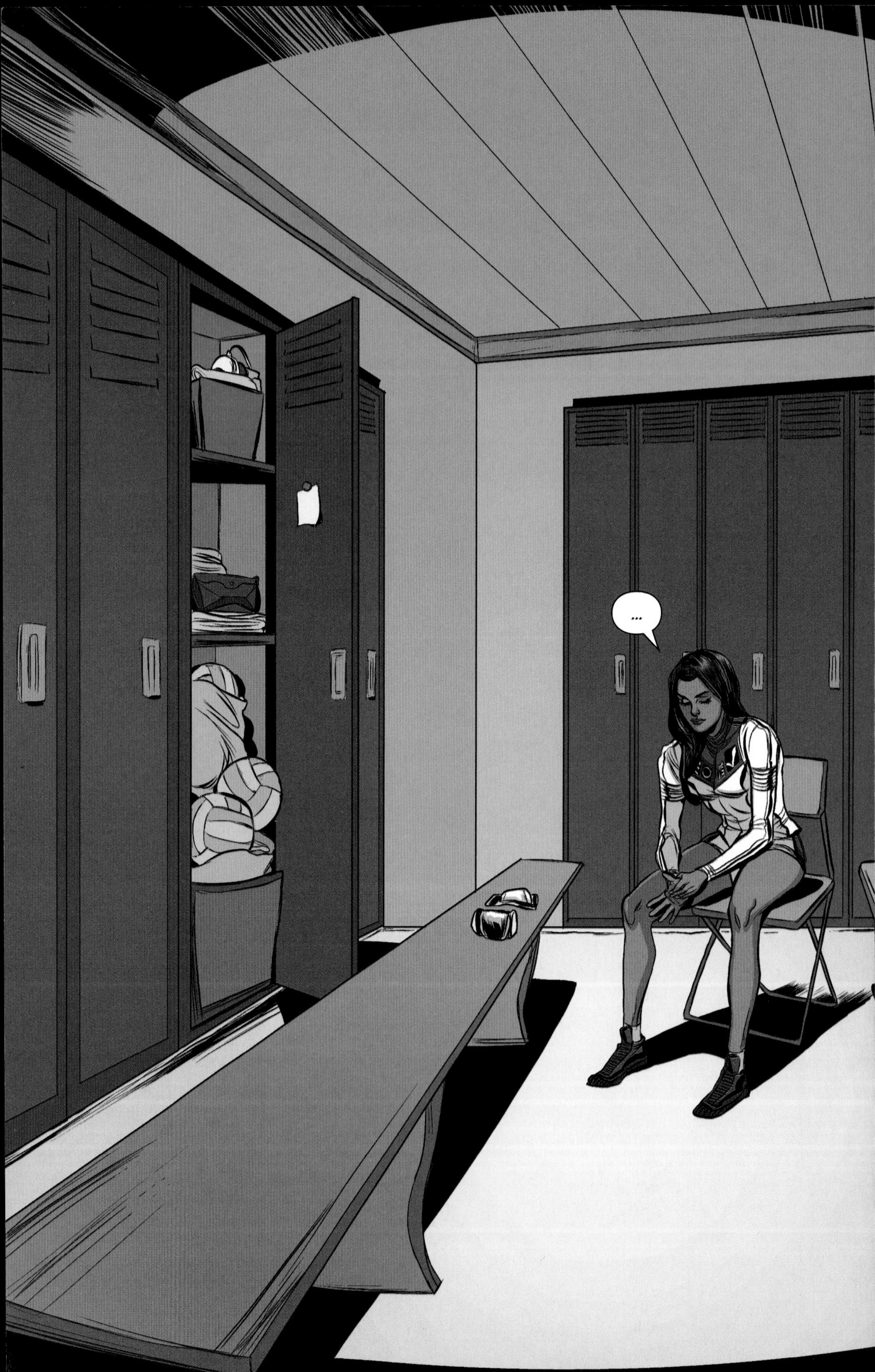
...

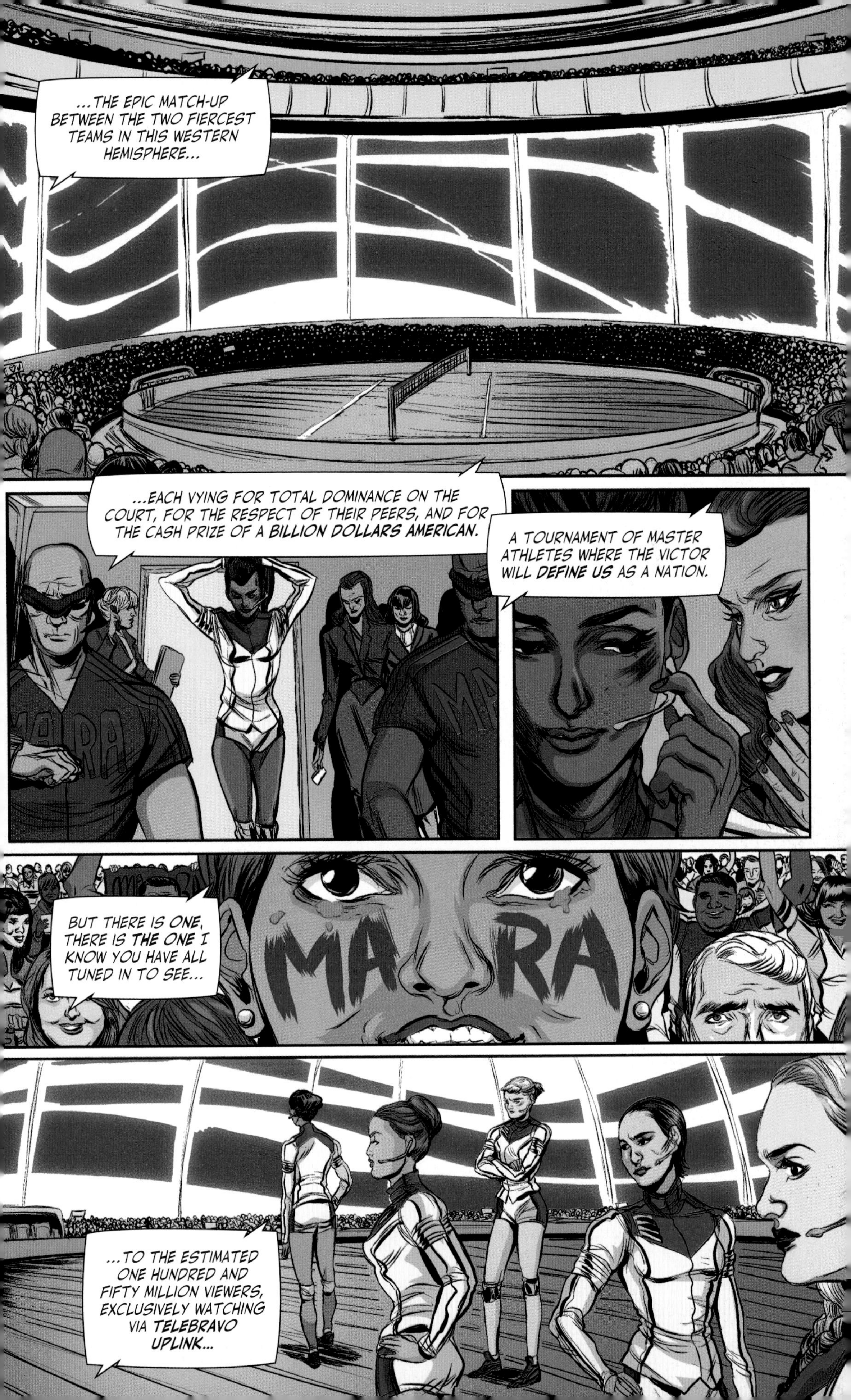
...THE EPIC MATCH-UP BETWEEN THE TWO FIERCEST TEAMS IN THIS WESTERN HEMISPHERE...
...EACH VYING FOR TOTAL DOMINANCE ON THE COURT, FOR THE RESPECT OF THEIR PEERS, AND FOR THE CASH PRIZE OF A **BILLION DOLLARS AMERICAN**.
MARA
A TOURNAMENT OF MASTER ATHLETES WHERE THE VICTOR WILL **DEFINE US** AS A NATION.
BUT THERE IS *ONE*, THERE IS **THE ONE** I KNOW YOU HAVE ALL TUNED IN TO SEE...
MA RA
...TO THE ESTIMATED ONE HUNDRED AND FIFTY MILLION VIEWERS, EXCLUSIVELY WATCHING VIA **TELEBRAVO UPLINK**...

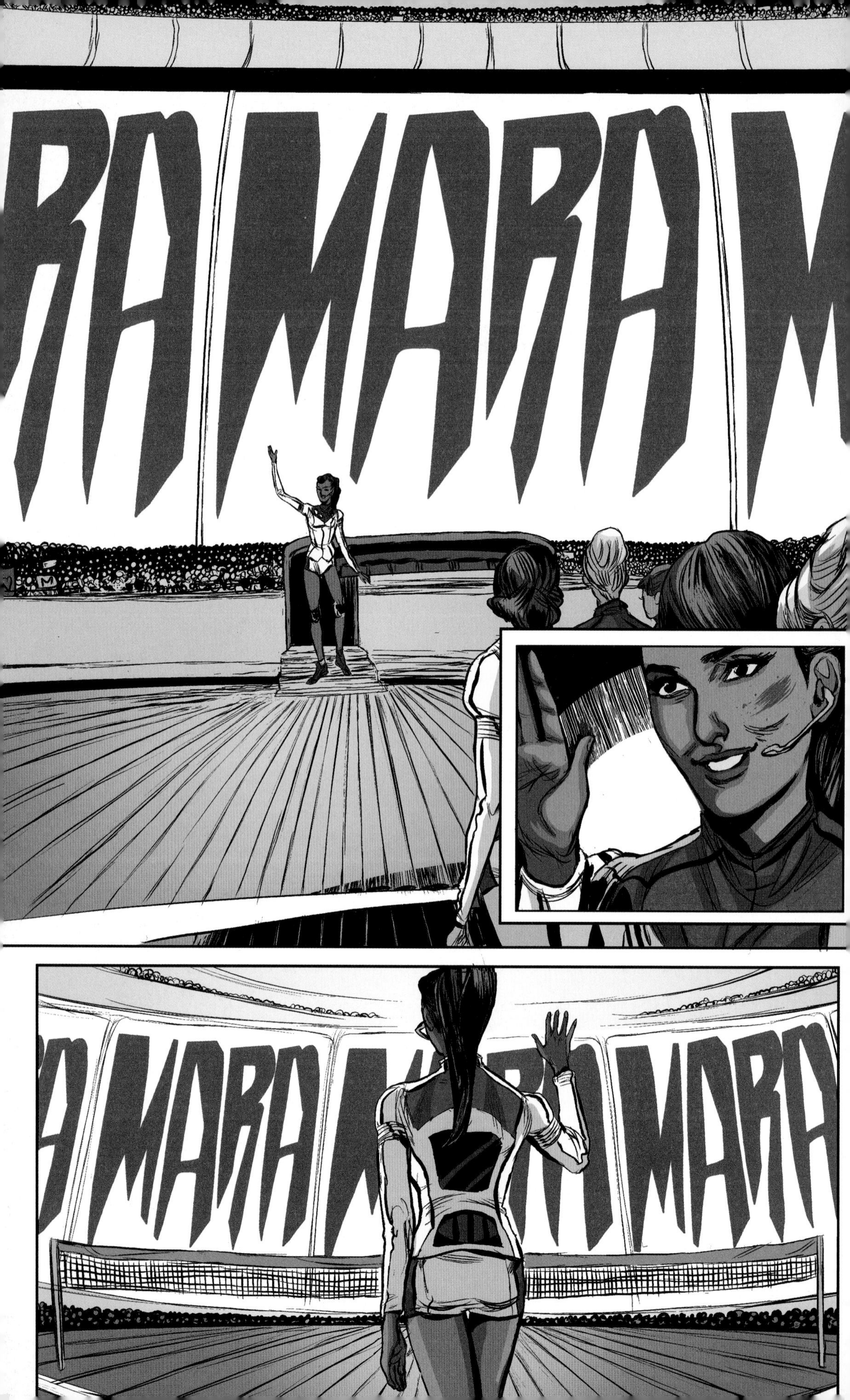
MARA
MARA
MARA

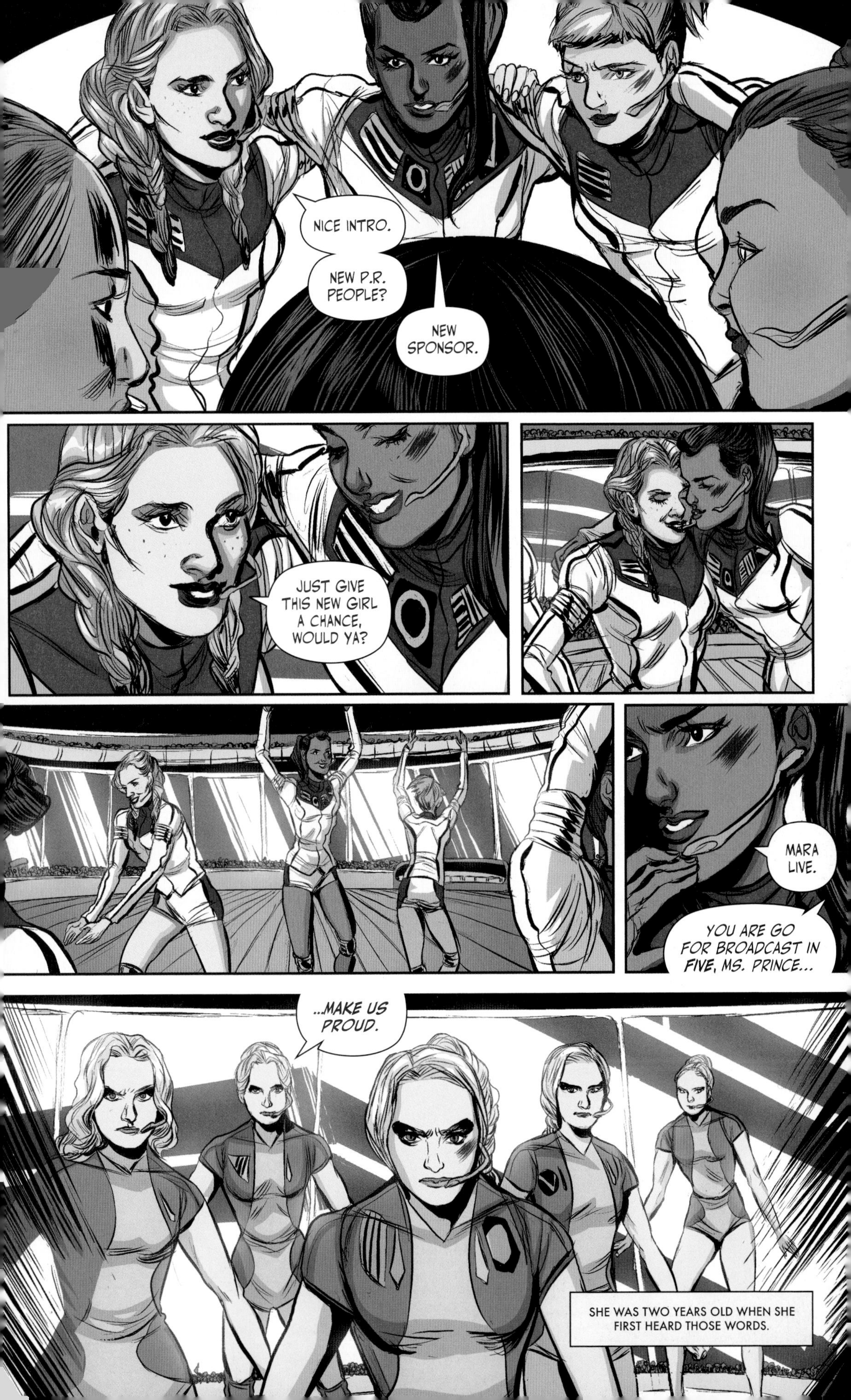
NICE INTRO.
NEW P.R. PEOPLE?
NEW SPONSOR.
JUST GIVE THIS NEW GIRL A CHANCE, WOULD YA?
MARA LIVE.
YOU ARE GO FOR BROADCAST IN FIVE, MS. PRINCE...
...MAKE US PROUD.
SHE WAS TWO YEARS OLD WHEN SHE FIRST HEARD THOSE WORDS.

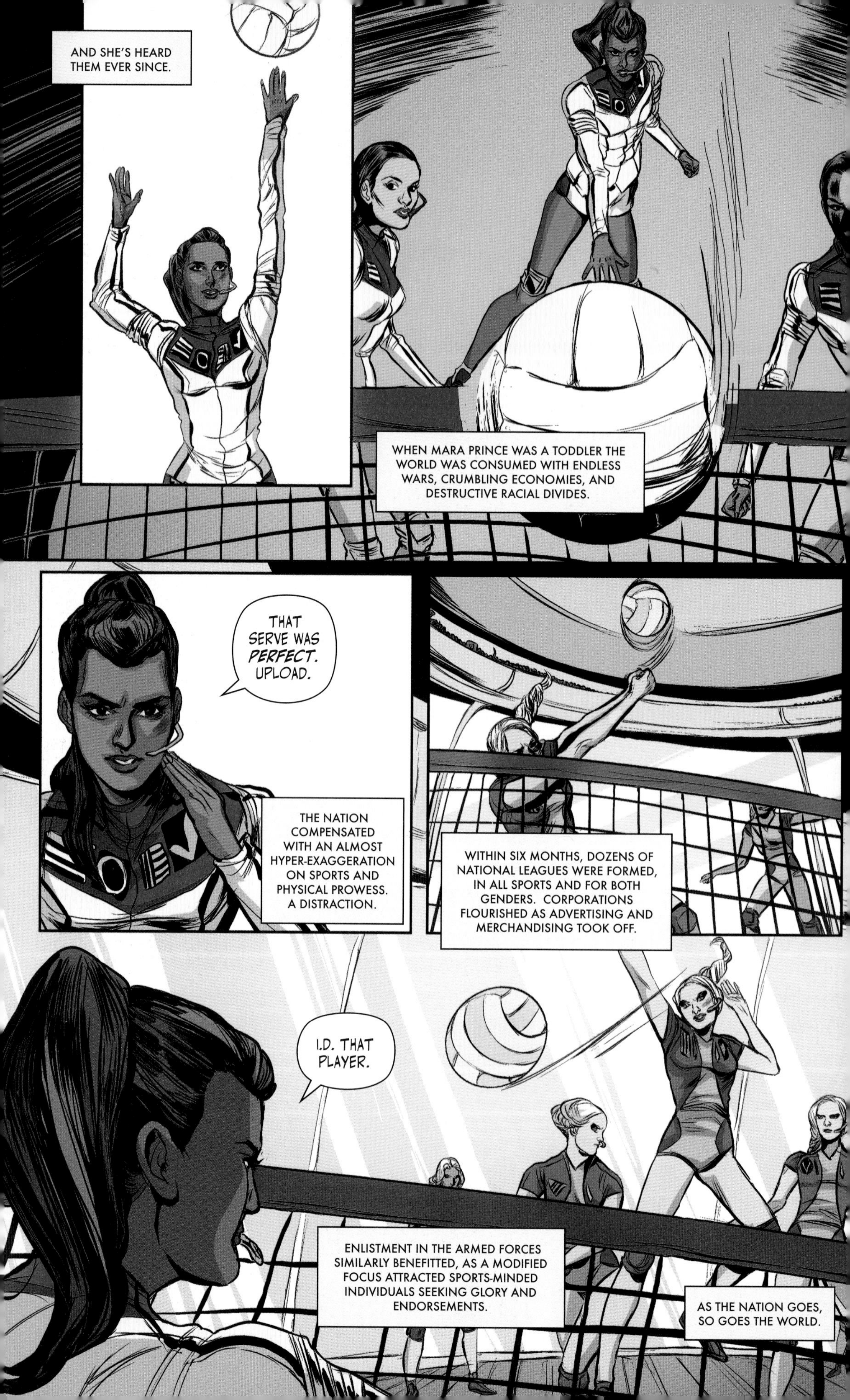
AND SHE'S HEARD THEM EVER SINCE.
WHEN MARA PRINCE WAS A TODDLER THE WORLD WAS CONSUMED WITH ENDLESS WARS, CRUMBLING ECONOMIES, AND DESTRUCTIVE RACIAL DIVIDES.
THAT SERVE WAS *PERFECT.* UPLOAD.
THE NATION COMPENSATED WITH AN ALMOST HYPER-EXAGGERATION ON SPORTS AND PHYSICAL PROWESS. A DISTRACTION.
WITHIN SIX MONTHS, DOZENS OF NATIONAL LEAGUES WERE FORMED, IN ALL SPORTS AND FOR BOTH GENDERS. CORPORATIONS FLOURISHED AS ADVERTISING AND MERCHANDISING TOOK OFF.
I.D. THAT PLAYER.
ENLISTMENT IN THE ARMED FORCES SIMILARLY BENEFITTED, AS A MODIFIED FOCUS ATTRACTED SPORTS-MINDED INDIVIDUALS SEEKING GLORY AND ENDORSEMENTS.
AS THE NATION GOES, SO GOES THE WORLD.

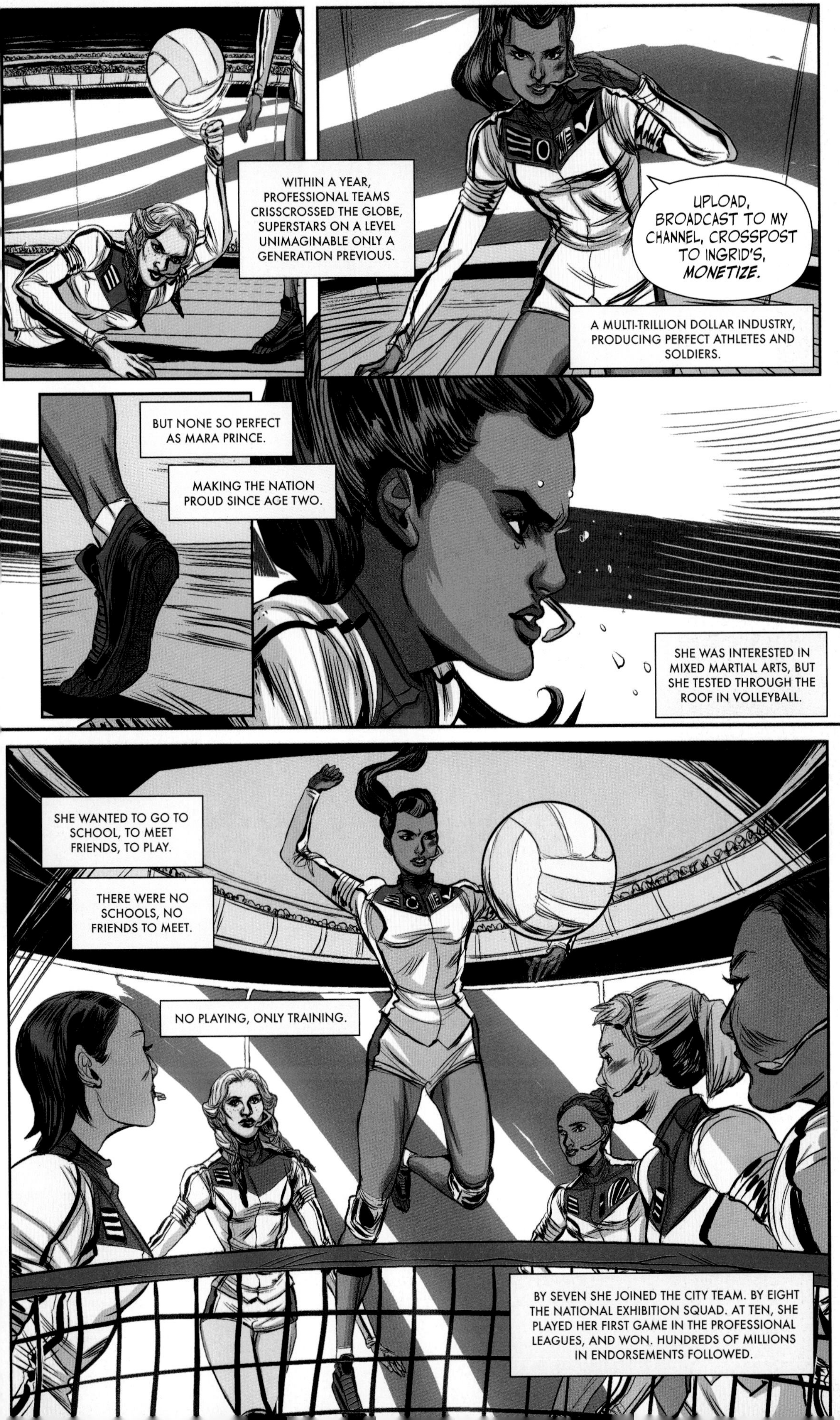
WITHIN A YEAR, PROFESSIONAL TEAMS CRISSCROSSED THE GLOBE, SUPERSTARS ON A LEVEL UNIMAGINABLE ONLY A GENERATION PREVIOUS.
UPLOAD, BROADCAST TO MY CHANNEL, CROSSPOST TO INGRID'S, *MONETIZE.*
A MULTI-TRILLION DOLLAR INDUSTRY, PRODUCING PERFECT ATHLETES AND SOLDIERS.
BUT NONE SO PERFECT AS MARA PRINCE.
MAKING THE NATION PROUD SINCE AGE TWO.
SHE WAS INTERESTED IN MIXED MARTIAL ARTS, BUT SHE TESTED THROUGH THE ROOF IN VOLLEYBALL.
SHE WANTED TO GO TO SCHOOL, TO MEET FRIENDS, TO PLAY.
THERE WERE NO SCHOOLS, NO FRIENDS TO MEET.
NO PLAYING, ONLY TRAINING.
BY SEVEN SHE JOINED THE CITY TEAM. BY EIGHT THE NATIONAL EXHIBITION SQUAD. AT TEN, SHE PLAYED HER FIRST GAME IN THE PROFESSIONAL LEAGUES, AND WON. HUNDREDS OF MILLIONS IN ENDORSEMENTS FOLLOWED.

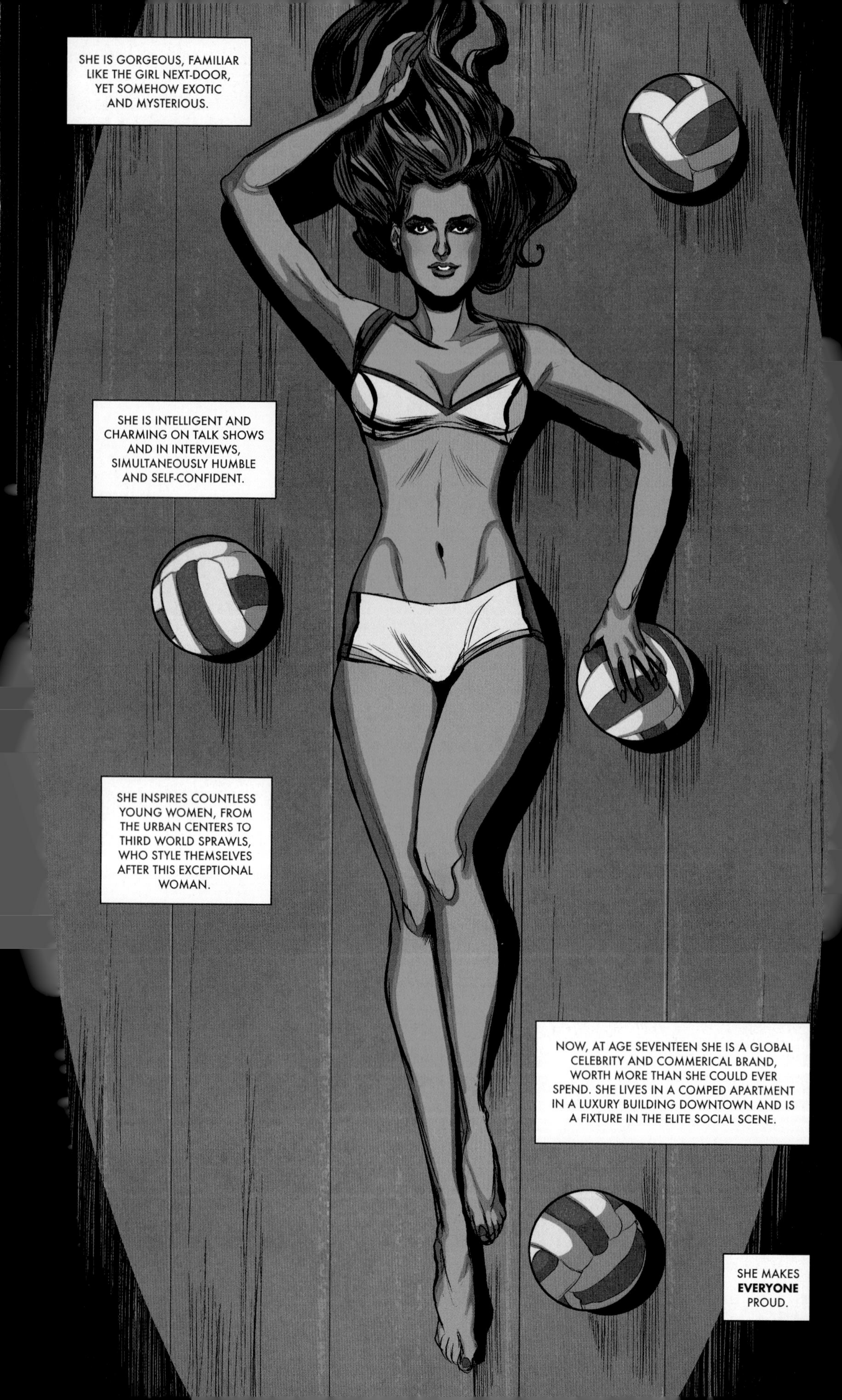
SHE IS GORGEOUS, FAMILIAR LIKE THE GIRL NEXT-DOOR, YET SOMEHOW EXOTIC AND MYSTERIOUS.
SHE IS INTELLIGENT AND CHARMING ON TALK SHOWS AND IN INTERVIEWS, SIMULTANEOUSLY HUMBLE AND SELF-CONFIDENT.
SHE INSPIRES COUNTLESS YOUNG WOMEN, FROM THE URBAN CENTERS TO THIRD WORLD SPRAWLS, WHO STYLE THEMSELVES AFTER THIS EXCEPTIONAL WOMAN.
NOW, AT AGE SEVENTEEN SHE IS A GLOBAL CELEBRITY AND COMMERICAL BRAND, WORTH MORE THAN SHE COULD EVER SPEND. SHE LIVES IN A COMPED APARTMENT IN A LUXURY BUILDING DOWNTOWN AND IS A FIXTURE IN THE ELITE SOCIAL SCENE.
SHE MAKES **EVERYONE** PROUD.

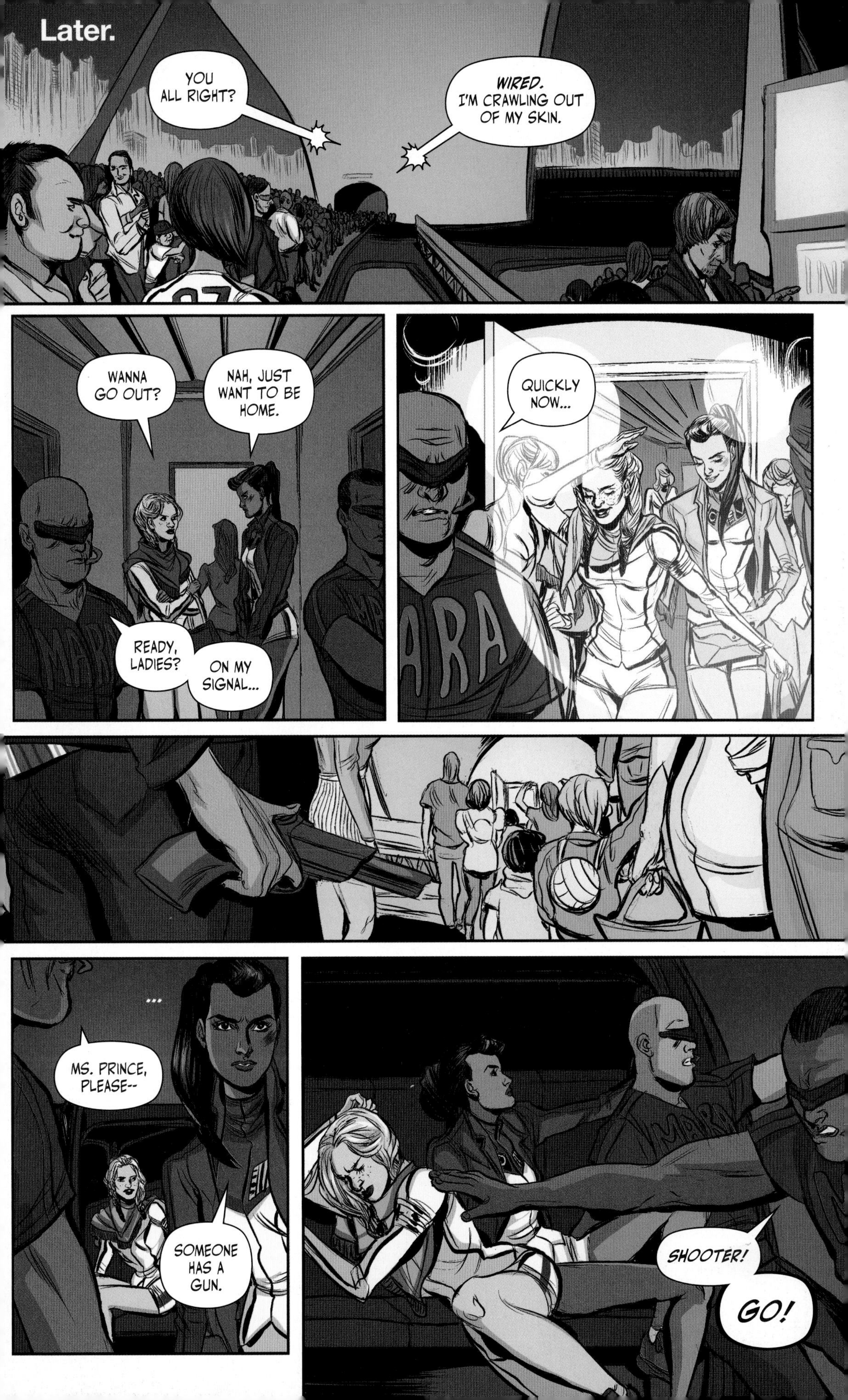
Later.
YOU ALL RIGHT?
WIRED. I'M CRAWLING OUT OF MY SKIN.
WANNA GO OUT?
NAH, JUST WANT TO BE HOME.
READY, LADIES?
ON MY SIGNAL...
QUICKLY NOW...
...
MS. PRINCE, PLEASE--
SOMEONE HAS A GUN.
SHOOTER!
GO!

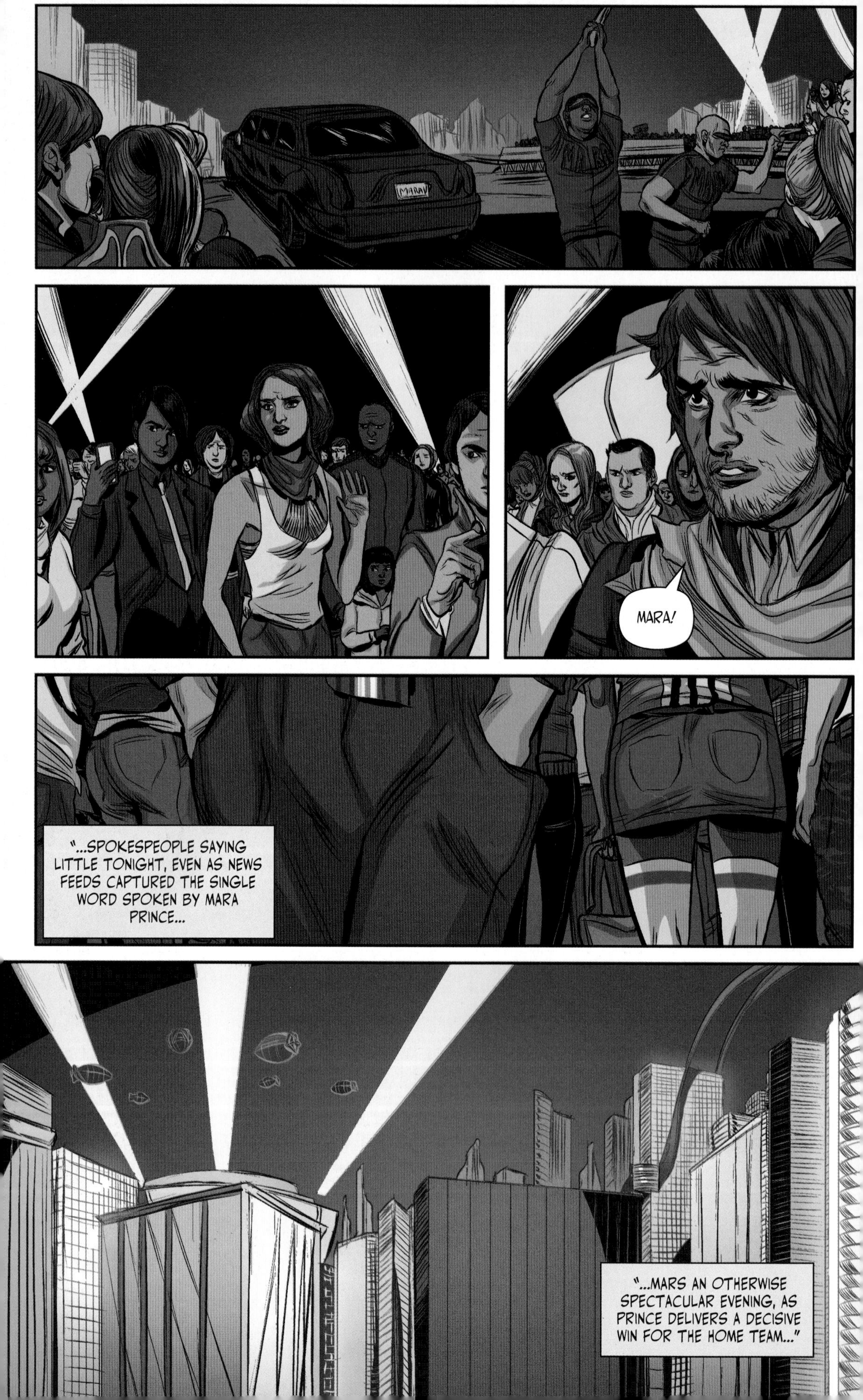
MARRA
MARA!
"...SPOKESPEOPLE SAYING LITTLE TONIGHT, EVEN AS NEWS FEEDS CAPTURED THE SINGLE WORD SPOKEN BY MARA PRINCE...
"...MARS AN OTHERWISE SPECTACULAR EVENING, AS PRINCE DELIVERS A DECISIVE WIN FOR THE HOME TEAM..."

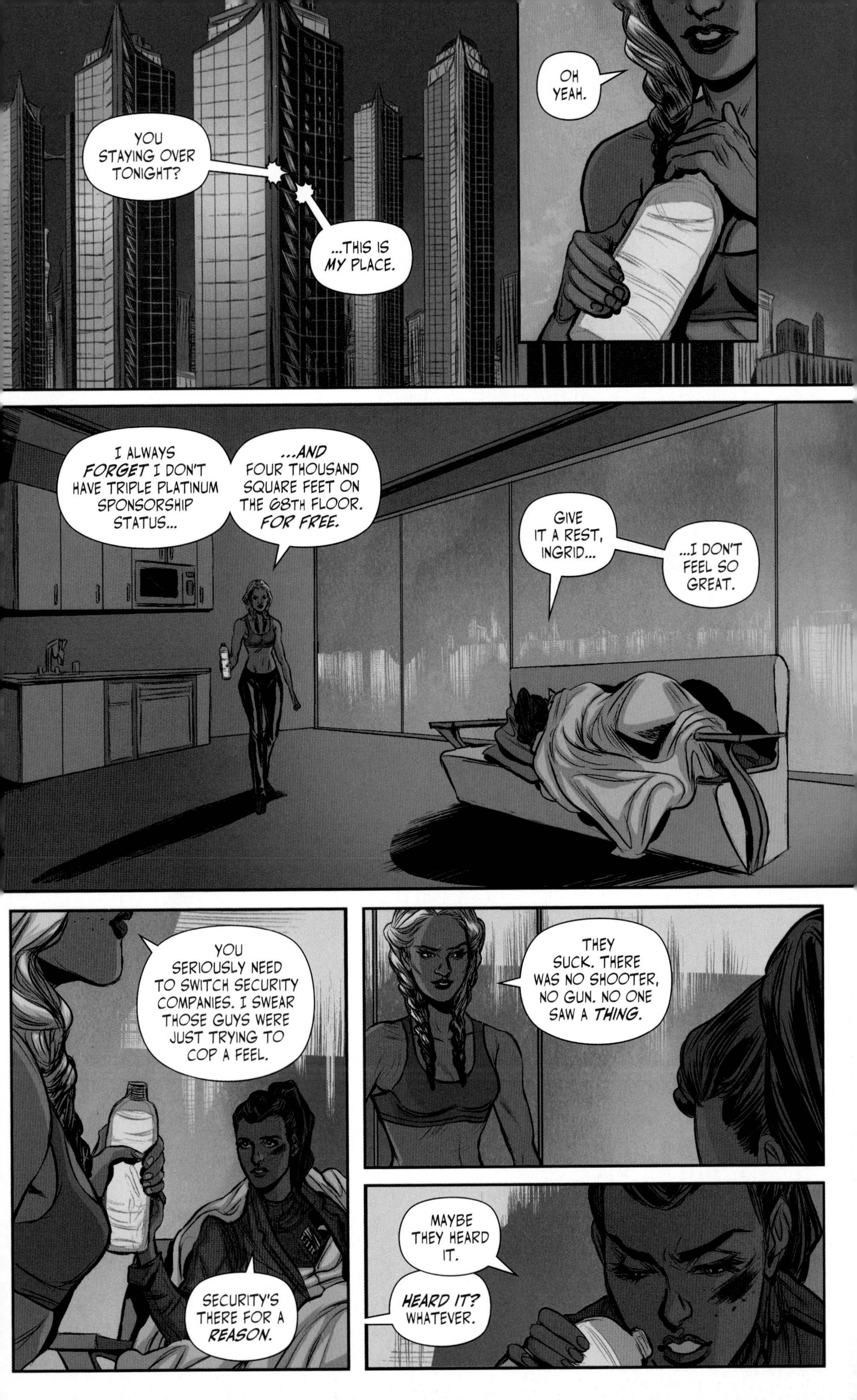
YOU STAYING OVER TONIGHT?
OH YEAH.
...THIS IS MY PLACE.
I ALWAYS FORGET I DON'T HAVE TRIPLE PLATINUM SPONSORSHIP STATUS...
...AND FOUR THOUSAND SQUARE FEET ON THE 68th FLOOR. FOR FREE.
GIVE IT A REST, INGRID...
...I DON'T FEEL SO GREAT.
YOU SERIOUSLY NEED TO SWITCH SECURITY COMPANIES. I SWEAR THOSE GUYS WERE JUST TRYING TO COP A FEEL.
SECURITY'S THERE FOR A REASON.
THEY SUCK. THERE WAS NO SHOOTER, NO GUN. NO ONE SAW A THING.
MAYBE THEY HEARD IT.
HEARD IT? WHATEVER.

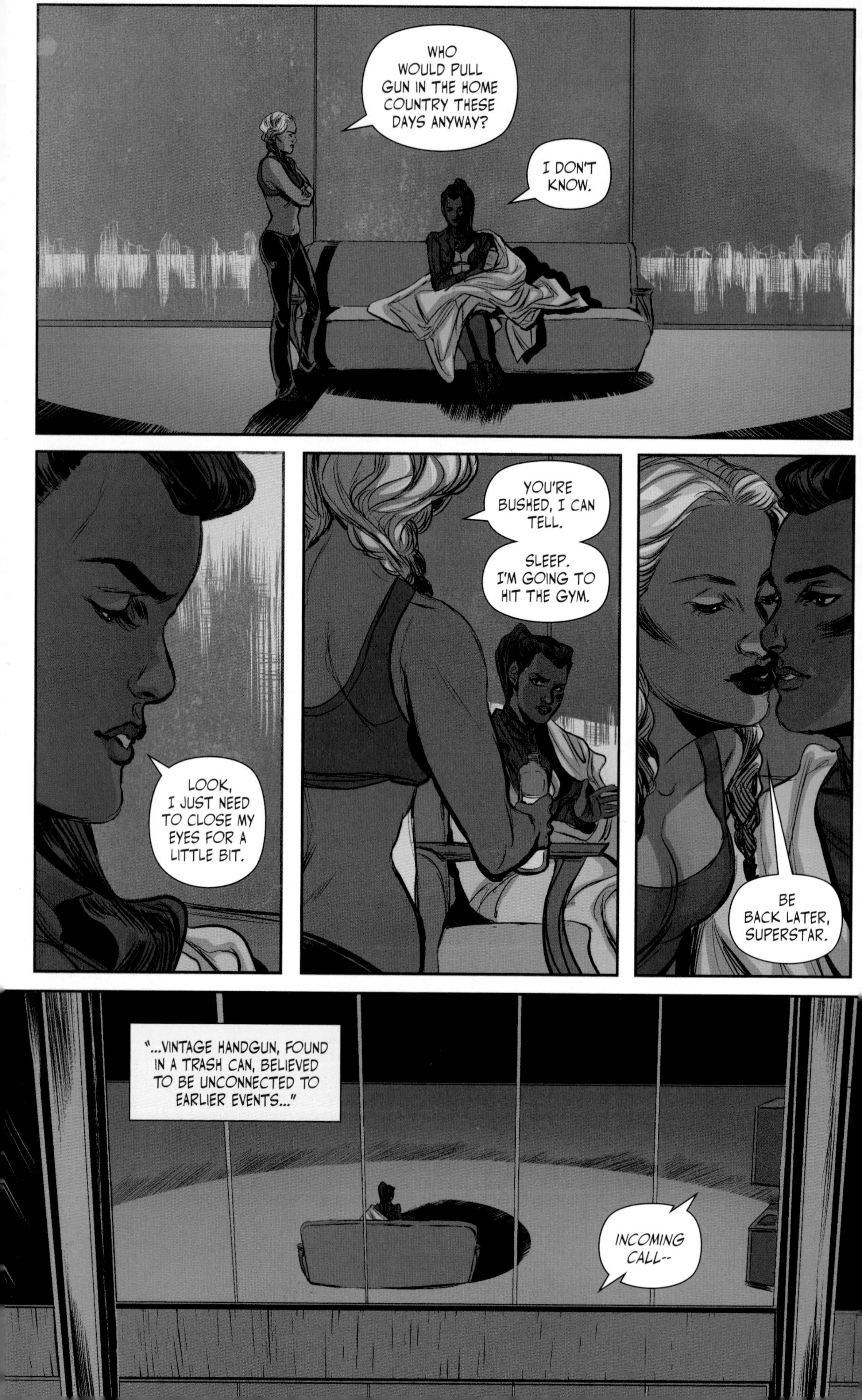
WHO WOULD PULL GUN IN THE HOME COUNTRY THESE DAYS ANYWAY?
I DON'T KNOW.
LOOK, I JUST NEED TO CLOSE MY EYES FOR A LITTLE BIT.
YOU'RE BUSHED, I CAN TELL.
SLEEP. I'M GOING TO HIT THE GYM.
BE BACK LATER, SUPERSTAR.
"...VINTAGE HANDGUN, FOUND IN A TRASH CAN, BELIEVED TO BE UNCONNECTED TO EARLIER EVENTS..."
INCOMING CALL--

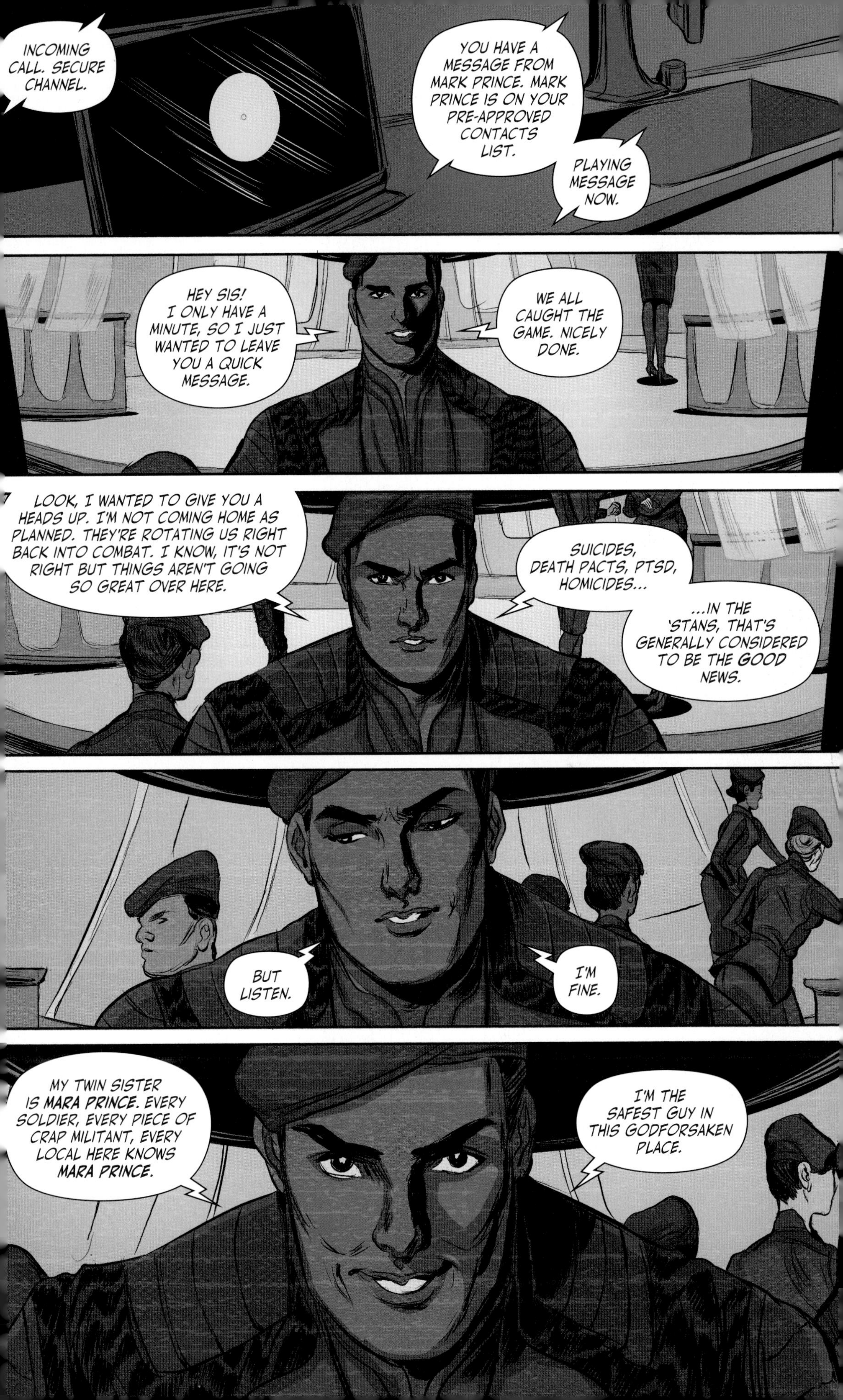
INCOMING CALL. SECURE CHANNEL.
YOU HAVE A MESSAGE FROM MARK PRINCE. MARK PRINCE IS ON YOUR PRE-APPROVED CONTACTS LIST.
PLAYING MESSAGE NOW.
HEY SIS! I ONLY HAVE A MINUTE, SO I JUST WANTED TO LEAVE YOU A QUICK MESSAGE.
WE ALL CAUGHT THE GAME. NICELY DONE.
LOOK, I WANTED TO GIVE YOU A HEADS UP. I'M NOT COMING HOME AS PLANNED. THEY'RE ROTATING US RIGHT BACK INTO COMBAT. I KNOW, IT'S NOT RIGHT BUT THINGS AREN'T GOING SO GREAT OVER HERE.
SUICIDES, DEATH PACTS, PTSD, HOMICIDES...
...IN THE 'STANS, THAT'S GENERALLY CONSIDERED TO BE THE GOOD NEWS.
BUT LISTEN.
I'M FINE.
MY TWIN SISTER IS MARA PRINCE. EVERY SOLDIER, EVERY PIECE OF CRAP MILITANT, EVERY LOCAL HERE KNOWS MARA PRINCE.
I'M THE SAFEST GUY IN THIS GODFORSAKEN PLACE.

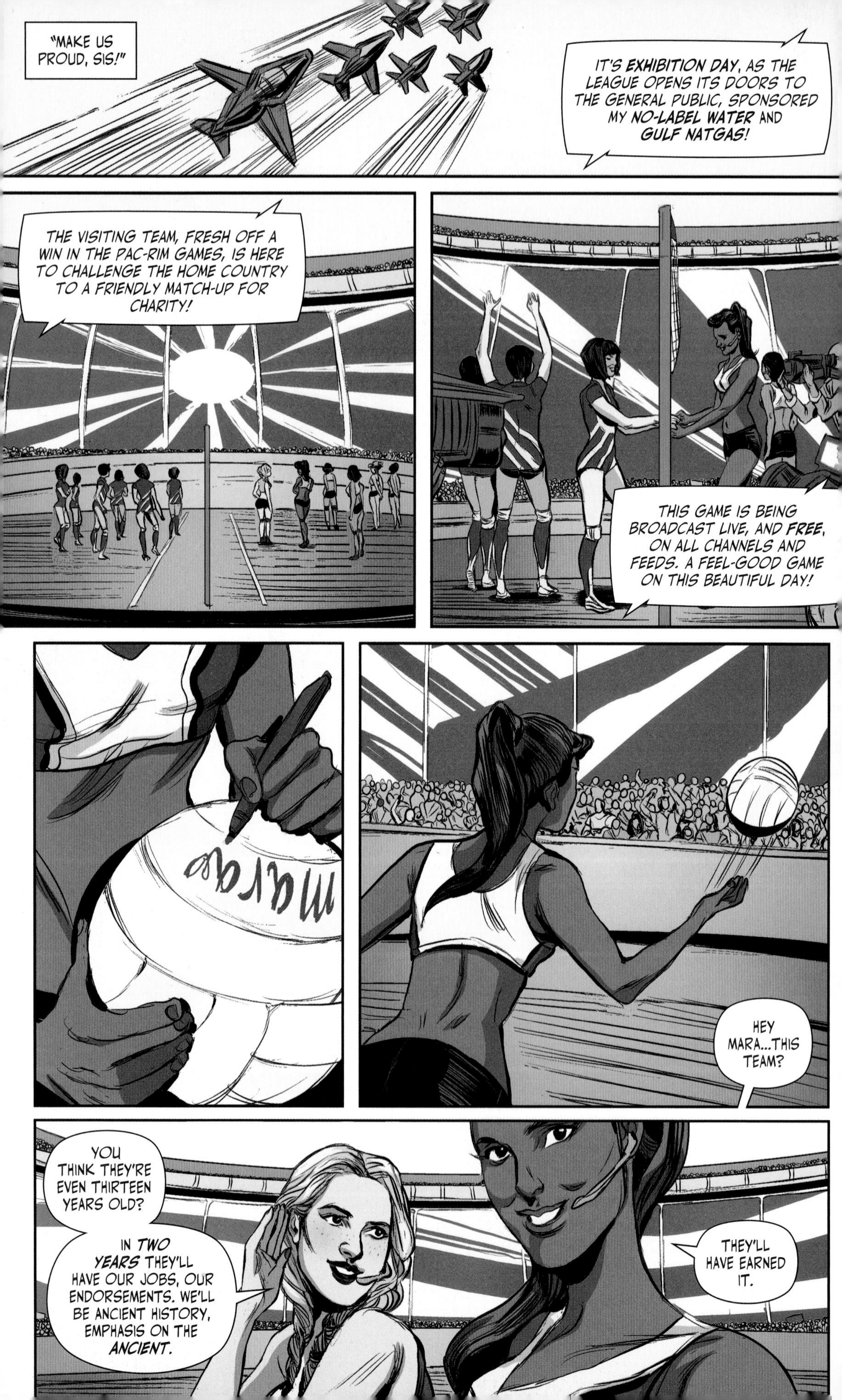
"MAKE US PROUD, SIS!"
IT'S **EXHIBITION DAY**, AS THE LEAGUE OPENS ITS DOORS TO THE GENERAL PUBLIC, SPONSORED MY **NO-LABEL WATER** AND **GULF NATGAS**!
THE VISITING TEAM, FRESH OFF A WIN IN THE PAC-RIM GAMES, IS HERE TO CHALLENGE THE HOME COUNTRY TO A FRIENDLY MATCH-UP FOR CHARITY!
THIS GAME IS BEING BROADCAST LIVE, AND **FREE**, ON ALL CHANNELS AND FEEDS. A FEEL-GOOD GAME ON THIS BEAUTIFUL DAY!
mara
HEY MARA...THIS TEAM?
YOU THINK THEY'RE EVEN THIRTEEN YEARS OLD?
IN ***TWO YEARS*** THEY'LL HAVE OUR JOBS, OUR ENDORSEMENTS. WE'LL BE ANCIENT HISTORY, EMPHASIS ON THE ***ANCIENT***.
THEY'LL HAVE EARNED IT.

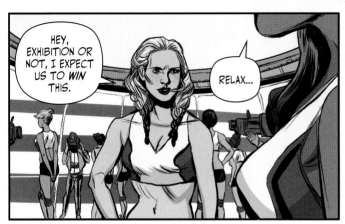

HEY, EXHIBITION OR NOT, I EXPECT US TO *WIN* THIS.

RELAX...

...IT'LL BE A BLOODBATH.

MS. PRINCE?

YES, SORRY, I'M HERE.

YOU ARE LIVE IN *FIVE* SECONDS, MS. PRINCE.

...

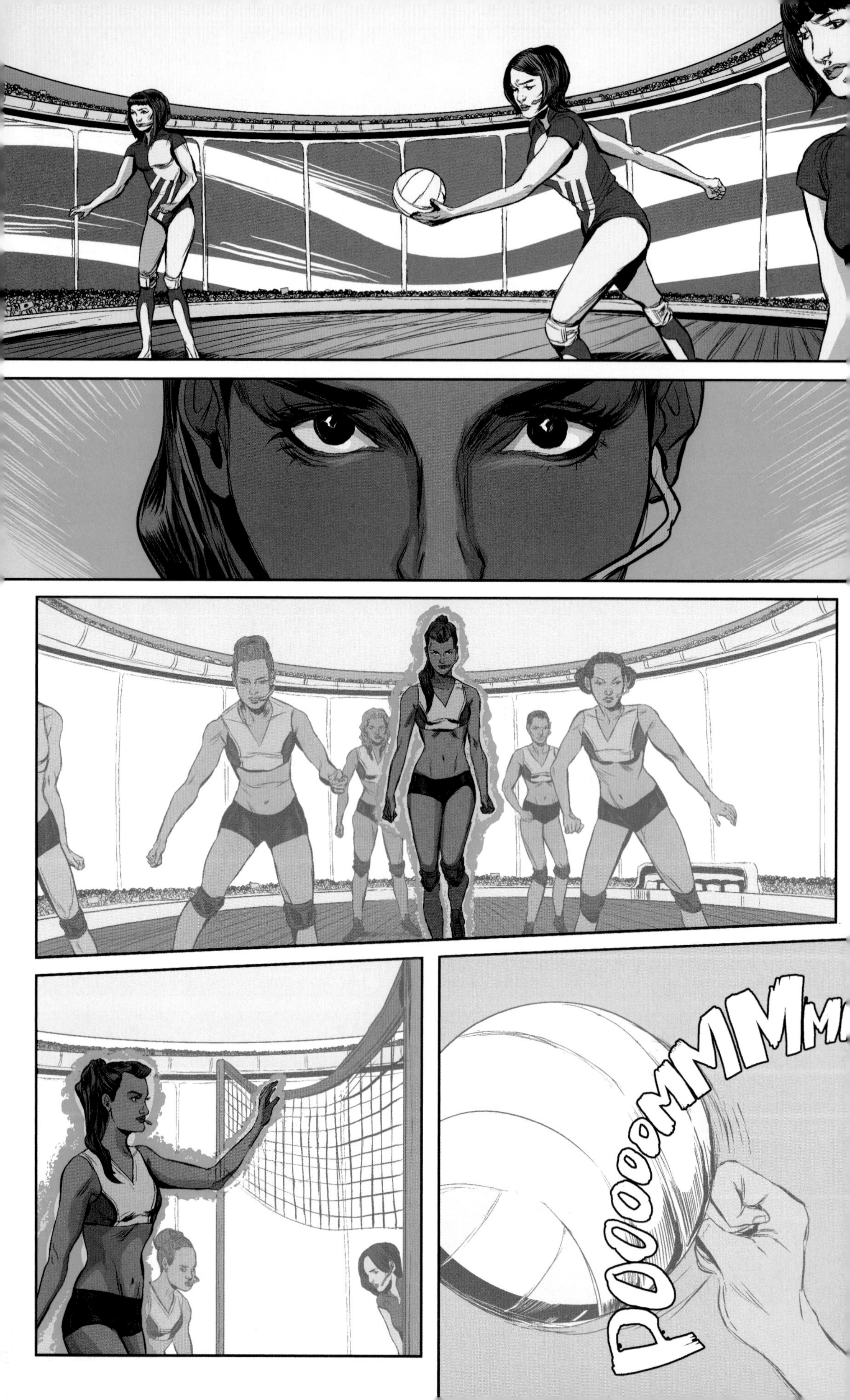
POOOOOMMMMM

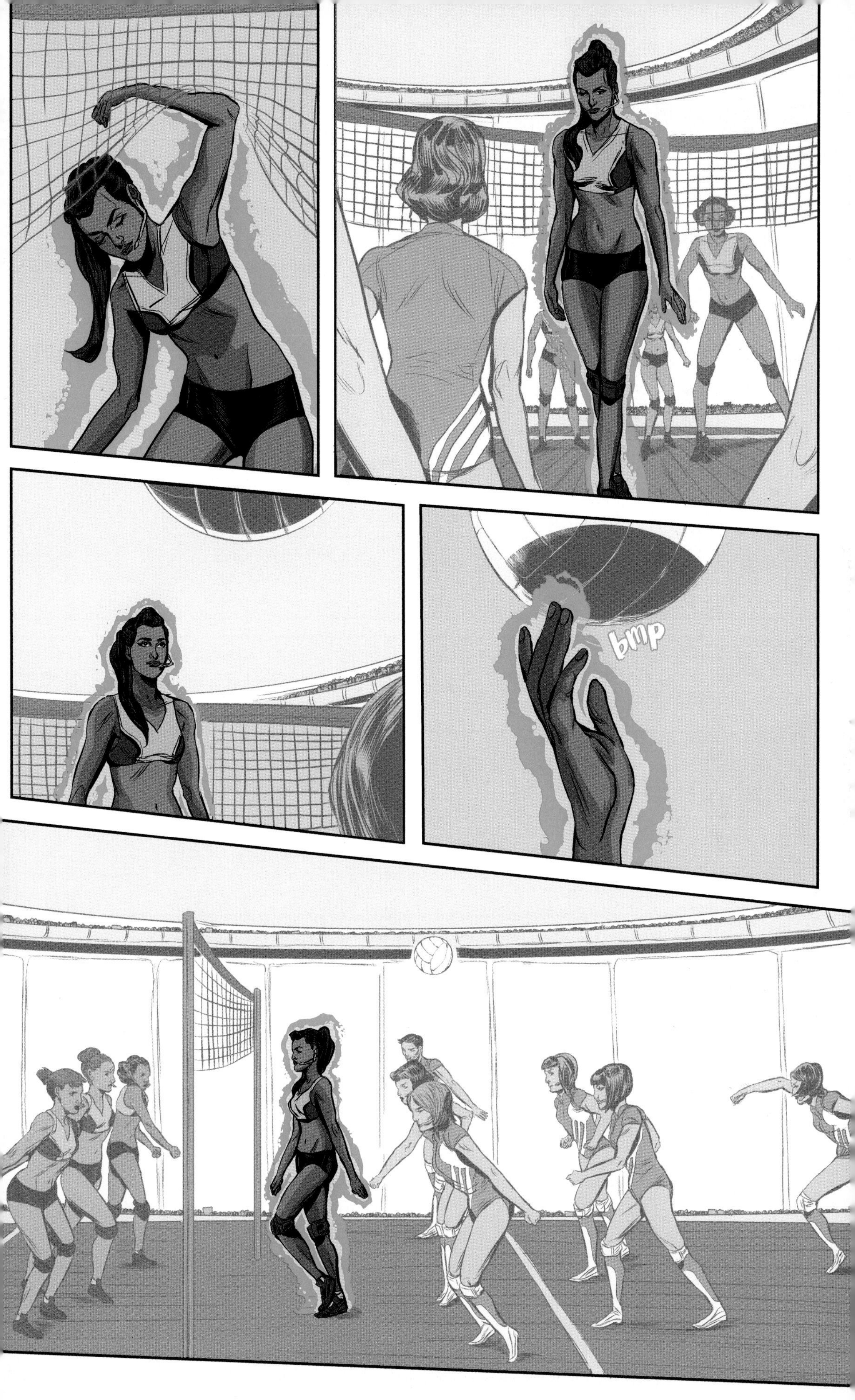
bmp

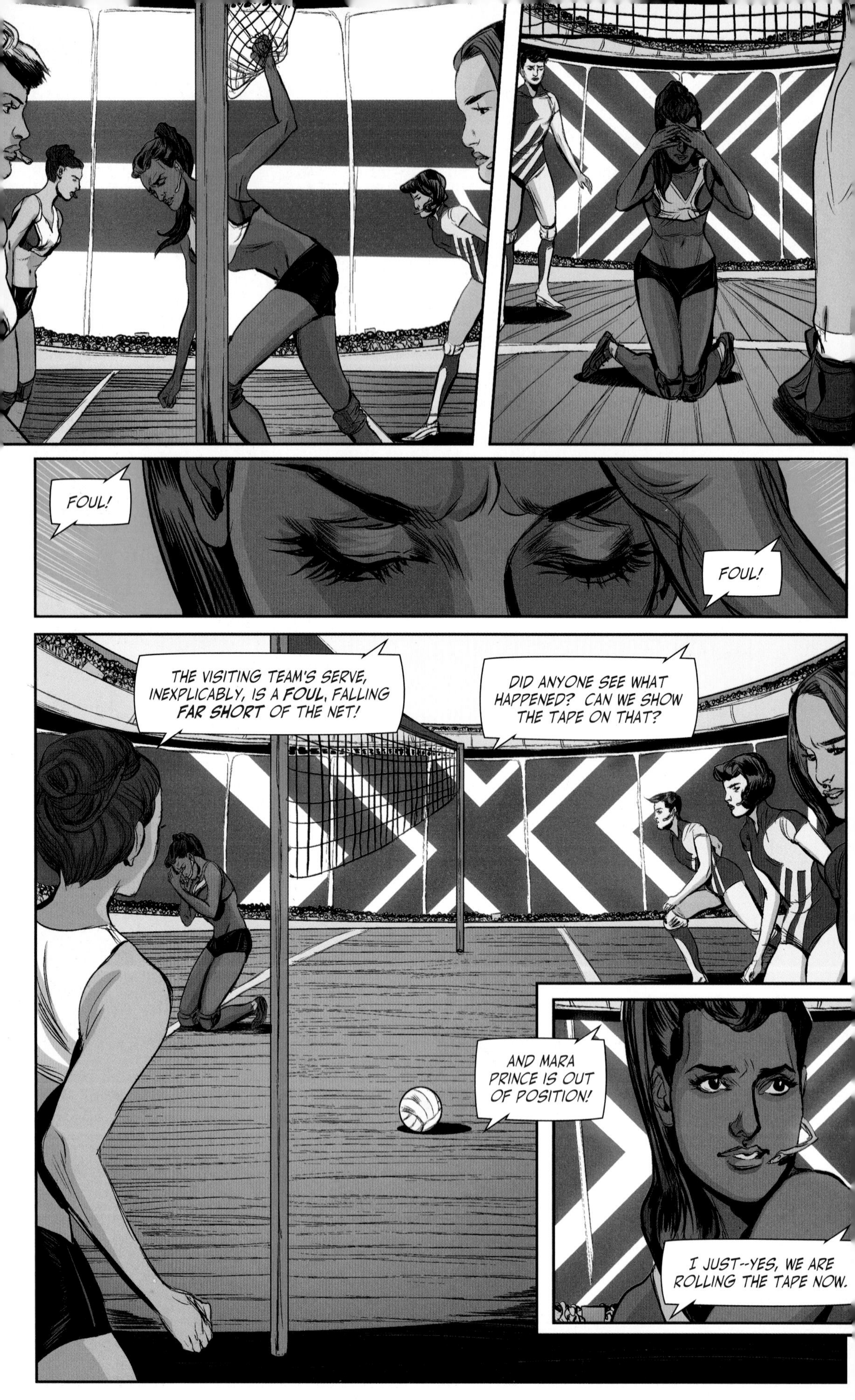
FOUL!
FOUL!
THE VISITING TEAM'S SERVE, INEXPLICABLY, IS A FOUL, FALLING FAR SHORT OF THE NET!
DID ANYONE SEE WHAT HAPPENED? CAN WE SHOW THE TAPE ON THAT?
AND MARA PRINCE IS OUT OF POSITION!
I JUST--YES, WE ARE ROLLING THE TAPE NOW.

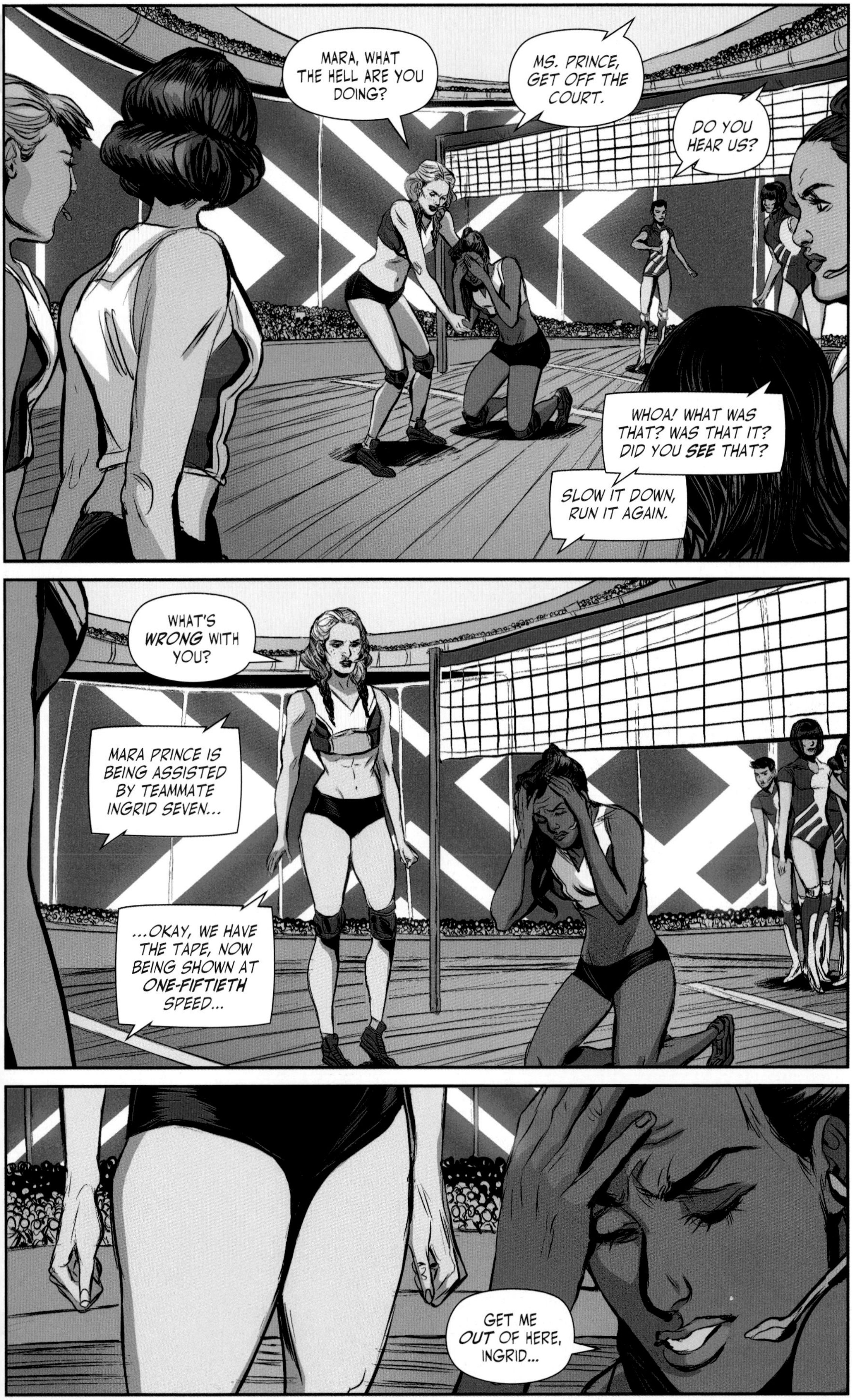
MARA, WHAT THE HELL ARE YOU DOING?
MS. PRINCE, GET OFF THE COURT.
DO YOU HEAR US?
WHOA! WHAT WAS THAT? WAS THAT IT? DID YOU SEE THAT?
SLOW IT DOWN, RUN IT AGAIN.
WHAT'S WRONG WITH YOU?
MARA PRINCE IS BEING ASSISTED BY TEAMMATE INGRID SEVEN...
...OKAY, WE HAVE THE TAPE, NOW BEING SHOWN AT ONE-FIFTIETH SPEED...
GET ME OUT OF HERE, INGRID...

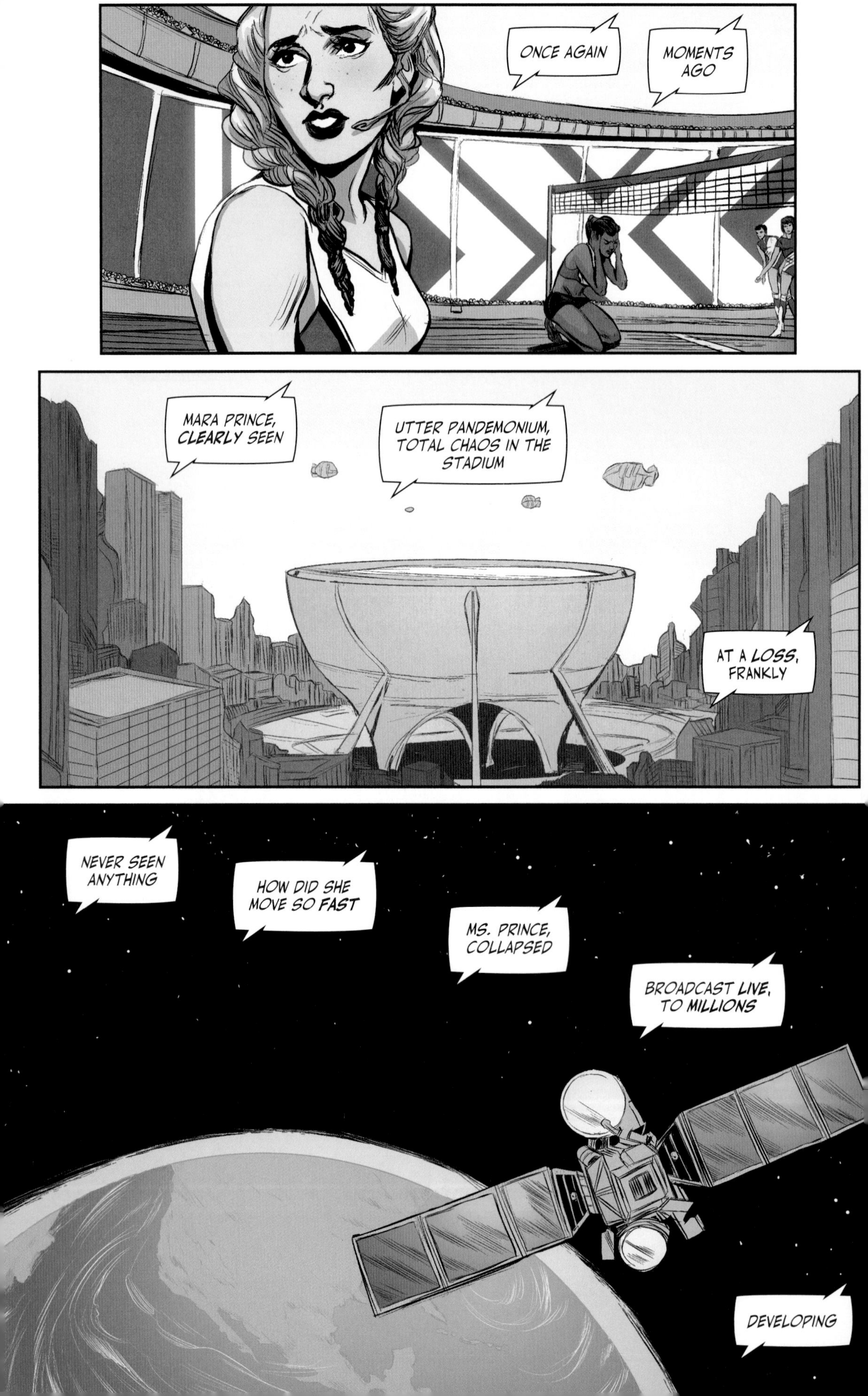
ONCE AGAIN
MOMENTS AGO
MARA PRINCE, CLEARLY SEEN
UTTER PANDEMONIUM, TOTAL CHAOS IN THE STADIUM
AT A LOSS, FRANKLY
NEVER SEEN ANYTHING
HOW DID SHE MOVE SO FAST
MS. PRINCE, COLLAPSED
BROADCAST LIVE, TO MILLIONS
DEVELOPING

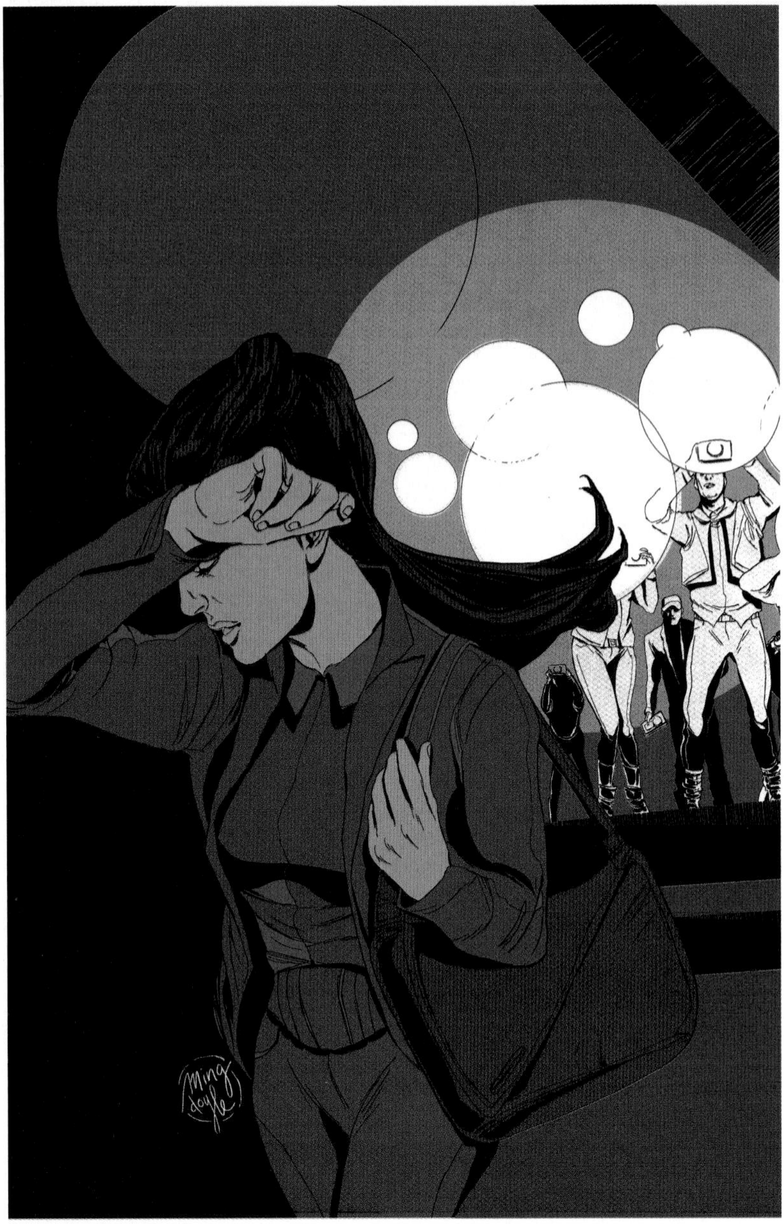
ming doyle

CHAPTER TWO

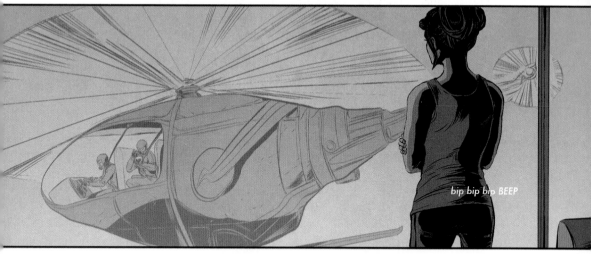

bip bip bip BEEP

bip bip b–

HELLO?

AS YOUR *PUBLICIST* I WOULD LIKE TO INFORM YOU THAT WE ARE NOW OFFICIALLY *TWENTY MINUTES* LATE.

COME DOWNSTAIRS AND *GET IN THE CAR,* MARA.

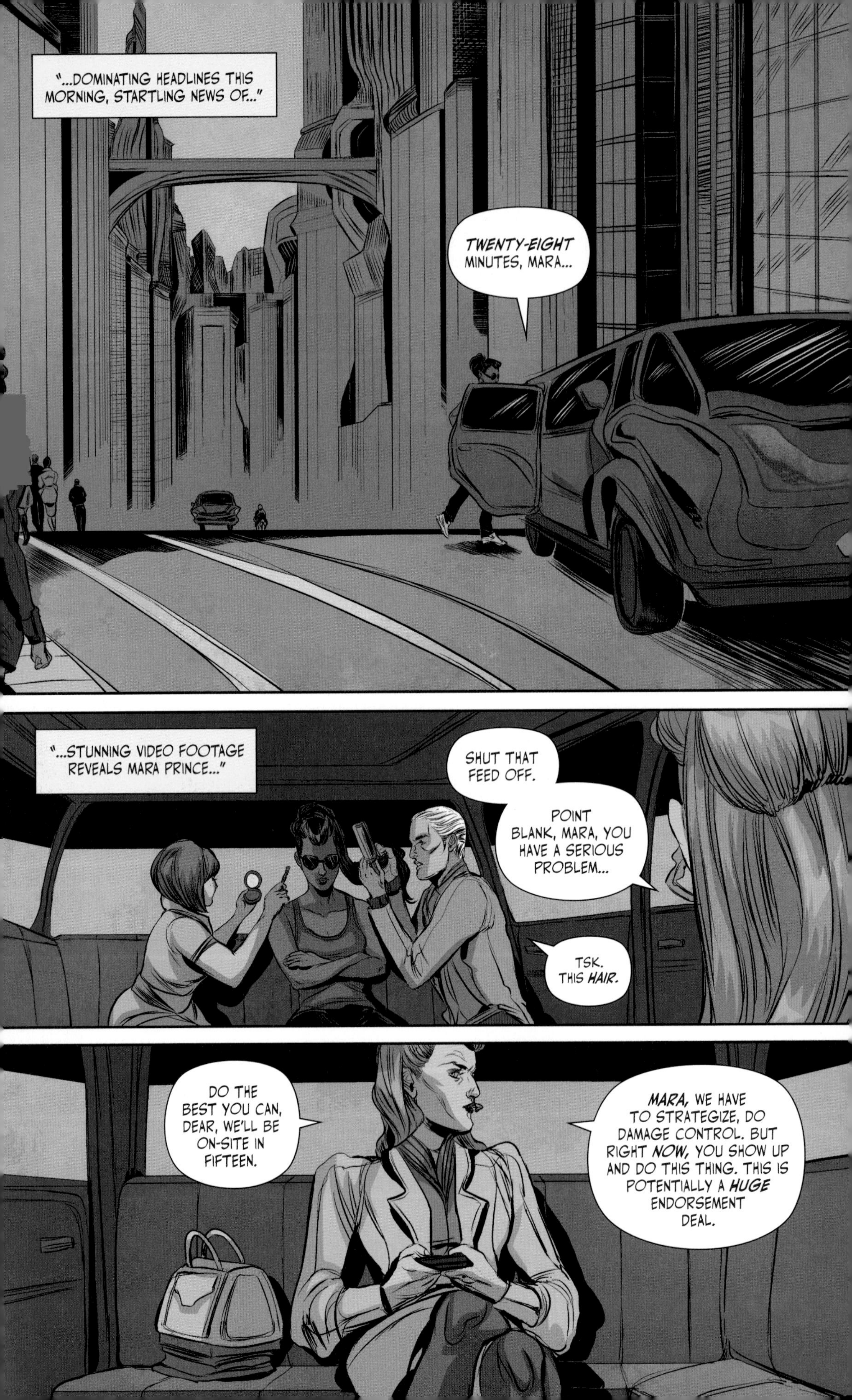
"...DOMINATING HEADLINES THIS MORNING, STARTLING NEWS OF..."
TWENTY-EIGHT MINUTES, MARA...
"...STUNNING VIDEO FOOTAGE REVEALS MARA PRINCE..."
SHUT THAT FEED OFF.
POINT BLANK, MARA, YOU HAVE A SERIOUS PROBLEM...
TSK. THIS HAIR.
MARA, WE HAVE TO STRATEGIZE, DO DAMAGE CONTROL. BUT RIGHT NOW, YOU SHOW UP AND DO THIS THING. THIS IS POTENTIALLY A HUGE ENDORSEMENT DEAL.
DO THE BEST YOU CAN, DEAR, WE'LL BE ON-SITE IN FIFTEEN.

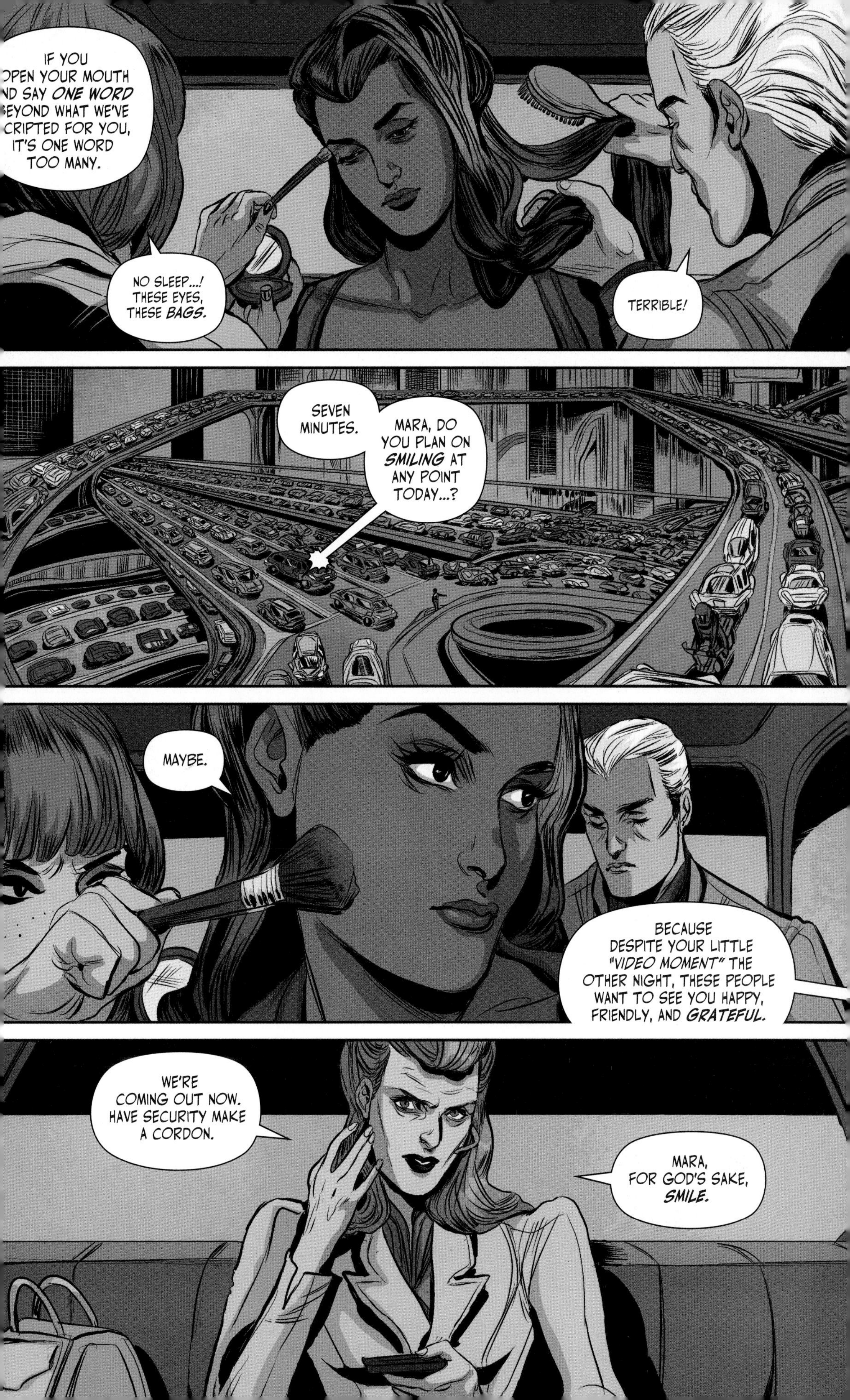
IF YOU OPEN YOUR MOUTH AND SAY ONE WORD BEYOND WHAT WE'VE SCRIPTED FOR YOU, IT'S ONE WORD TOO MANY.
NO SLEEP...! THESE EYES, THESE BAGS.
TERRIBLE!
SEVEN MINUTES.
MARA, DO YOU PLAN ON SMILING AT ANY POINT TODAY...?
MAYBE.
BECAUSE DESPITE YOUR LITTLE "VIDEO MOMENT" THE OTHER NIGHT, THESE PEOPLE WANT TO SEE YOU HAPPY, FRIENDLY, AND GRATEFUL.
WE'RE COMING OUT NOW. HAVE SECURITY MAKE A CORDON.
MARA, FOR GOD'S SAKE, SMILE.

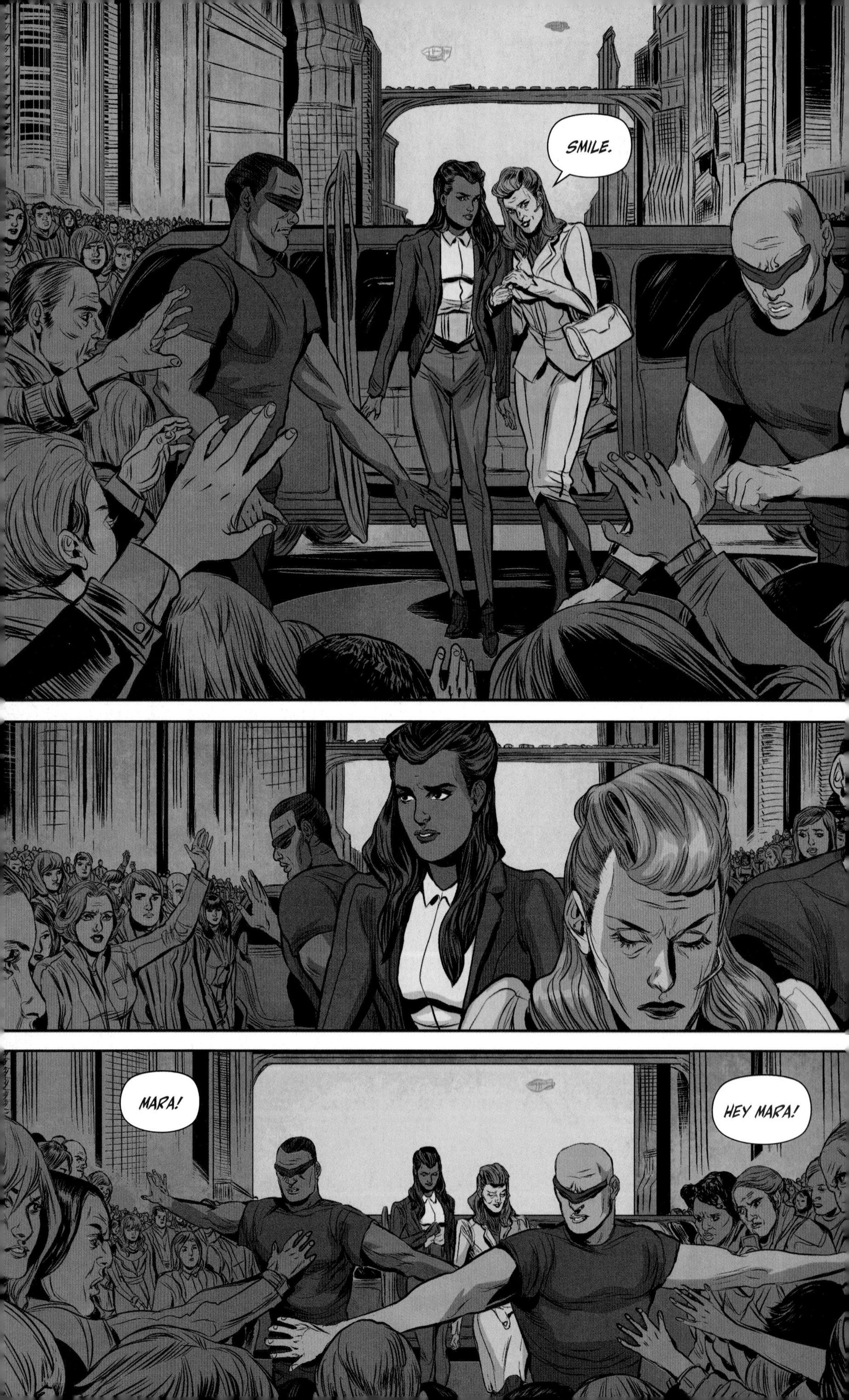
SMILE.
MARA!
HEY MARA!

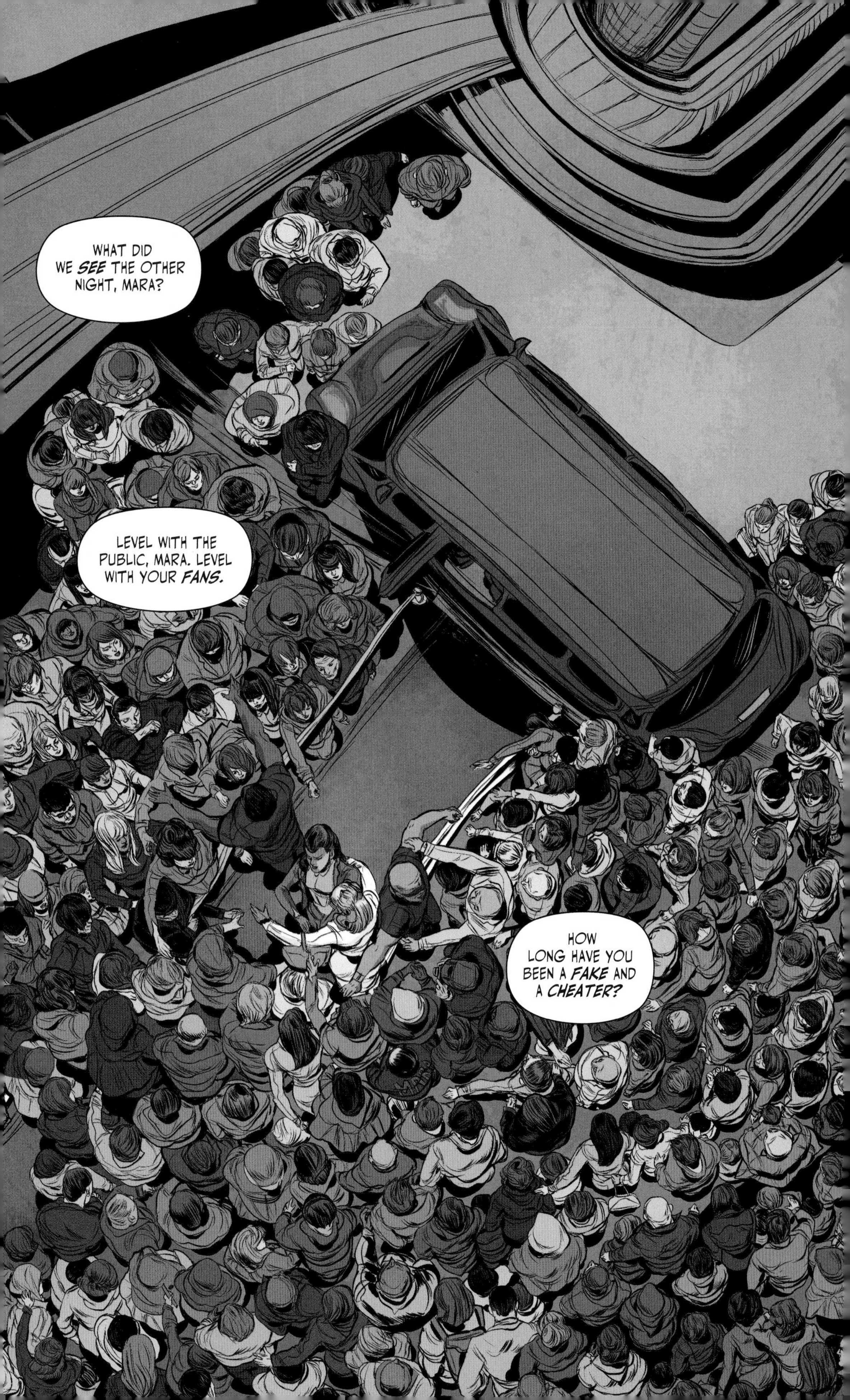
WHAT DID WE SEE THE OTHER NIGHT, MARA?
LEVEL WITH THE PUBLIC, MARA. LEVEL WITH YOUR FANS.
HOW LONG HAVE YOU BEEN A FAKE AND A CHEATER?

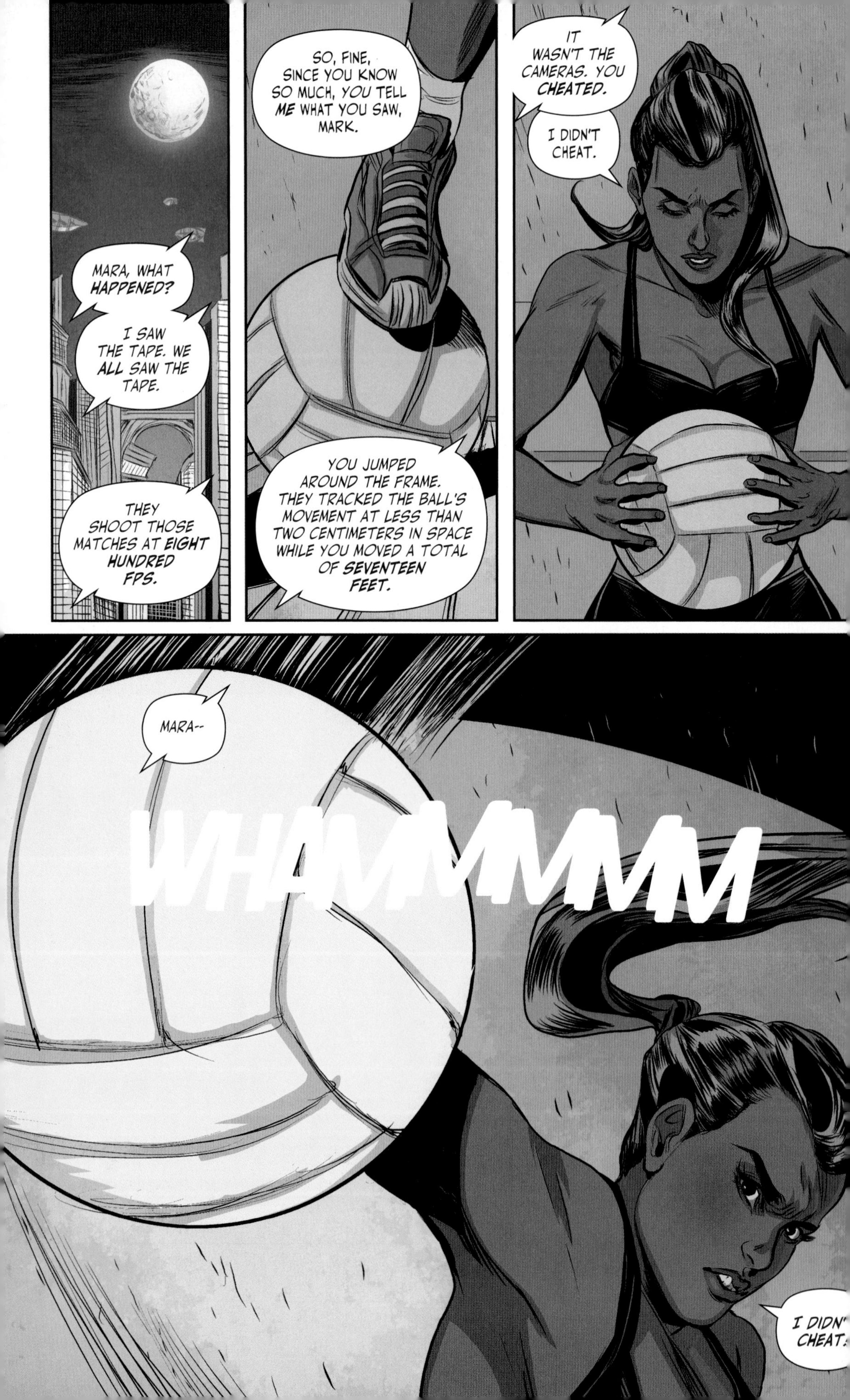
MARA, WHAT HAPPENED?
I SAW THE TAPE. WE ALL SAW THE TAPE.
THEY SHOOT THOSE MATCHES AT EIGHT HUNDRED FPS.
SO, FINE, SINCE YOU KNOW SO MUCH, YOU TELL ME WHAT YOU SAW, MARK.
YOU JUMPED AROUND THE FRAME. THEY TRACKED THE BALL'S MOVEMENT AT LESS THAN TWO CENTIMETERS IN SPACE WHILE YOU MOVED A TOTAL OF SEVENTEEN FEET.
IT WASN'T THE CAMERAS. YOU CHEATED.
I DIDN'T CHEAT.
MARA--
WHAMMMMM
I DIDN' CHEAT.

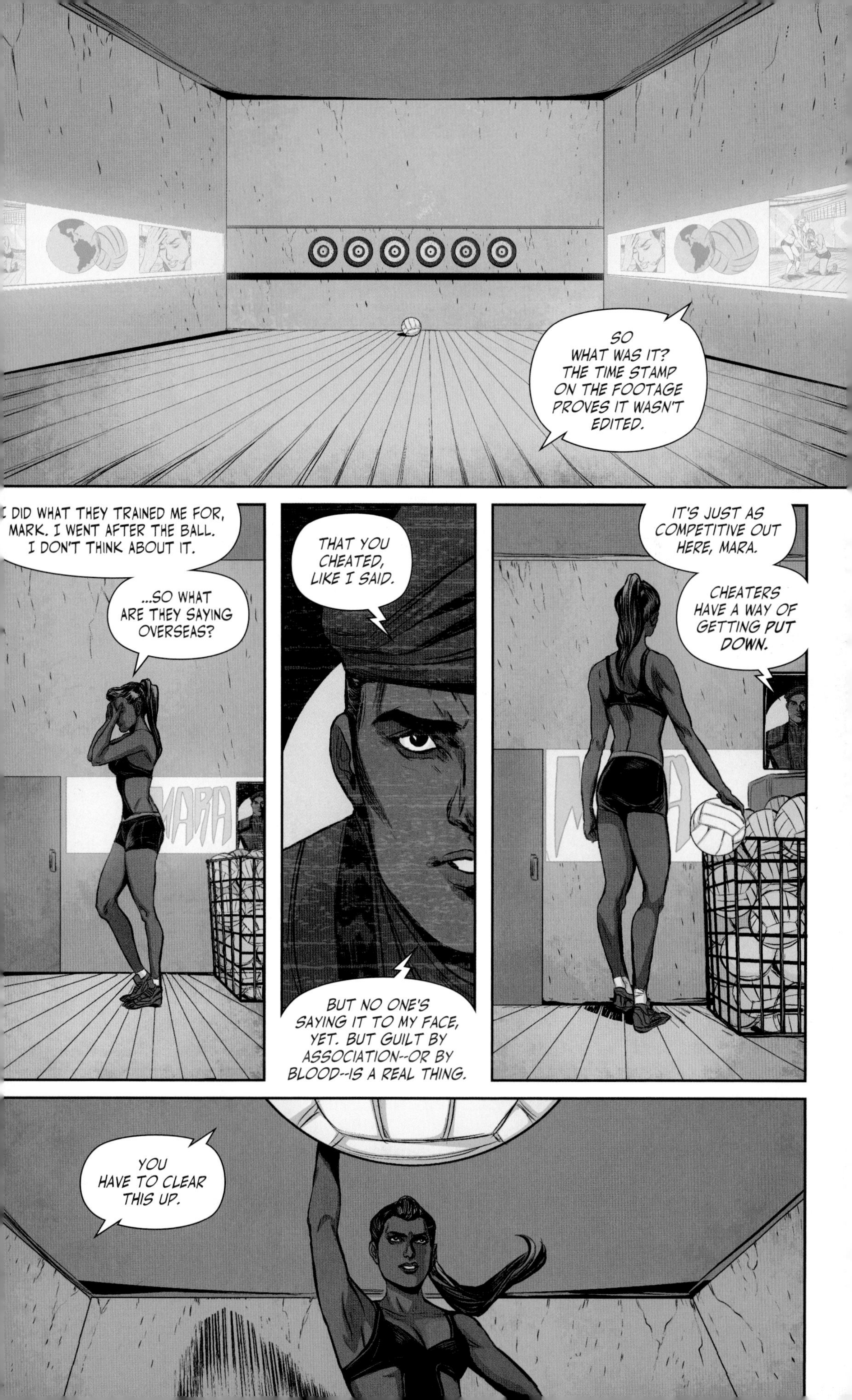
SO WHAT WAS IT? THE TIME STAMP ON THE FOOTAGE PROVES IT WASN'T EDITED.
I DID WHAT THEY TRAINED ME FOR, MARK. I WENT AFTER THE BALL. I DON'T THINK ABOUT IT.
...SO WHAT ARE THEY SAYING OVERSEAS?
MARA
THAT YOU CHEATED, LIKE I SAID.
BUT NO ONE'S SAYING IT TO MY FACE, YET. BUT GUILT BY ASSOCIATION--OR BY BLOOD--IS A REAL THING.
IT'S JUST AS COMPETITIVE OUT HERE, MARA.
CHEATERS HAVE A WAY OF GETTING PUT DOWN.
YOU HAVE TO CLEAR THIS UP.

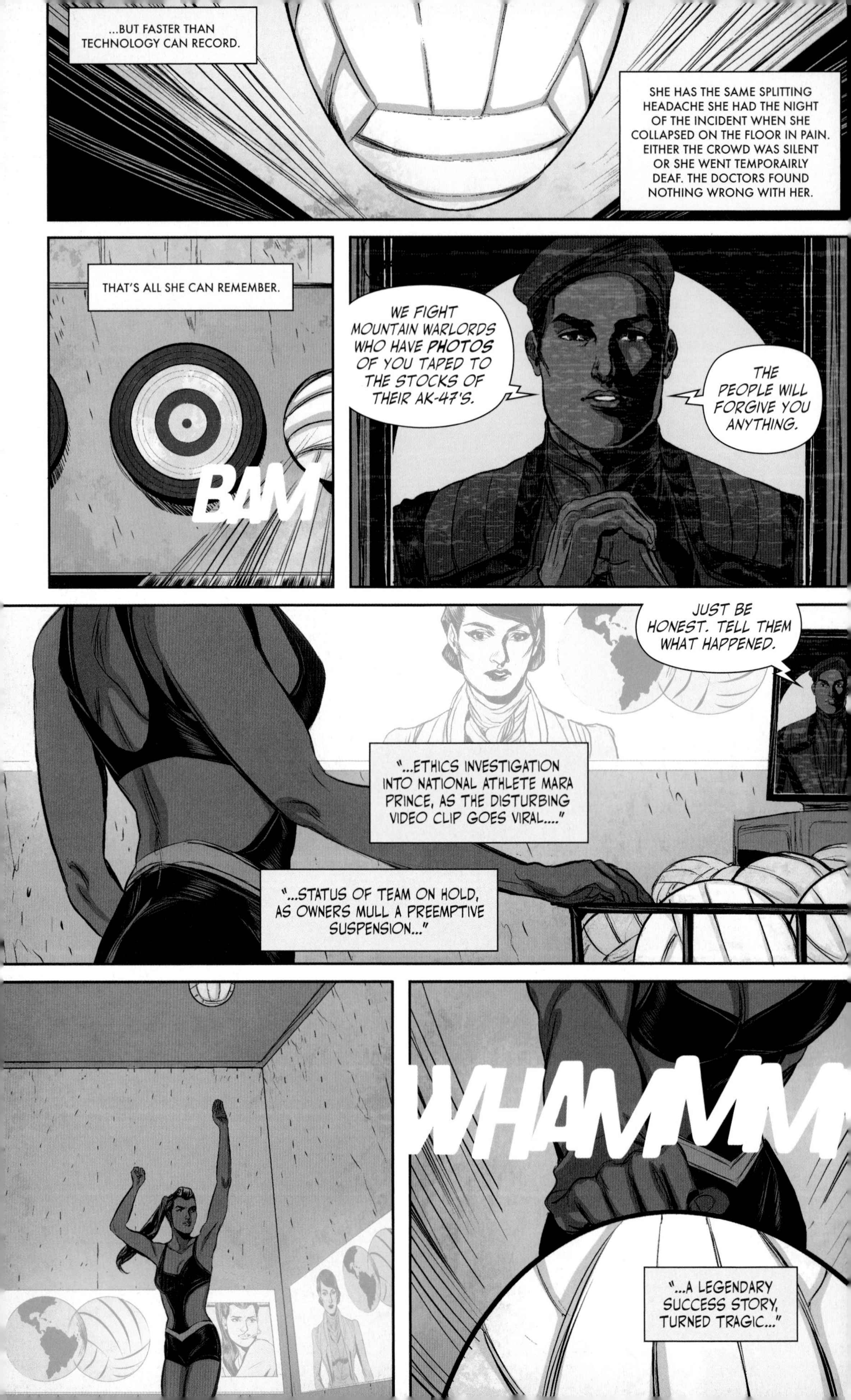

...BUT FASTER THAN TECHNOLOGY CAN RECORD.
SHE HAS THE SAME SPLITTING HEADACHE SHE HAD THE NIGHT OF THE INCIDENT WHEN SHE COLLAPSED ON THE FLOOR IN PAIN. EITHER THE CROWD WAS SILENT OR SHE WENT TEMPORAIRLY DEAF. THE DOCTORS FOUND NOTHING WRONG WITH HER.
THAT'S ALL SHE CAN REMEMBER.
BAM
WE FIGHT MOUNTAIN WARLORDS WHO HAVE PHOTOS OF YOU TAPED TO THE STOCKS OF THEIR AK-47'S.
THE PEOPLE WILL FORGIVE YOU ANYTHING.
JUST BE HONEST. TELL THEM WHAT HAPPENED.
"...ETHICS INVESTIGATION INTO NATIONAL ATHLETE MARA PRINCE, AS THE DISTURBING VIDEO CLIP GOES VIRAL...."
"...STATUS OF TEAM ON HOLD, AS OWNERS MULL A PREEMPTIVE SUSPENSION..."
WHAMMM
"...A LEGENDARY SUCCESS STORY, TURNED TRAGIC..."

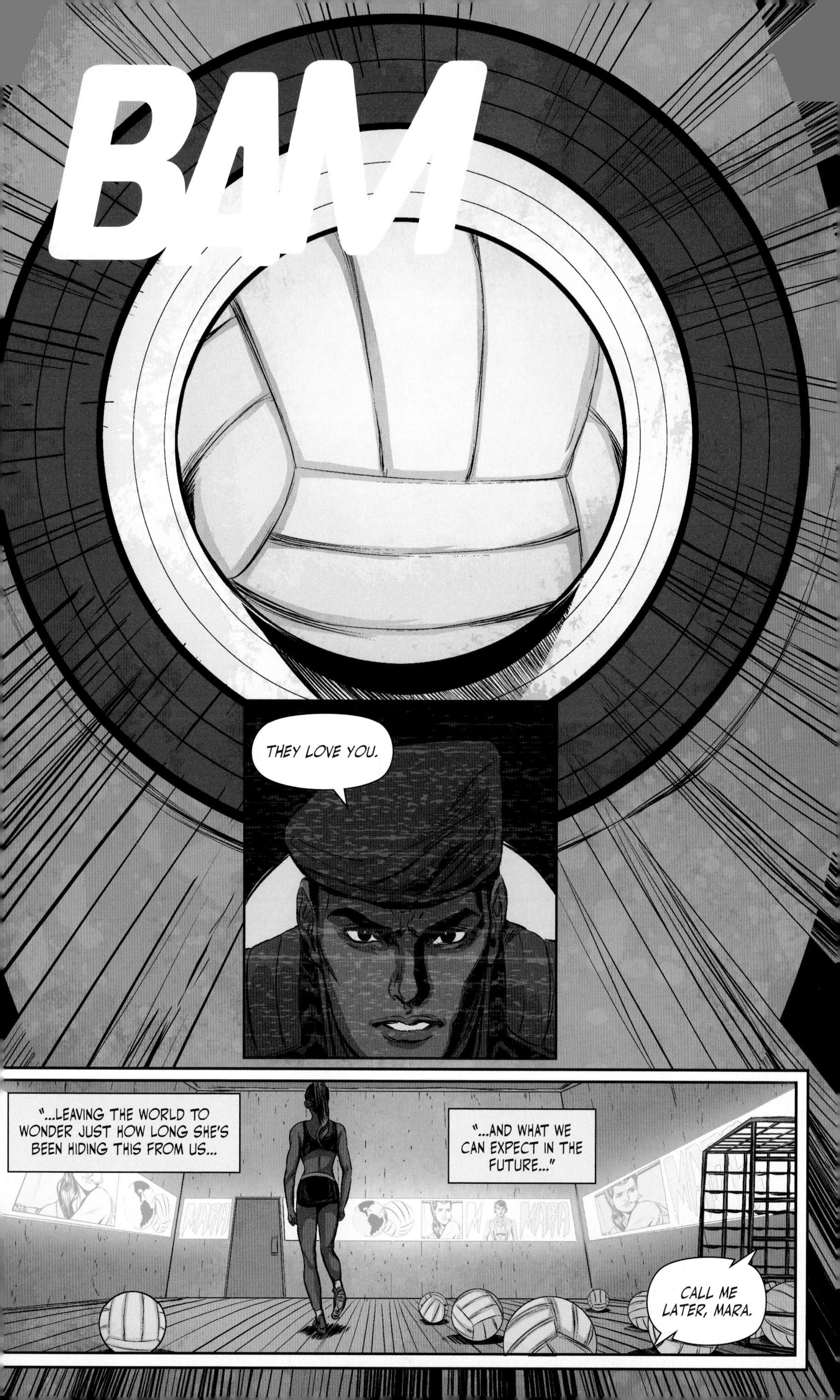
BAM
THEY LOVE YOU.
"...LEAVING THE WORLD TO WONDER JUST HOW LONG SHE'S BEEN HIDING THIS FROM US...
"...AND WHAT WE CAN EXPECT IN THE FUTURE..."
CALL ME LATER, MARA.

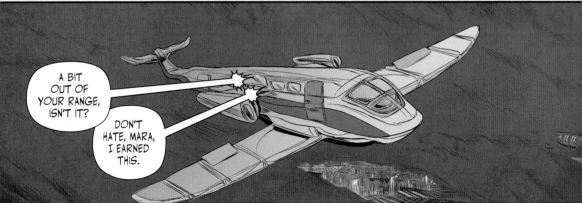

A BIT OUT OF YOUR RANGE, ISN'T IT?

DON'T HATE, MARA, I EARNED THIS.

LITERALLY. MEET CORPJET, MY NEW SPONSOR.

I LOVE ENDORSEMENT SEASON. YOU MUST BE *SWAMPED* WITH OFFERS.

YEAH, *"THE USUAL"* MEANING A HUNDRED MILLION, PROBABLY.

WHAT'S THE ADVANTAGE OF SIGNING WITH BIG AGRA?

TRAVEL PERKS, MOSTLY. GOOD HOTEL ROOMS. BIG PER DIEMS.

SCORE. *DONE.*

DETROIT AUTO? *DONE.*

WHO ARE YOU TAKING ON?

IT'S MOSTLY RENEWALS.

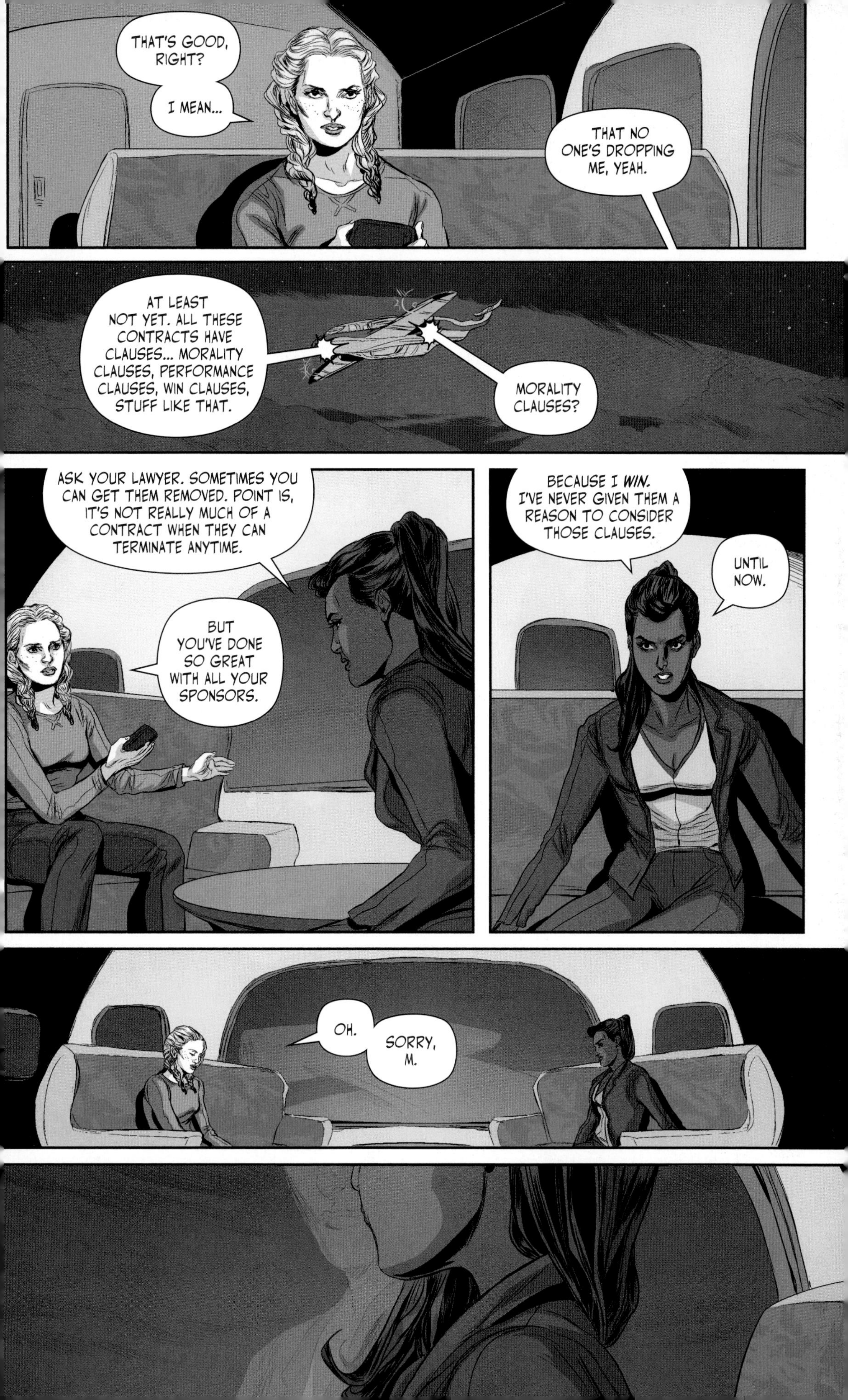
THAT'S GOOD, RIGHT?
I MEAN...
THAT NO ONE'S DROPPING ME, YEAH.
AT LEAST NOT YET. ALL THESE CONTRACTS HAVE CLAUSES... MORALITY CLAUSES, PERFORMANCE CLAUSES, WIN CLAUSES, STUFF LIKE THAT.
MORALITY CLAUSES?
ASK YOUR LAWYER. SOMETIMES YOU CAN GET THEM REMOVED. POINT IS, IT'S NOT REALLY MUCH OF A CONTRACT WHEN THEY CAN TERMINATE ANYTIME.
BUT YOU'VE DONE SO GREAT WITH ALL YOUR SPONSORS.
BECAUSE I *WIN.* I'VE NEVER GIVEN THEM A REASON TO CONSIDER THOSE CLAUSES.
UNTIL NOW.
OH.
SORRY, M.

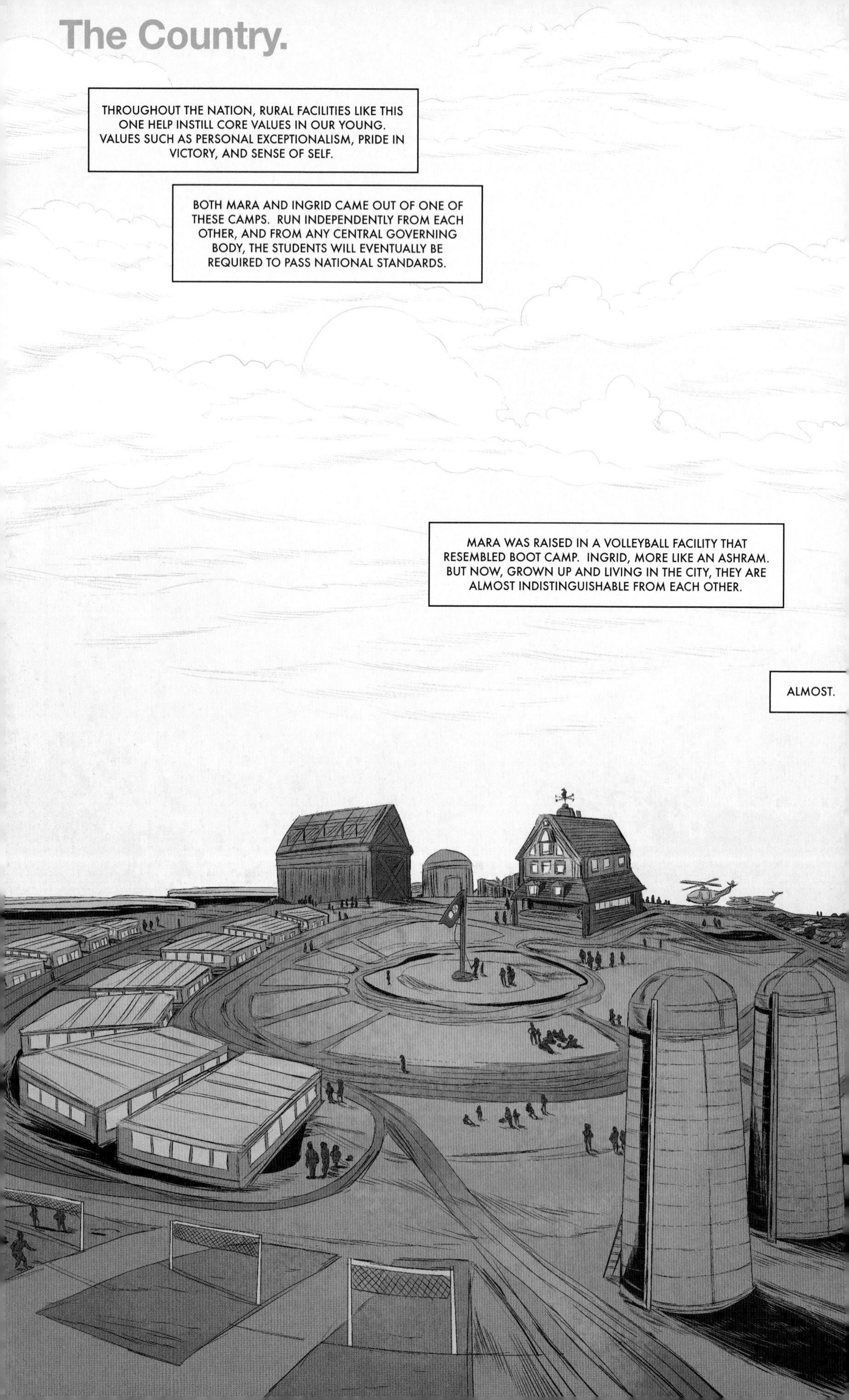
The Country.
THROUGHOUT THE NATION, RURAL FACILITIES LIKE THIS ONE HELP INSTILL CORE VALUES IN OUR YOUNG. VALUES SUCH AS PERSONAL EXCEPTIONALISM, PRIDE IN VICTORY, AND SENSE OF SELF.
BOTH MARA AND INGRID CAME OUT OF ONE OF THESE CAMPS. RUN INDEPENDENTLY FROM EACH OTHER, AND FROM ANY CENTRAL GOVERNING BODY, THE STUDENTS WILL EVENTUALLY BE REQUIRED TO PASS NATIONAL STANDARDS.
MARA WAS RAISED IN A VOLLEYBALL FACILITY THAT RESEMBLED BOOT CAMP. INGRID, MORE LIKE AN ASHRAM. BUT NOW, GROWN UP AND LIVING IN THE CITY, THEY ARE ALMOST INDISTINGUISHABLE FROM EACH OTHER.
ALMOST.

BUT BOTH ARE SPONSORED BY A SPORTSWEAR CORPORATION THAT PRIDES ITSELF ON OUTREACH, AND SO THEY MAKE TRI-ANNUAL RETREATS TO THESE CAMPS FOR SHORT RESIDENCES.

IT'S A MASSIVE SUCCESS.

EVERY SINGLE GIRL HERE WANTS TO BE INGRID OR MARA. IT'S, LITERALLY, THE ENTIRETY OF THEIR LIFE'S AMBITION.

FOR TWO WEEKS, THE STAR ATHLETES WILL TRAIN WITH AND TALK TO THE GIRLS, RUNNING DRILLS AND GIVING CAREER ADVICE. TELLING WAR STORIES AND CAUTIONARY TALES.

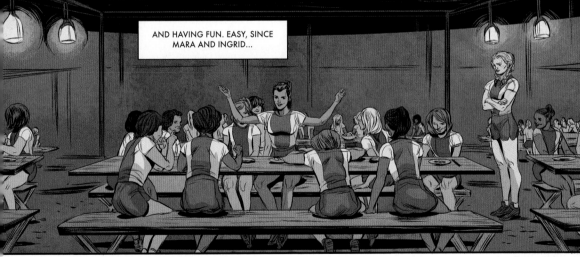

AND HAVING FUN. EASY, SINCE MARA AND INGRID...

...ARE BARELY OUT OF CHILDHOOD THEMSELVES.

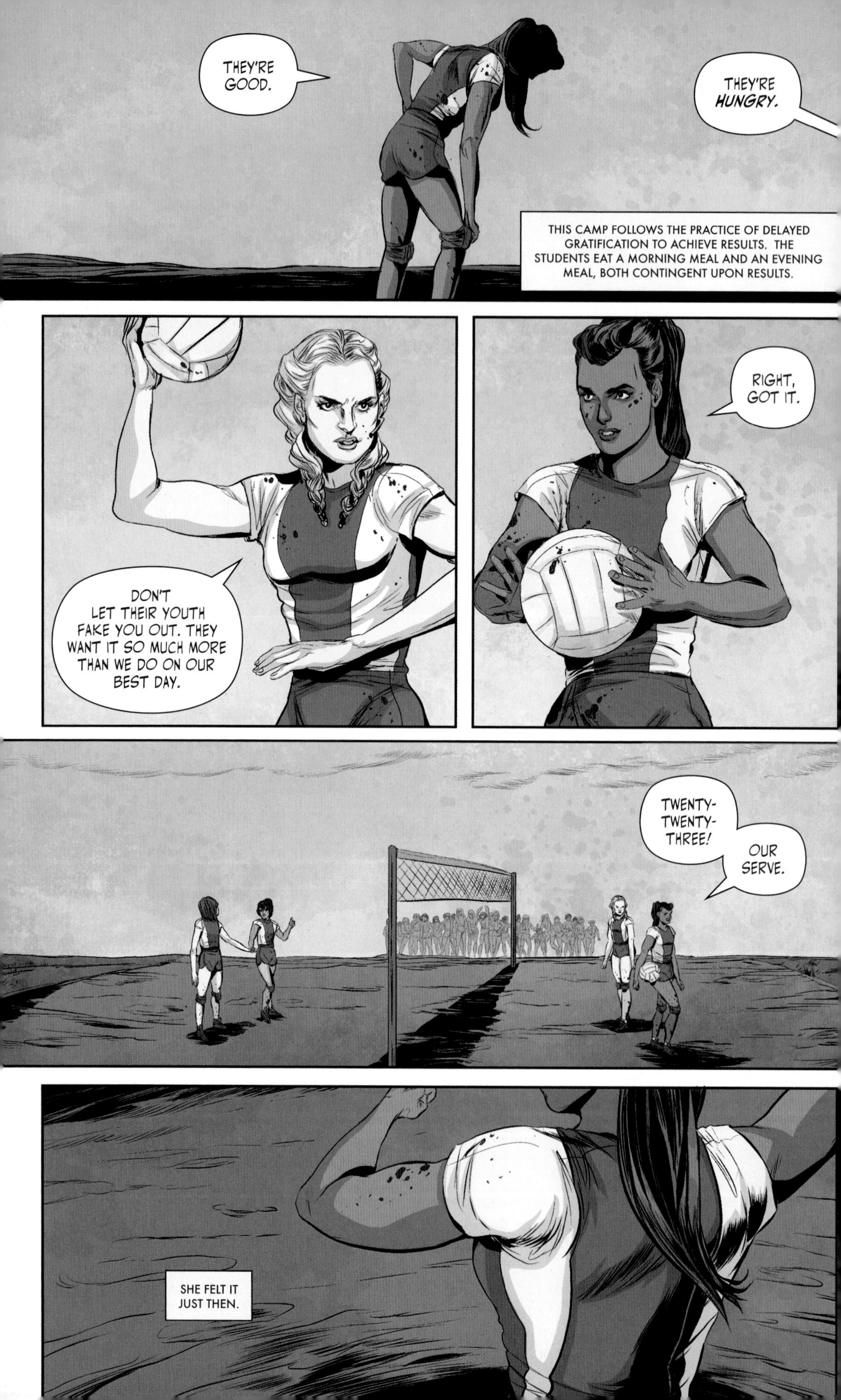
THEY'RE GOOD.
THEY'RE *HUNGRY.*
THIS CAMP FOLLOWS THE PRACTICE OF DELAYED GRATIFICATION TO ACHIEVE RESULTS. THE STUDENTS EAT A MORNING MEAL AND AN EVENING MEAL, BOTH CONTINGENT UPON RESULTS.
DON'T LET THEIR YOUTH FAKE YOU OUT. THEY WANT IT SO MUCH MORE THAN WE DO ON OUR BEST DAY.
RIGHT, GOT IT.
TWENTY-TWENTY-THREE!
OUR SERVE.
SHE FELT IT JUST THEN.

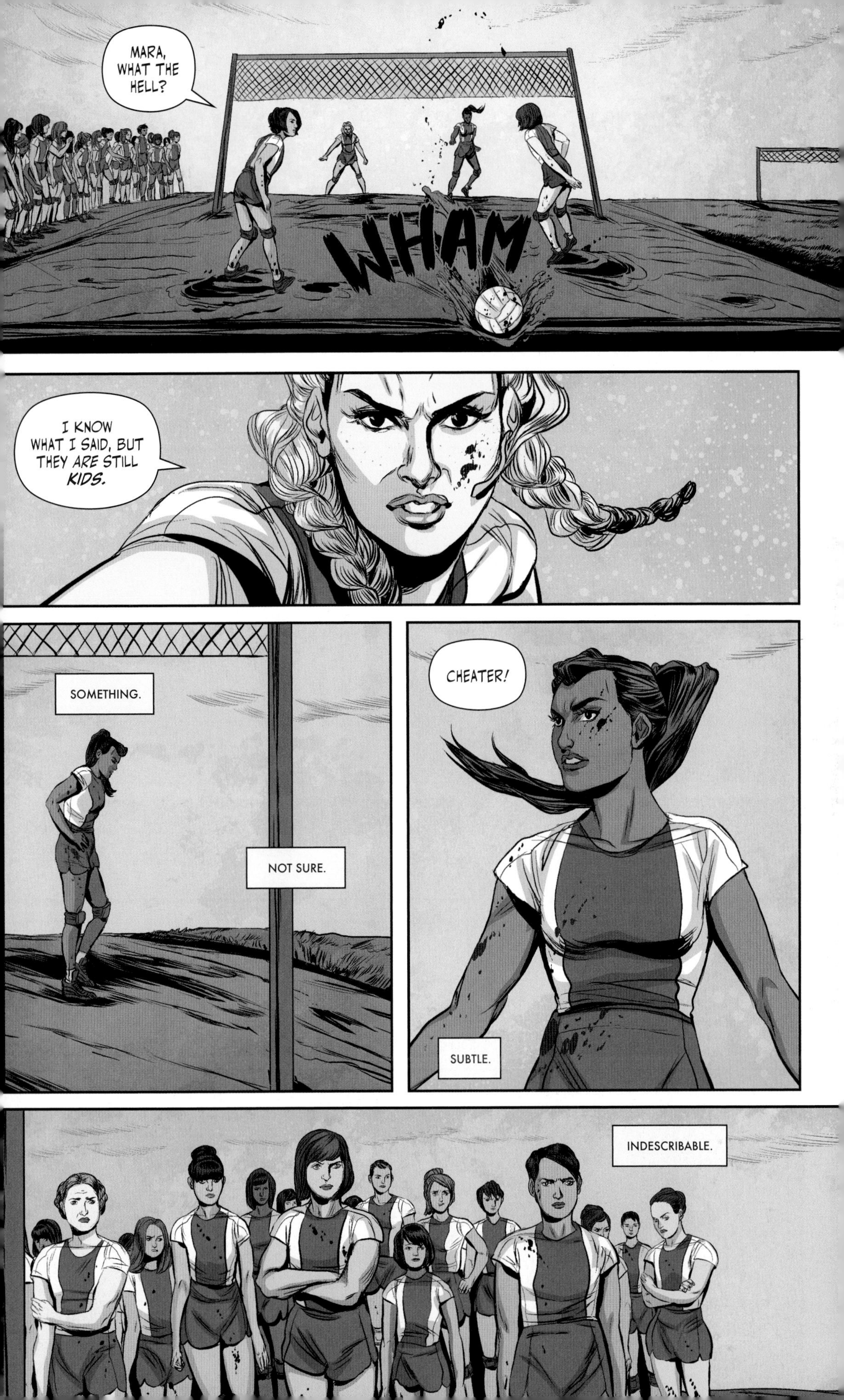
MARA, WHAT THE HELL?
WHAM
I KNOW WHAT I SAID, BUT THEY ARE STILL KIDS.
SOMETHING.
NOT SURE.
CHEATER!
SUBTLE.
INDESCRIBABLE.

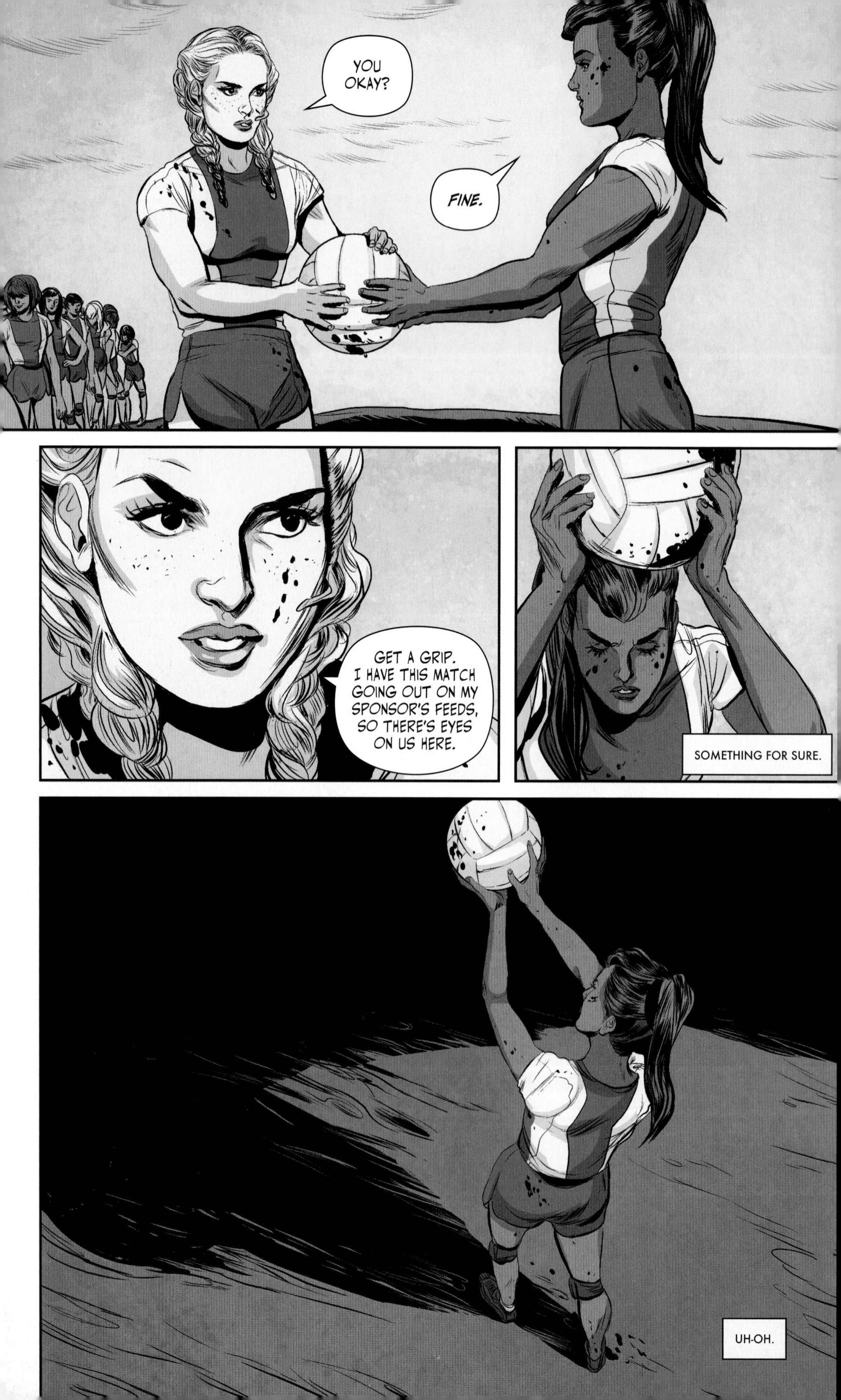

YOU OKAY?
FINE.
GET A GRIP. I HAVE THIS MATCH GOING OUT ON MY SPONSOR'S FEEDS, SO THERE'S EYES ON US HERE.
SOMETHING FOR SURE.
UH-OH.

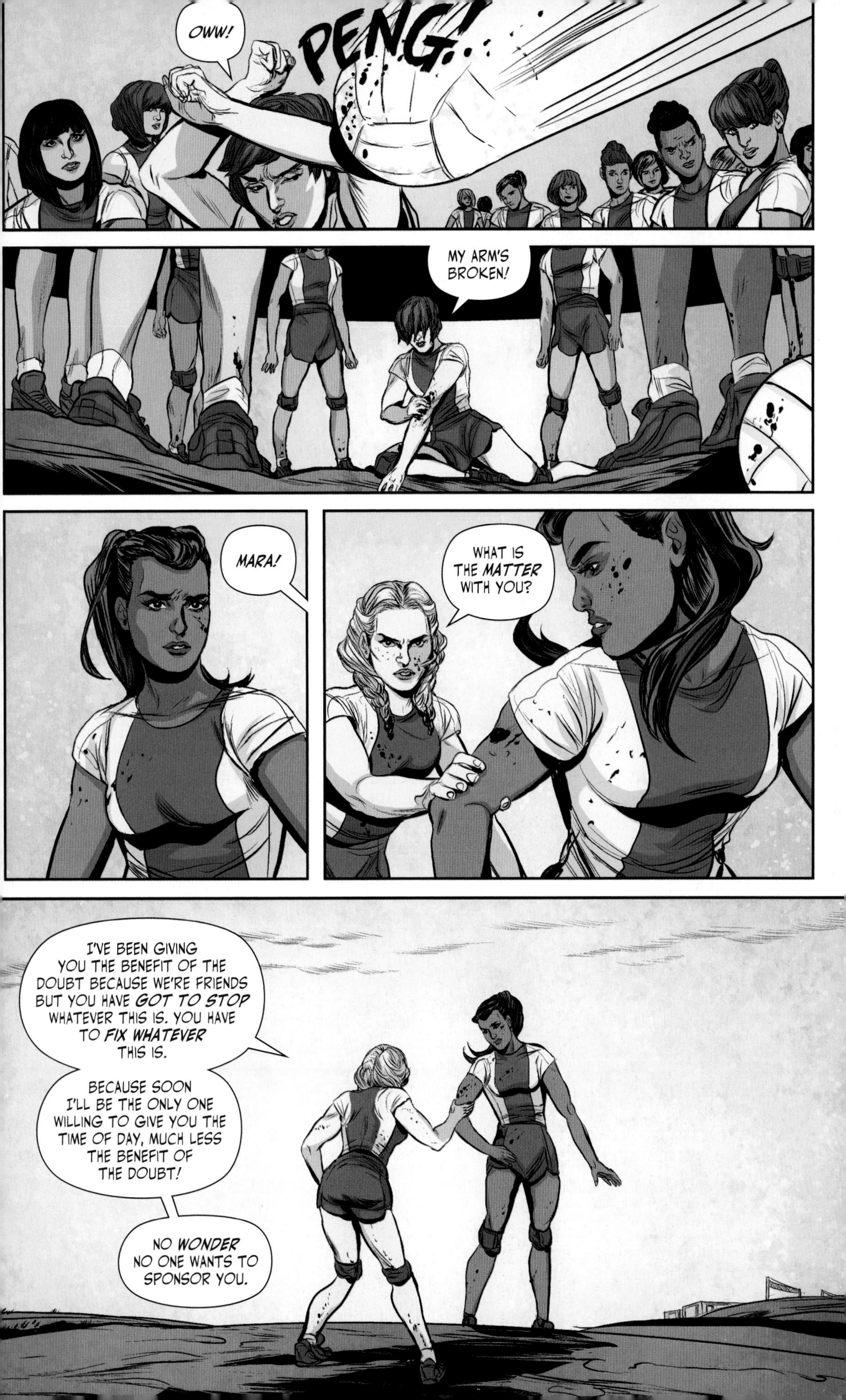
OWW!
PENG!
MY ARM'S BROKEN!
MARA!
WHAT IS THE MATTER WITH YOU?
I'VE BEEN GIVING YOU THE BENEFIT OF THE DOUBT BECAUSE WE'RE FRIENDS BUT YOU HAVE GOT TO STOP WHATEVER THIS IS. YOU HAVE TO FIX WHATEVER THIS IS.
BECAUSE SOON I'LL BE THE ONLY ONE WILLING TO GIVE YOU THE TIME OF DAY, MUCH LESS THE BENEFIT OF THE DOUBT!
NO WONDER NO ONE WANTS TO SPONSOR YOU.

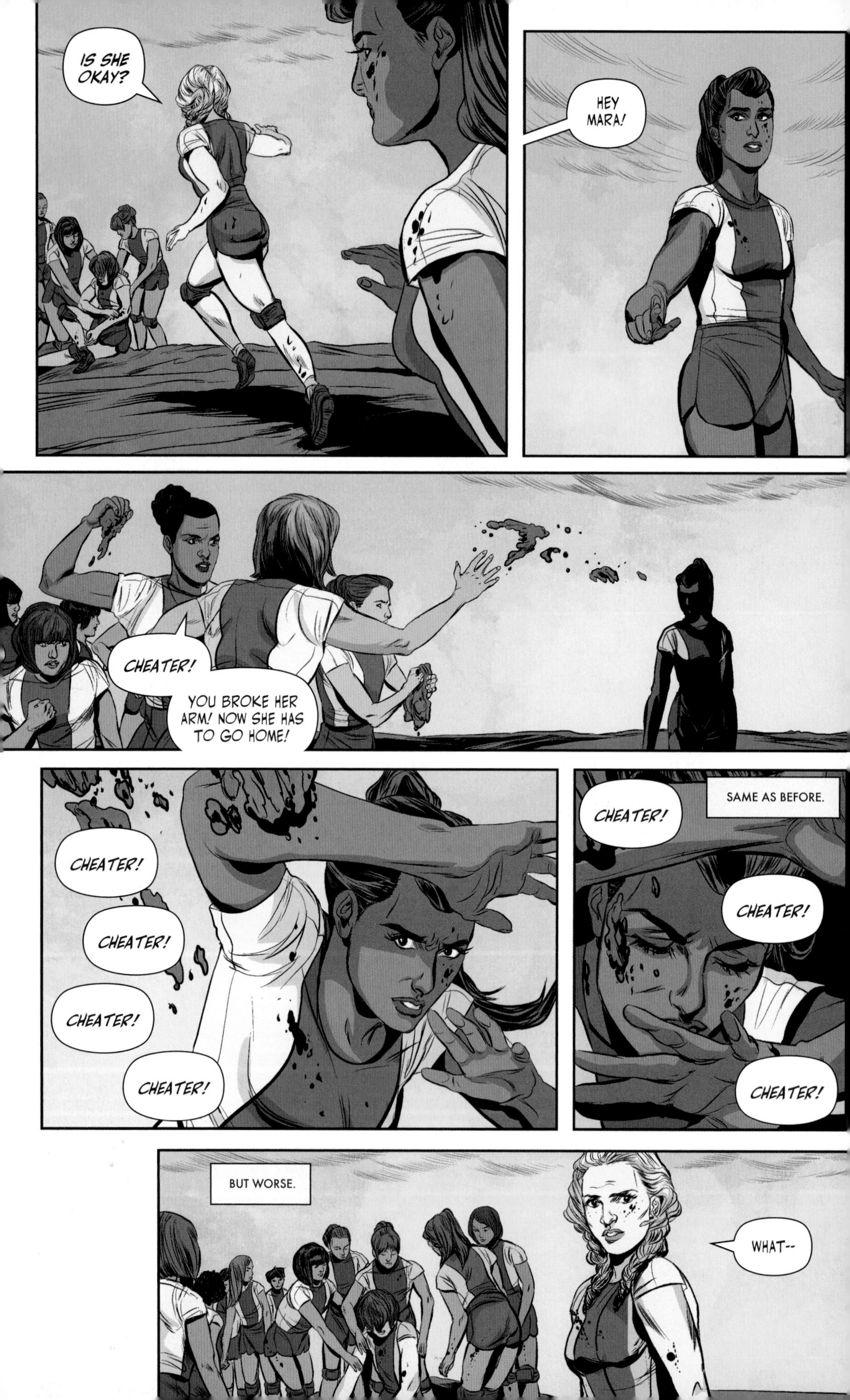
IS SHE OKAY?
HEY MARA!
CHEATER!
YOU BROKE HER ARM! NOW SHE HAS TO GO HOME!
CHEATER!
CHEATER!
CHEATER!
CHEATER!
SAME AS BEFORE.
CHEATER!
CHEATER!
CHEATER!
BUT WORSE.
WHAT--

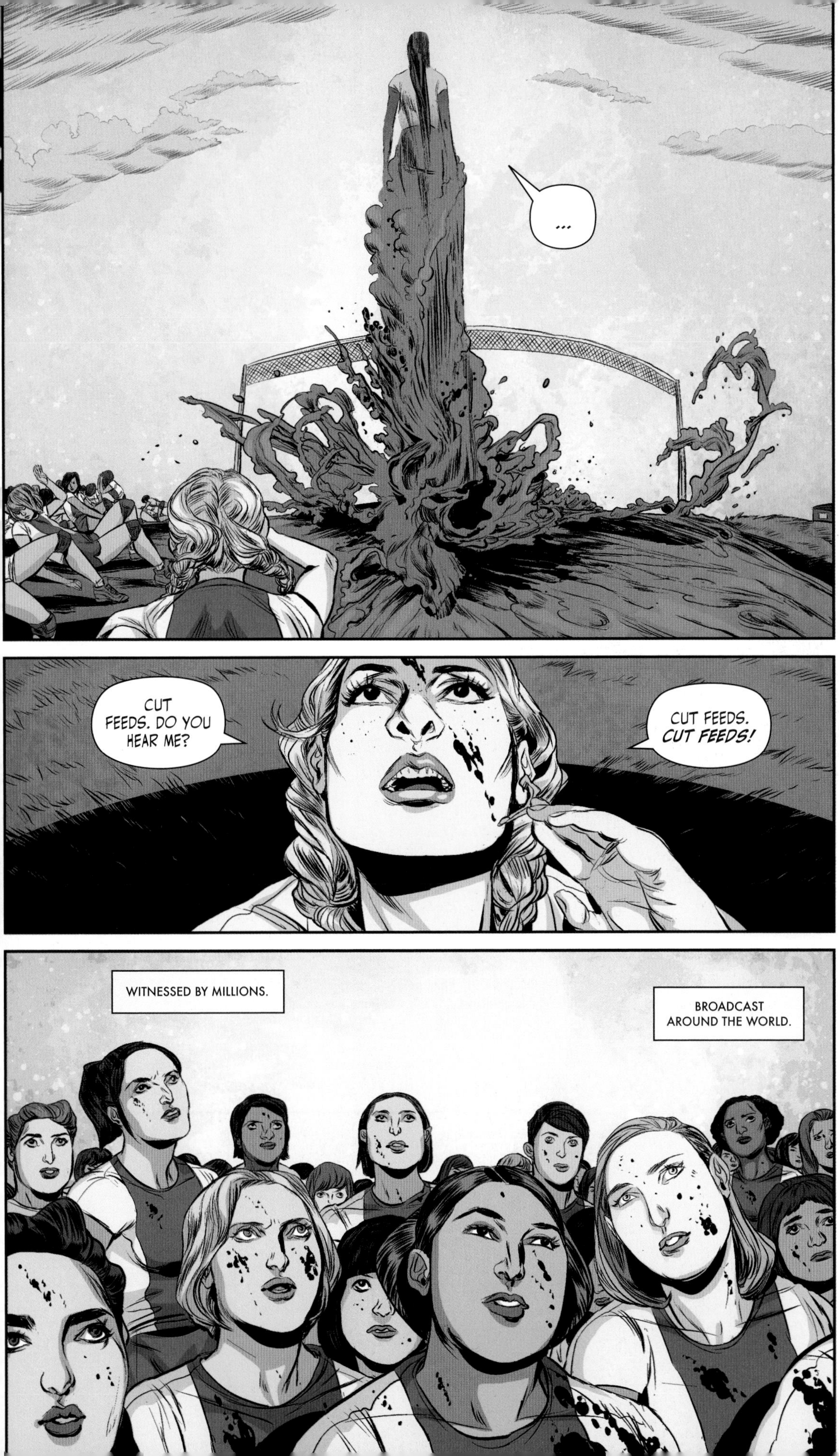
...
CUT FEEDS. DO YOU HEAR ME?
CUT FEEDS. *CUT FEEDS!*
WITNESSED BY MILLIONS.
BROADCAST AROUND THE WORLD.

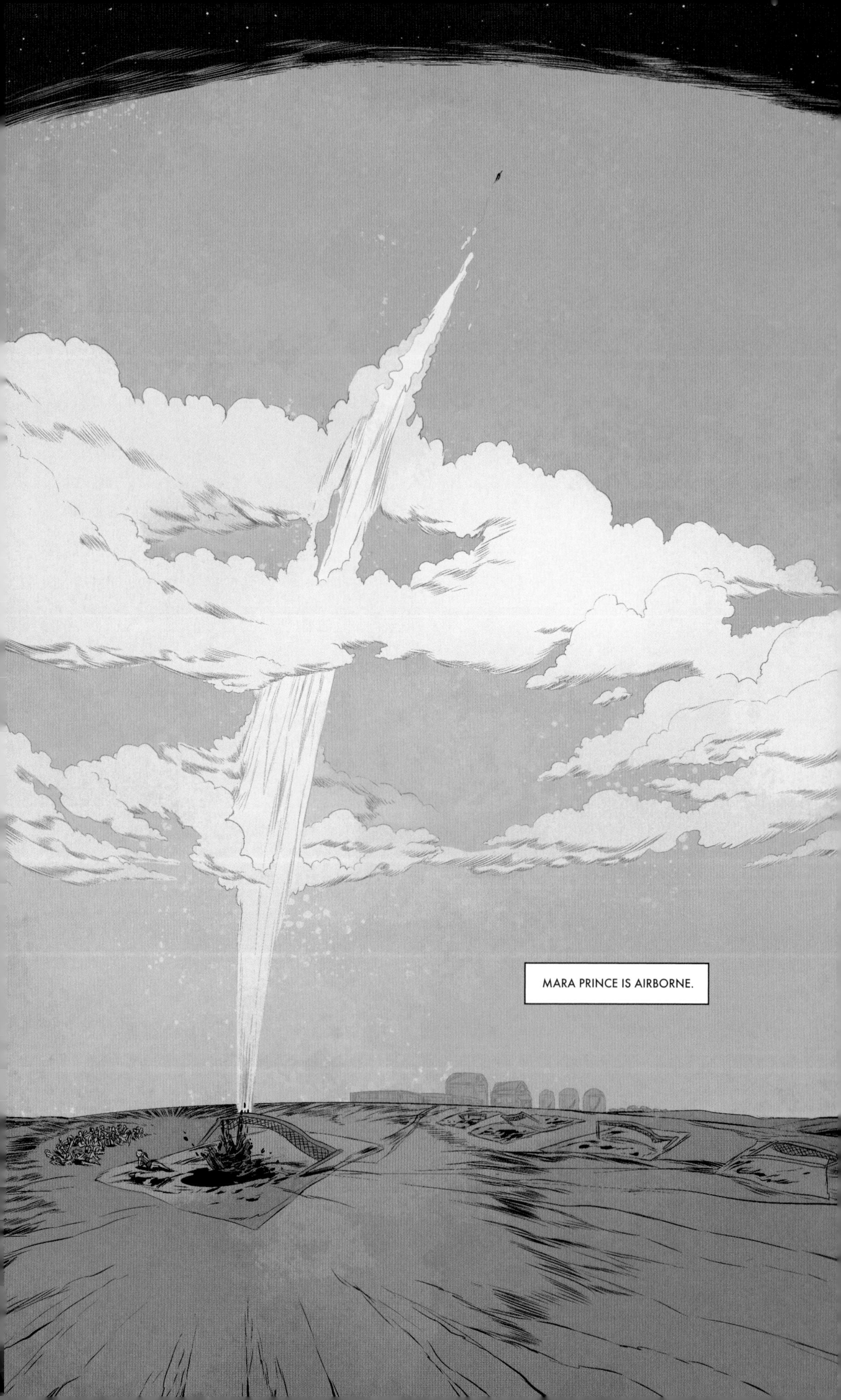
MARA PRINCE IS AIRBORNE.

CHAPTER THREE

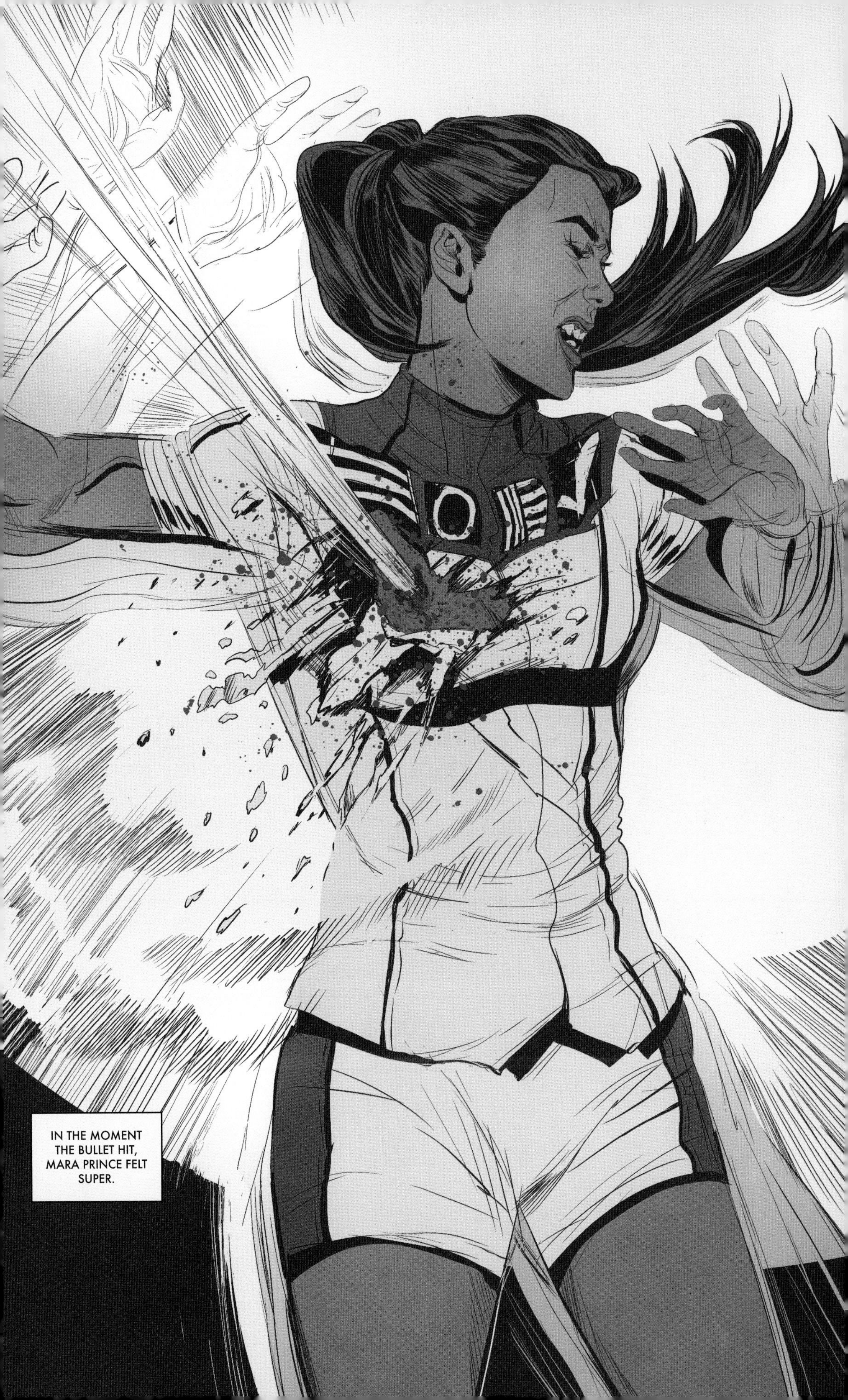
IN THE MOMENT THE BULLET HIT, MARA PRINCE FELT SUPER.

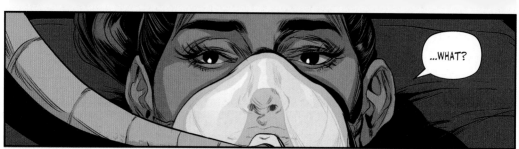

...WHAT?

INGRID?

WHAT IS IT? WHAT HAPPENED?

MARA, LOOK DOWN.

YOU WERE HIT WITH A .308 CALIBER BULLET, FIRED FROM A HUNTING RIFLE. THEY FOUND THE SHOOTER AND THE WEAPON.

THE BULLET WAS ON THE GROUND AT YOUR FEET. IT WAS ALL REAL, MARA, IT ALL HAPPENED.

AND YOU *DIDN'T* DIE.

HOW IS THAT *POSSIBLE?* WHEN IS THIS ALL GOING TO BE *EXPLAINED?*

...

WHY ISN'T THE AMBULANCE MOVING?

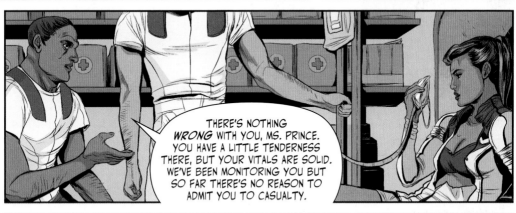

THERE'S NOTHING *WRONG* WITH YOU, MS. PRINCE. YOU HAVE A LITTLE TENDERNESS THERE, BUT YOUR VITALS ARE SOLID. WE'VE BEEN MONITORING YOU BUT SO FAR THERE'S NO REASON TO ADMIT YOU TO CASUALTY.

TAKE HER ANYWAY!

NO...

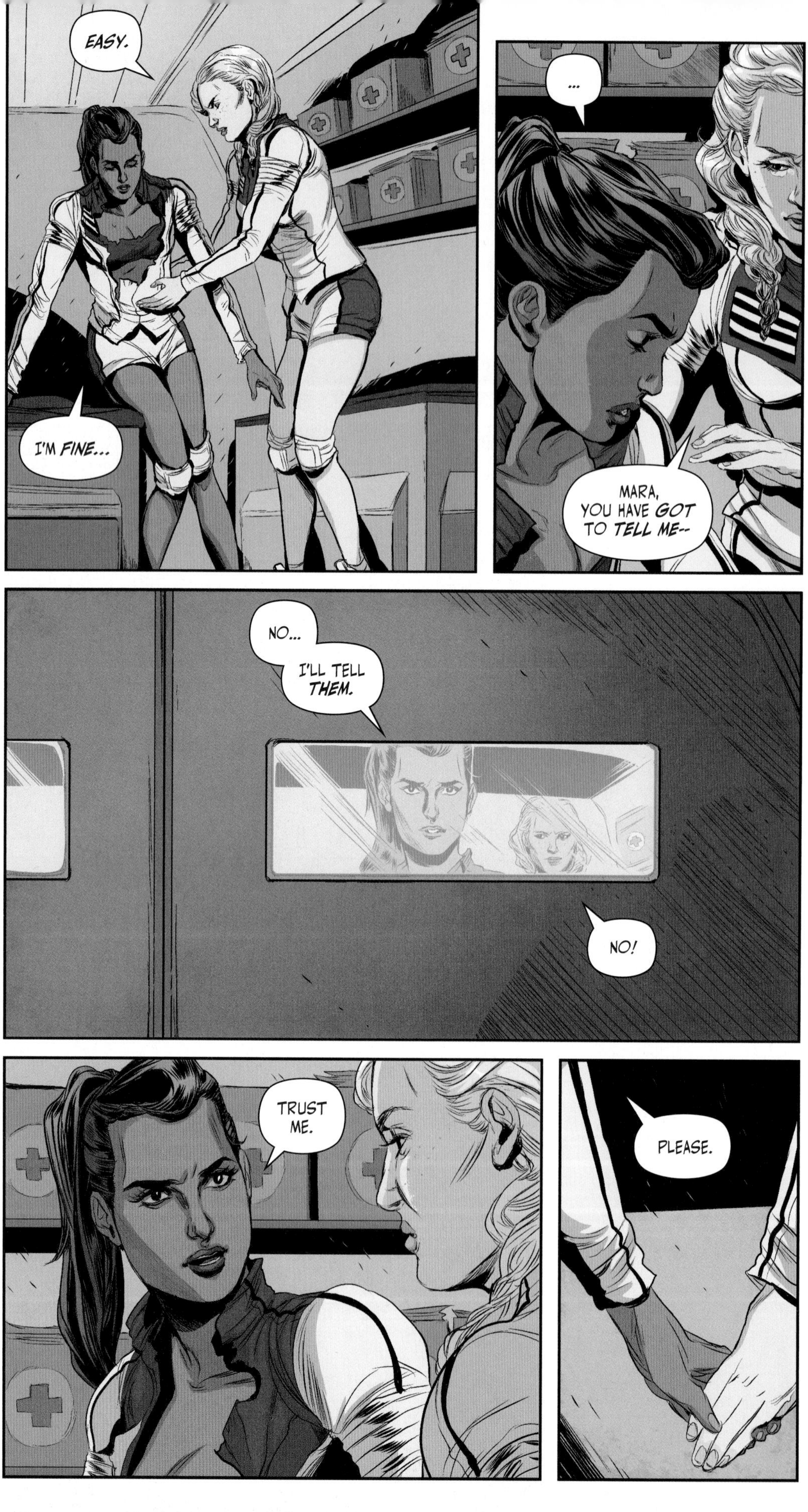

EASY.
I'M FINE...
...
MARA, YOU HAVE GOT TO TELL ME--
NO...
I'LL TELL THEM.
NO!
TRUST ME.
PLEASE.

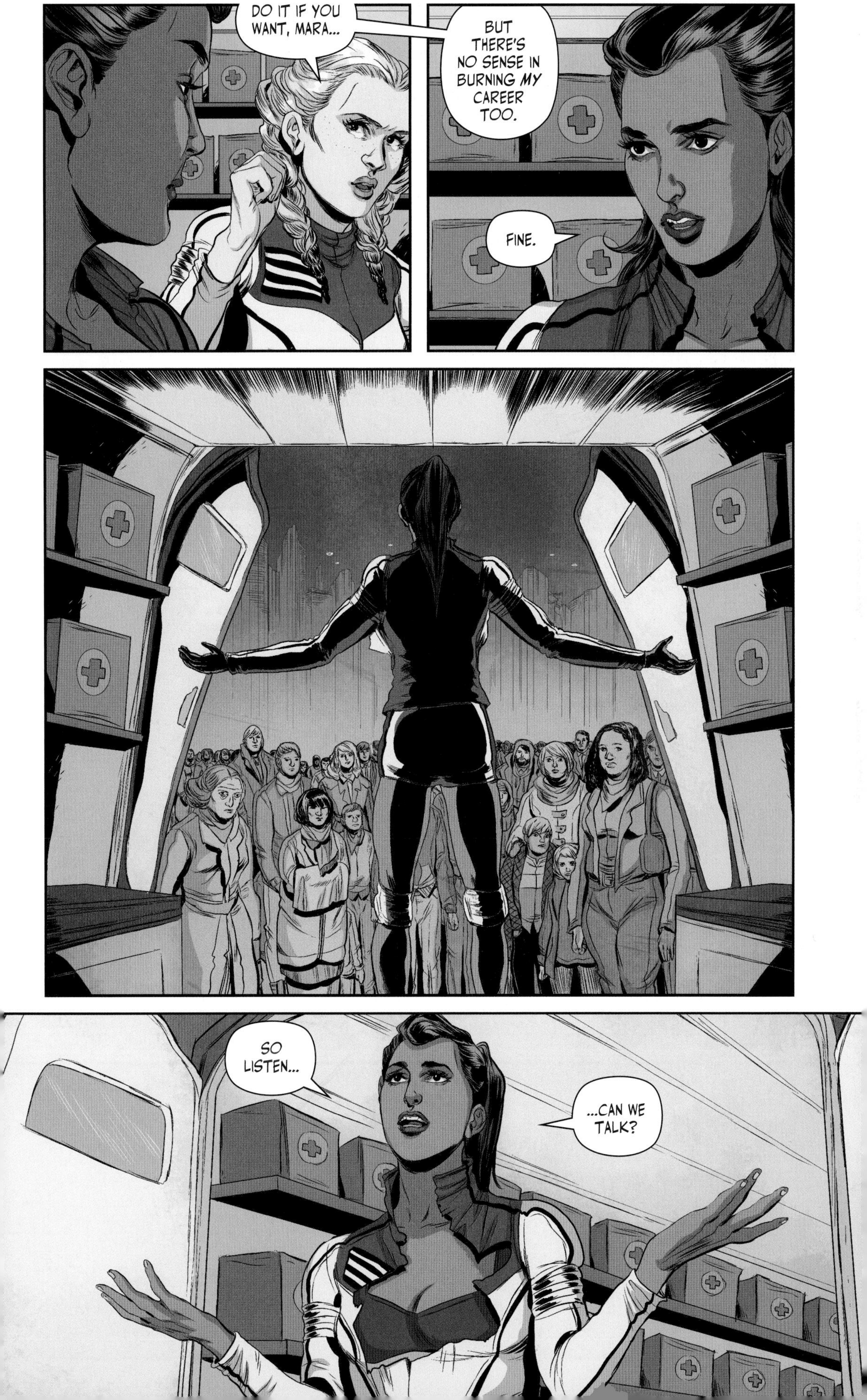
DO IT IF YOU WANT, MARA...
BUT THERE'S NO SENSE IN BURNING *MY* CAREER TOO.
FINE.
SO LISTEN...
...CAN WE TALK?

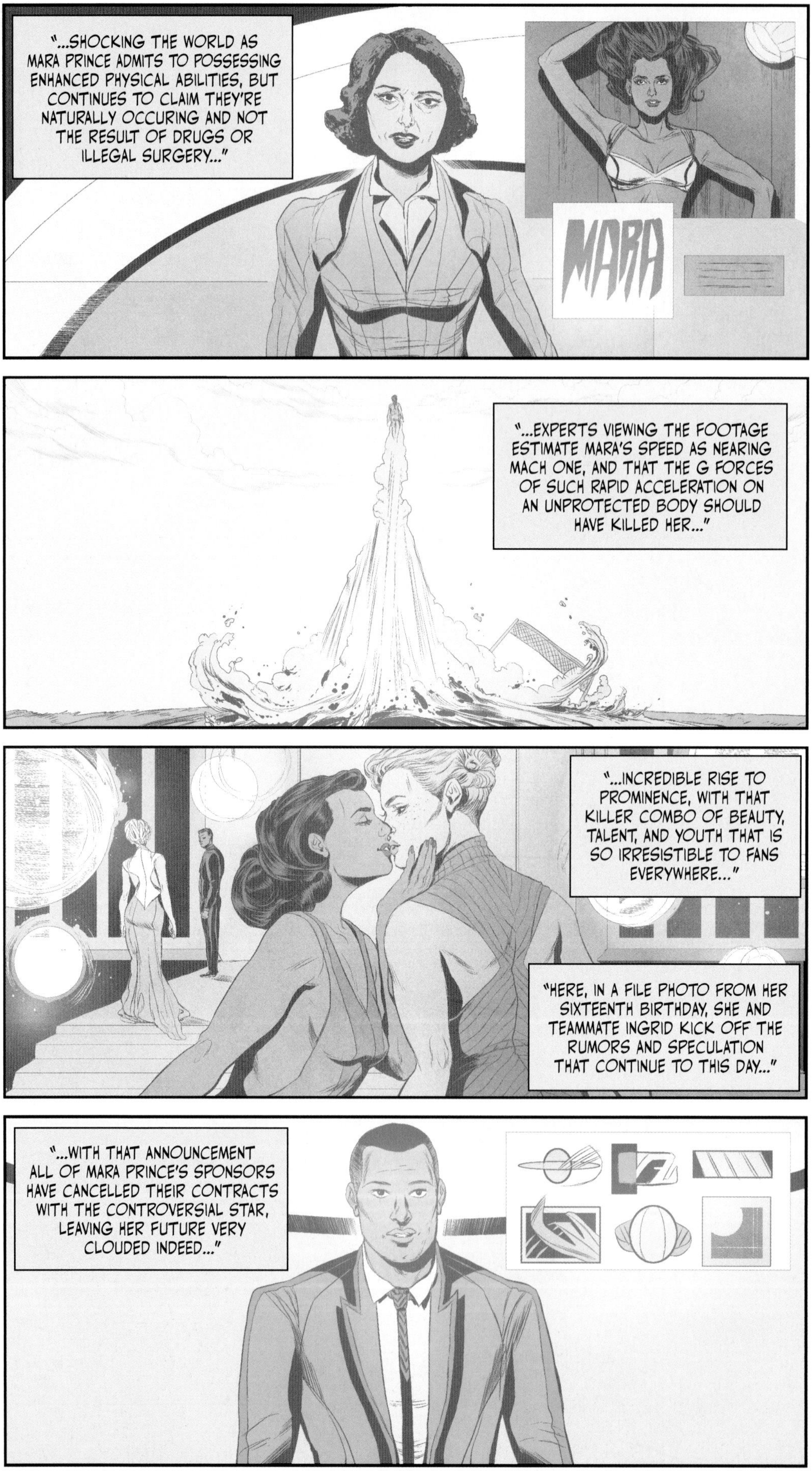
"...SHOCKING THE WORLD AS MARA PRINCE ADMITS TO POSSESSING ENHANCED PHYSICAL ABILITIES, BUT CONTINUES TO CLAIM THEY'RE NATURALLY OCCURING AND NOT THE RESULT OF DRUGS OR ILLEGAL SURGERY..."
MARA
"...EXPERTS VIEWING THE FOOTAGE ESTIMATE MARA'S SPEED AS NEARING MACH ONE, AND THAT THE G FORCES OF SUCH RAPID ACCELERATION ON AN UNPROTECTED BODY SHOULD HAVE KILLED HER..."
"...INCREDIBLE RISE TO PROMINENCE, WITH THAT KILLER COMBO OF BEAUTY, TALENT, AND YOUTH THAT IS SO IRRESISTIBLE TO FANS EVERYWHERE..."
"HERE, IN A FILE PHOTO FROM HER SIXTEENTH BIRTHDAY, SHE AND TEAMMATE INGRID KICK OFF THE RUMORS AND SPECULATION THAT CONTINUE TO THIS DAY..."
"...WITH THAT ANNOUNCEMENT ALL OF MARA PRINCE'S SPONSORS HAVE CANCELLED THEIR CONTRACTS WITH THE CONTROVERSIAL STAR, LEAVING HER FUTURE VERY CLOUDED INDEED..."

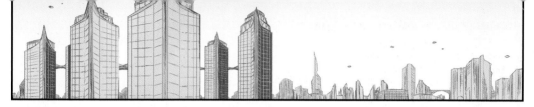

Earlier.

IS INGRID THERE?

THIS IS MARA PRINCE.

OKAY, THANKS.

klik

DIAL MANAGEMENT.

HELLO? HEY, THIS IS MARA. DID INGRID COME IN THIS MORNING? NO?

OKAY, ANY--OH, OKAY, THANKS.

klik

DIAL STAR THREE SIX OH.

HELLO? HI, MRS. ALDER, IT'S MARA.

HAVE YOU HEARD FROM INGRID? NO, NO, NOTHING HAPPENED.

I JUST--

...

NO PROBLEM. I'LL HAVE HER CALL YOU NEXT TIME I SEE HER.

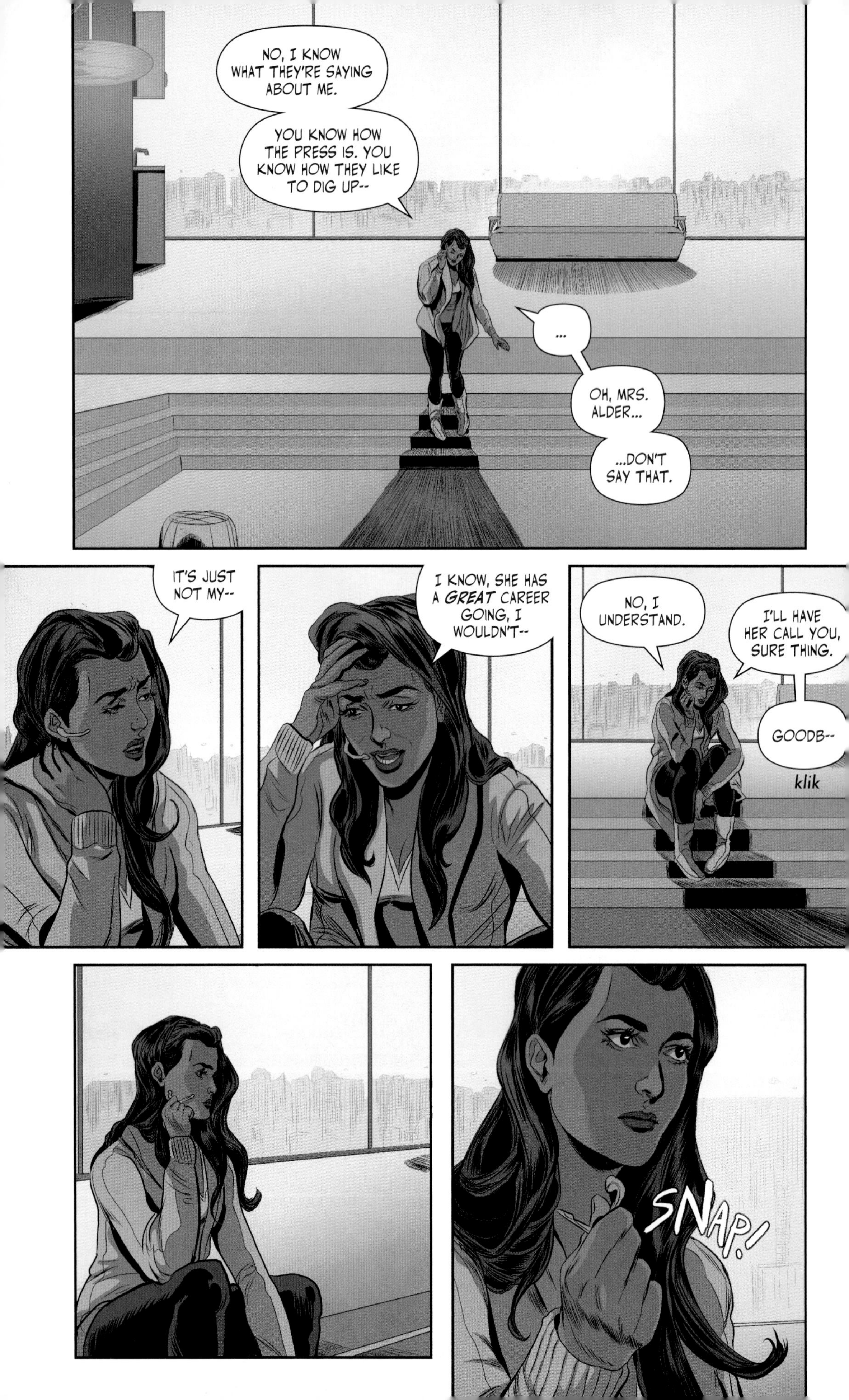
NO, I KNOW WHAT THEY'RE SAYING ABOUT ME.
YOU KNOW HOW THE PRESS IS. YOU KNOW HOW THEY LIKE TO DIG UP--
...
OH, MRS. ALDER...
...DON'T SAY THAT.
IT'S JUST NOT MY--
I KNOW, SHE HAS A GREAT CAREER GOING, I WOULDN'T--
NO, I UNDERSTAND.
I'LL HAVE HER CALL YOU, SURE THING.
GOODB--
klik
SNAP!

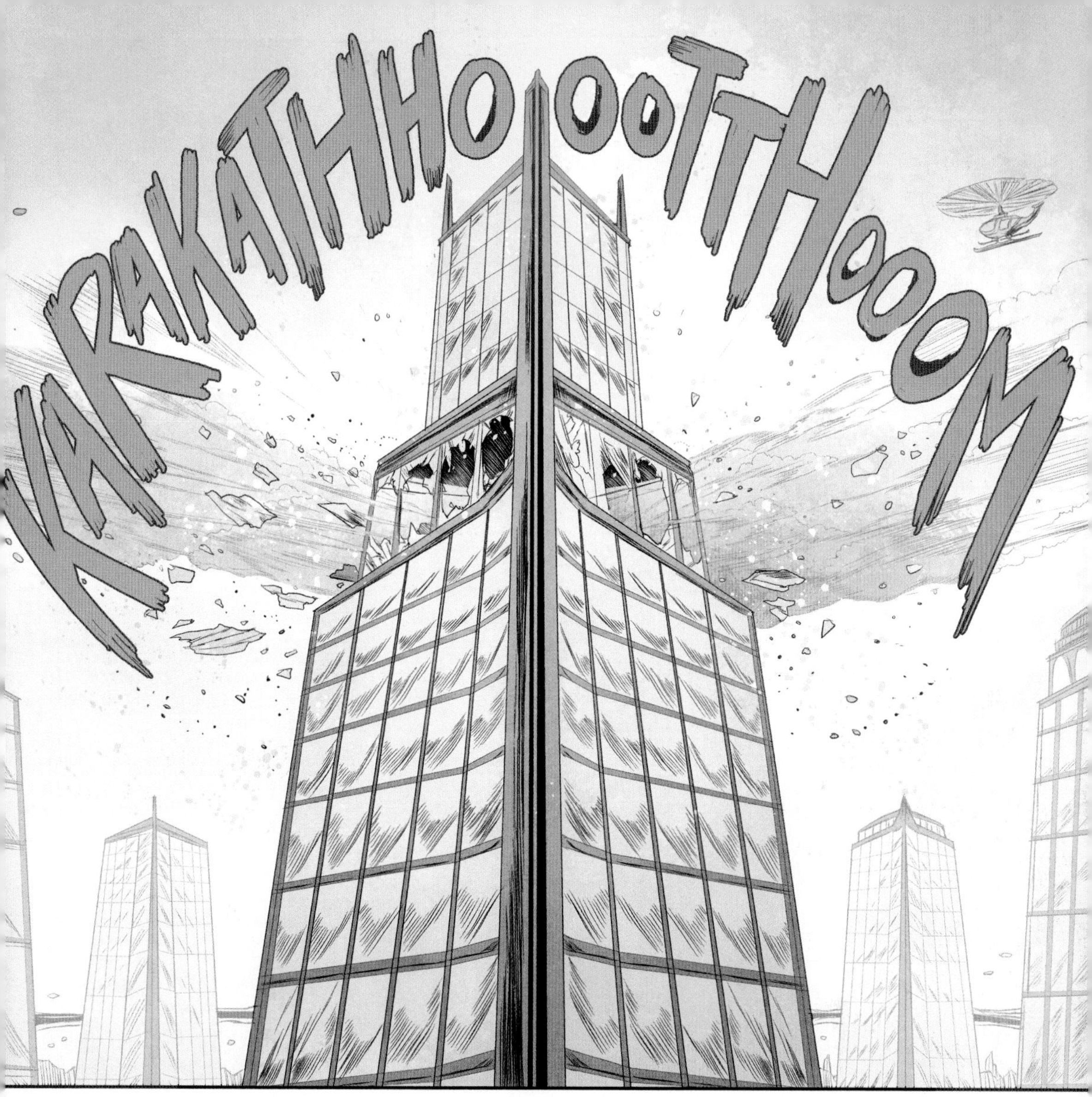
KARAKATHHOOOOTTHOOOOM

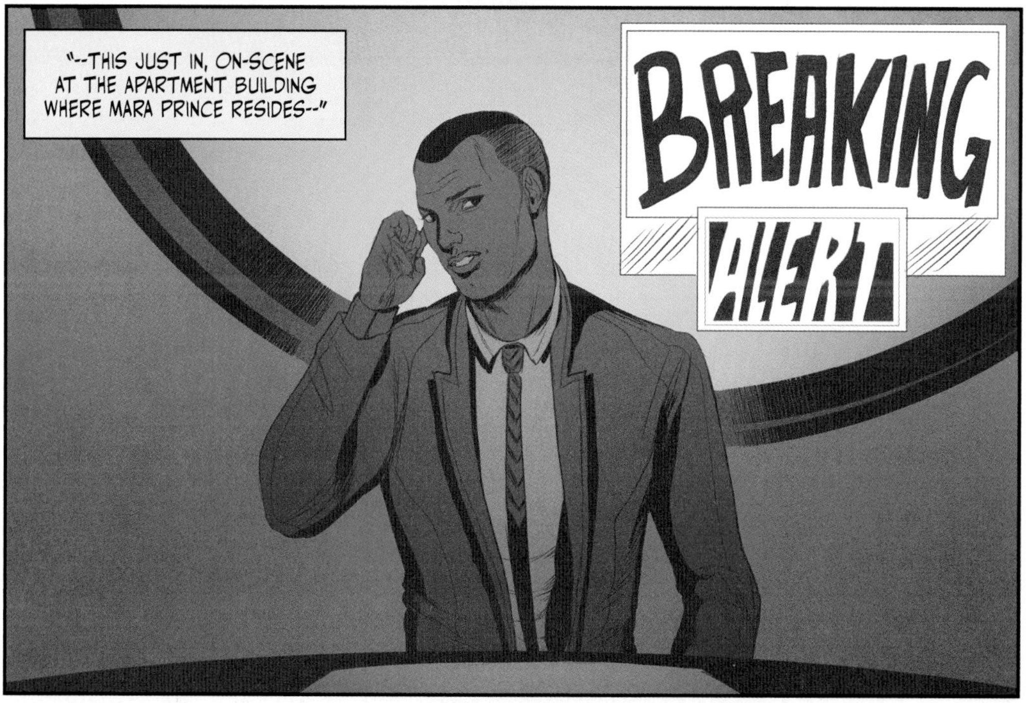
"--THIS JUST IN, ON-SCENE AT THE APARTMENT BUILDING WHERE MARA PRINCE RESIDES--"
BREAKING
ALERT

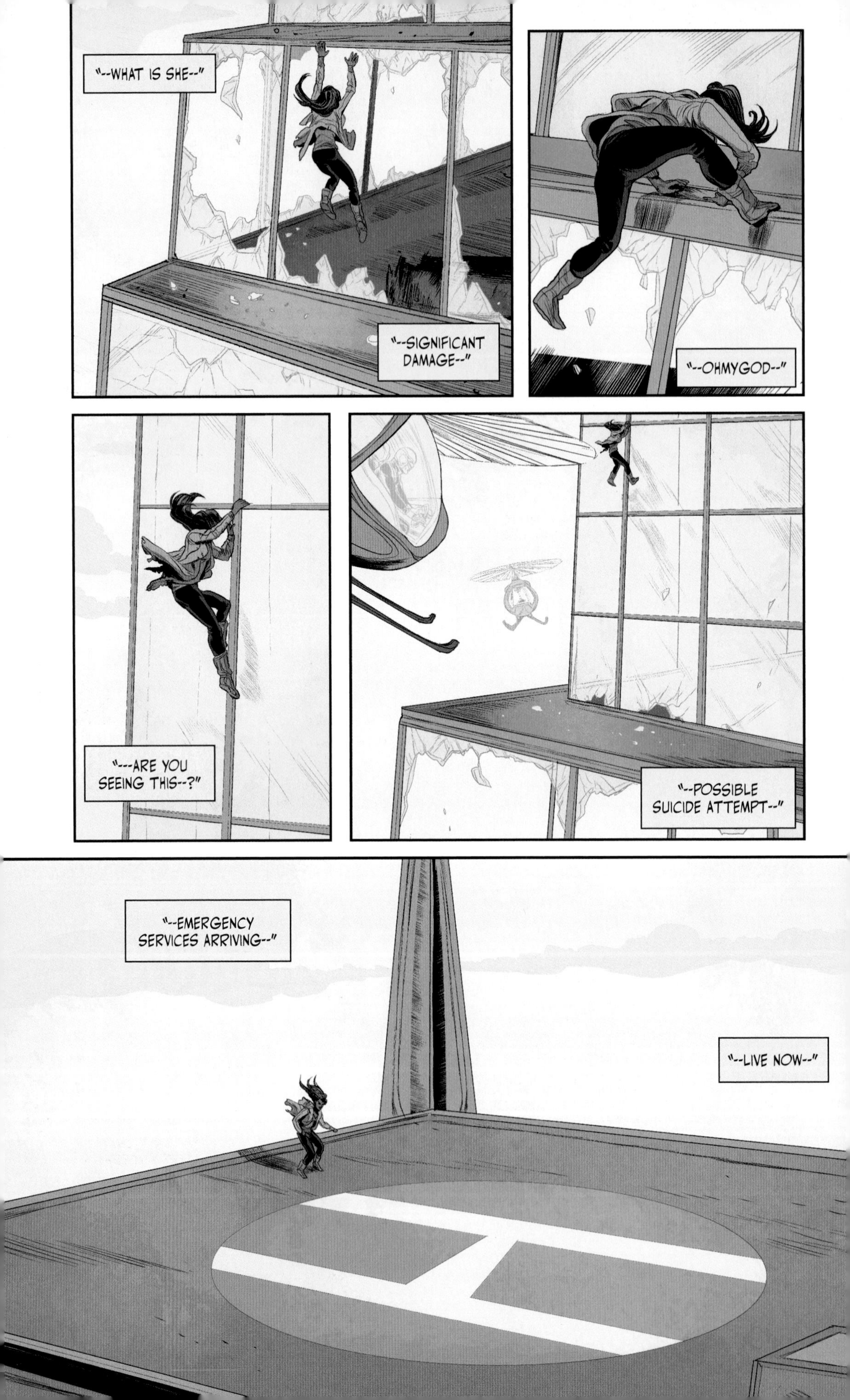
"--WHAT IS SHE--"
"--SIGNIFICANT DAMAGE--"
"--OHMYGOD--"
"---ARE YOU SEEING THIS--?"
"--POSSIBLE SUICIDE ATTEMPT--"
"--EMERGENCY SERVICES ARRIVING--"
"--LIVE NOW--"

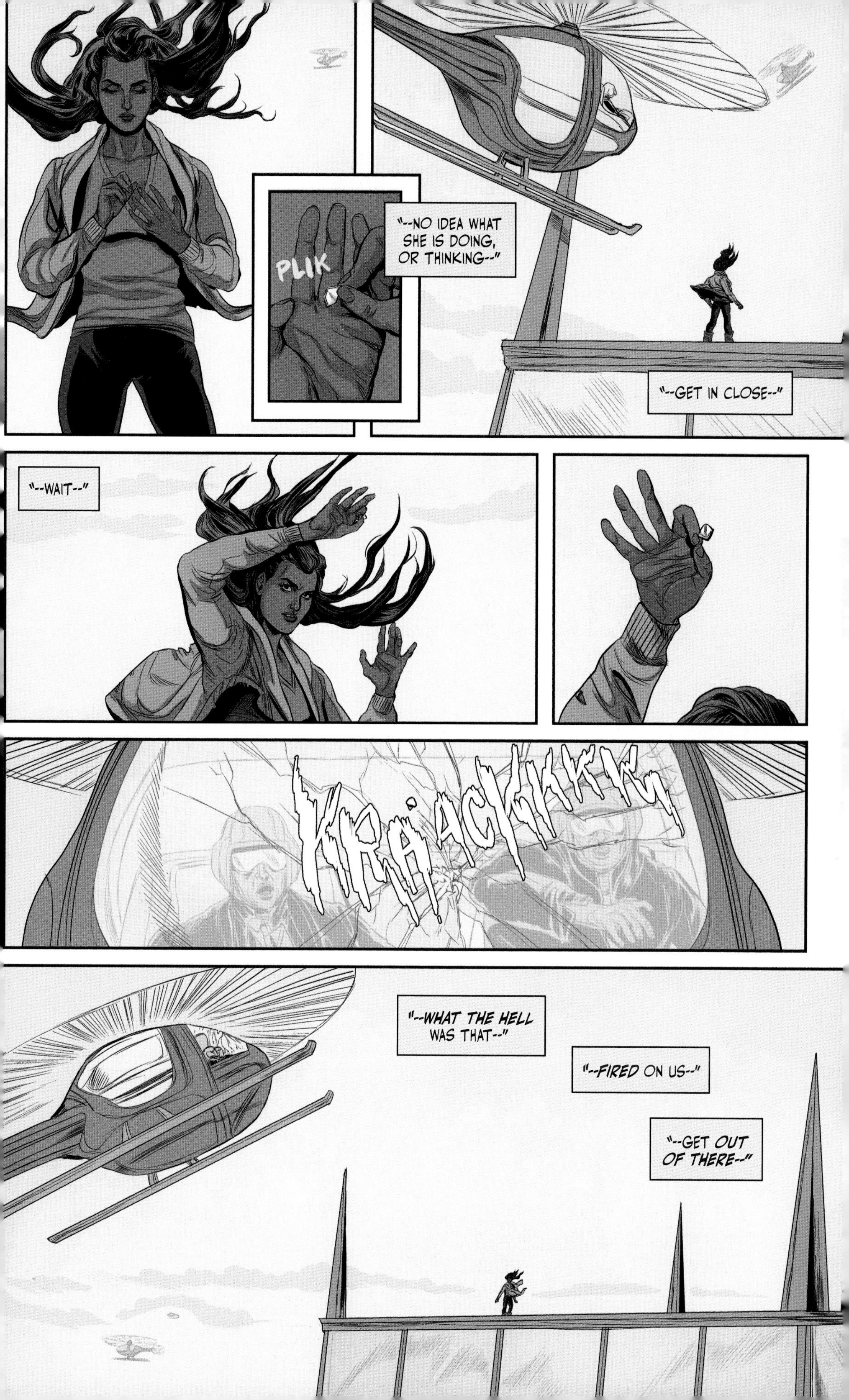

PLIK
"--NO IDEA WHAT SHE IS DOING, OR THINKING--"
"--GET IN CLOSE--"
"--WAIT--"
KRAACKKKK
"--WHAT THE HELL WAS THAT--"
"--FIRED ON US--"
"--GET OUT OF THERE--"

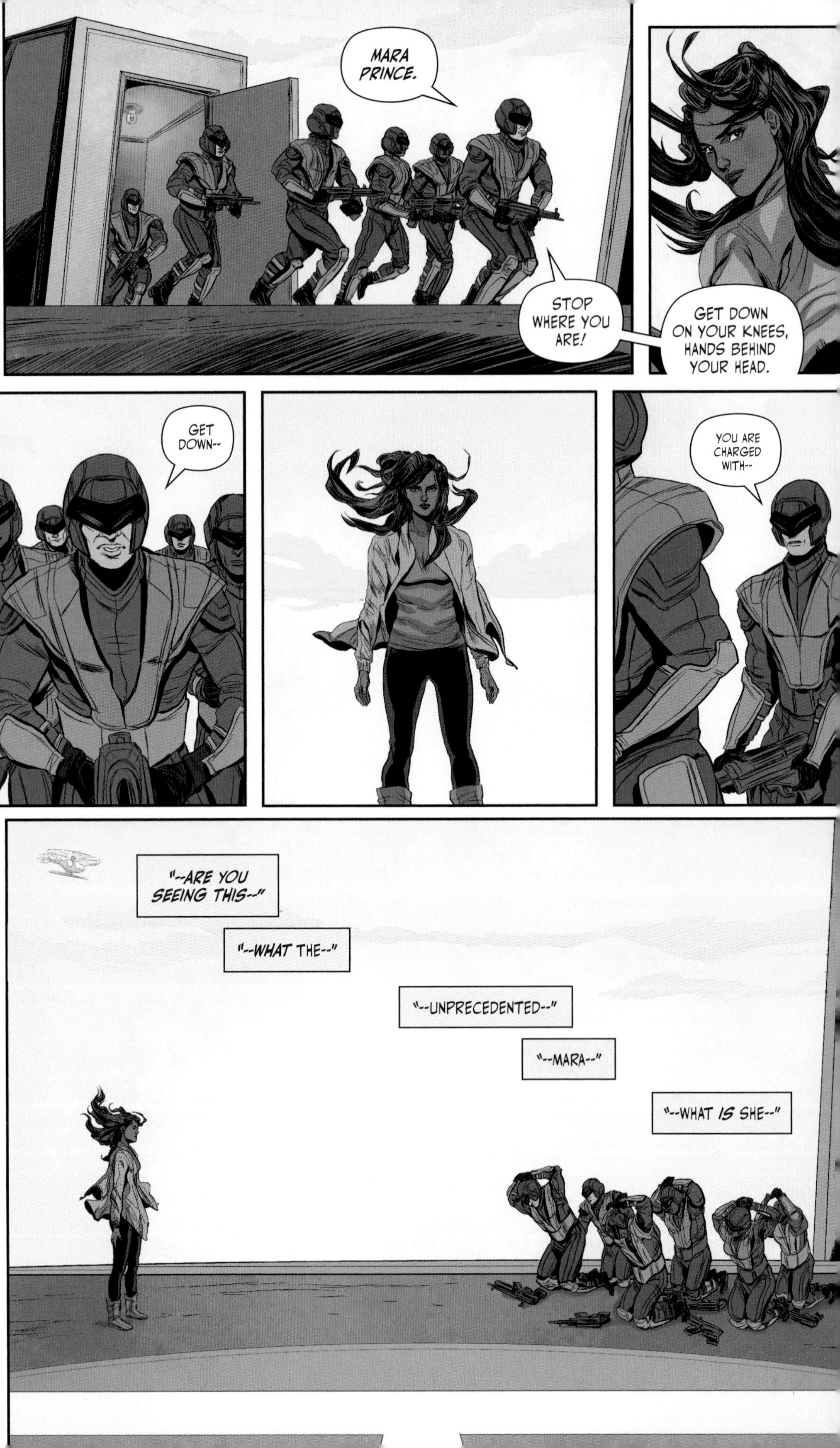
MARA PRINCE.
STOP WHERE YOU ARE!
GET DOWN ON YOUR KNEES, HANDS BEHIND YOUR HEAD.
GET DOWN--
YOU ARE CHARGED WITH--
"--ARE YOU SEEING THIS--"
"--WHAT THE--"
"--UNPRECEDENTED--"
"--MARA--"
"--WHAT IS SHE--"

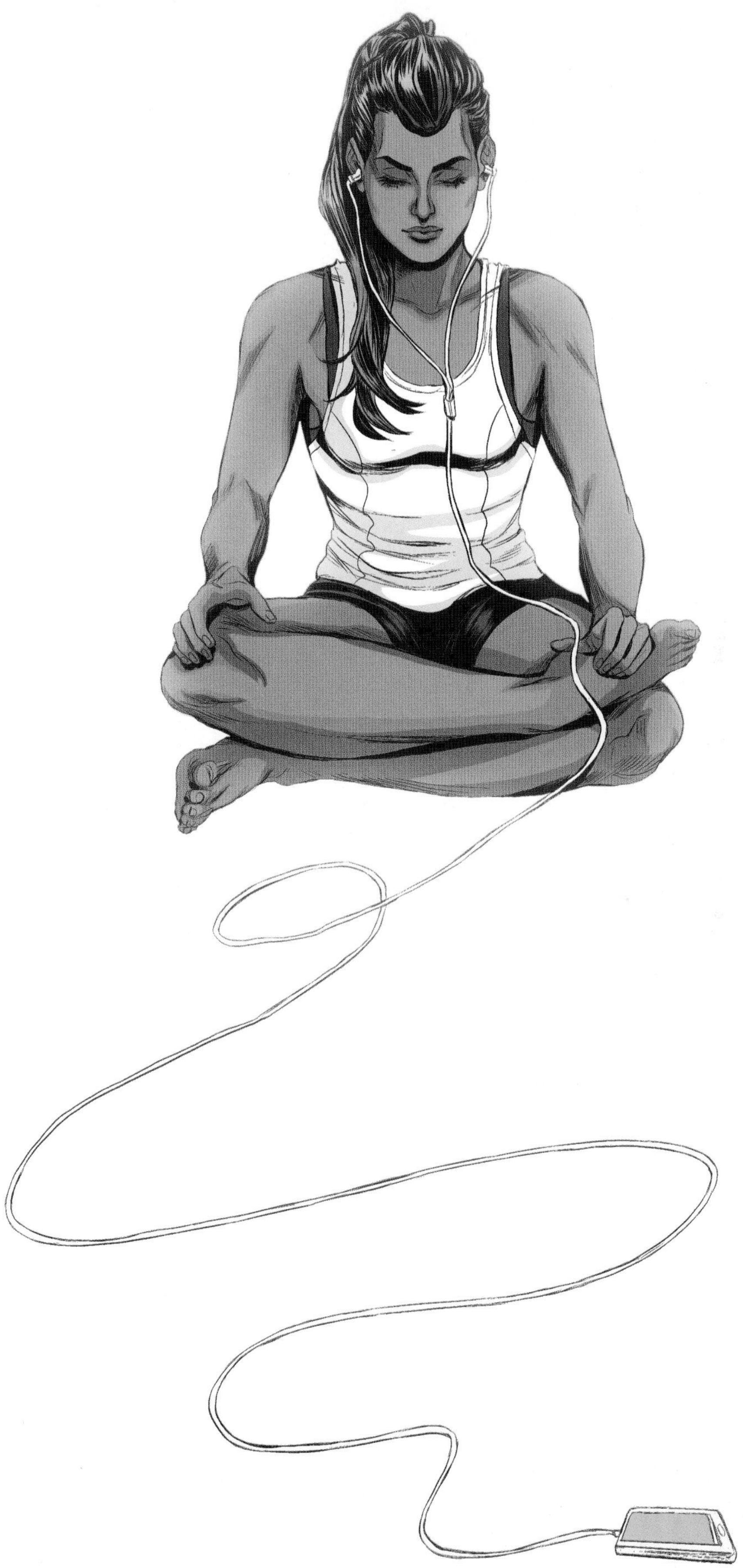

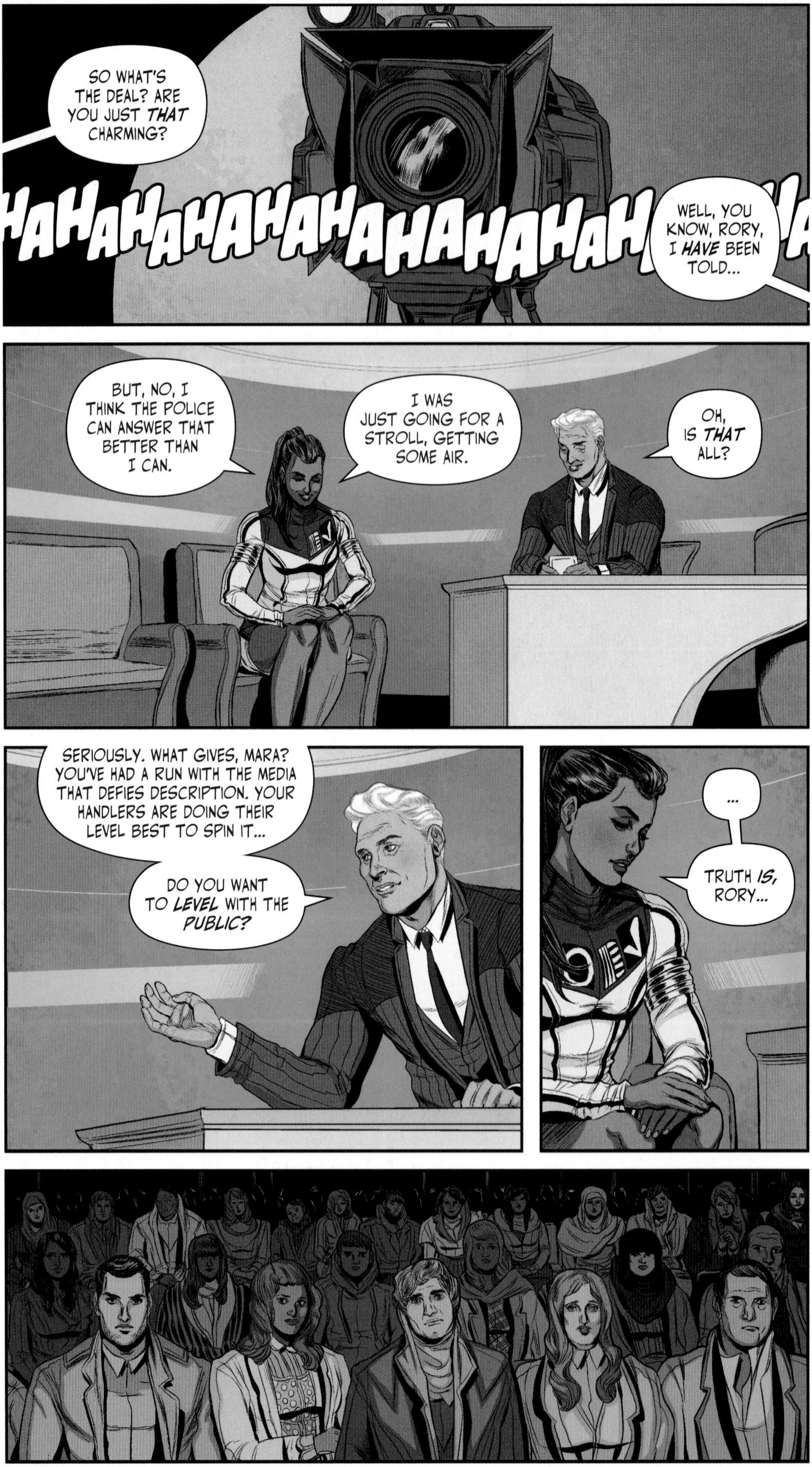
SO WHAT'S THE DEAL? ARE YOU JUST *THAT* CHARMING?
HAHAHAHAHAHAHAHAHAHAHAHAH
WELL, YOU KNOW, RORY, I *HAVE* BEEN TOLD...
BUT, NO, I THINK THE POLICE CAN ANSWER THAT BETTER THAN I CAN.
I WAS JUST GOING FOR A STROLL, GETTING SOME AIR.
OH, IS *THAT* ALL?
SERIOUSLY. WHAT GIVES, MARA? YOU'VE HAD A RUN WITH THE MEDIA THAT DEFIES DESCRIPTION. YOUR HANDLERS ARE DOING THEIR LEVEL BEST TO SPIN IT...
DO YOU WANT TO *LEVEL* WITH THE *PUBLIC?*
...
TRUTH *IS,* RORY...

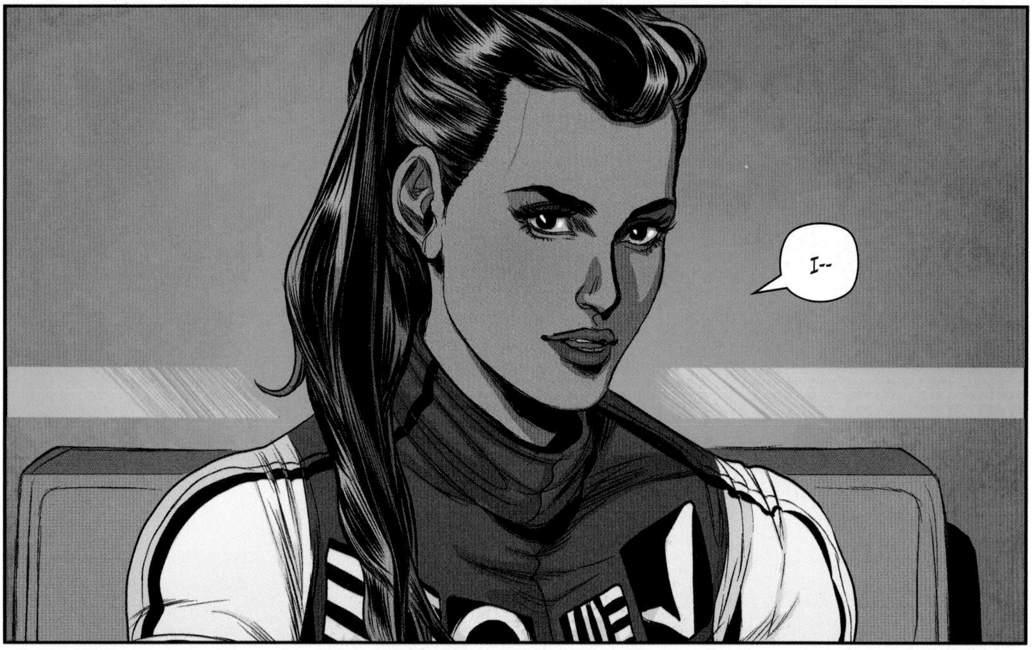
I--

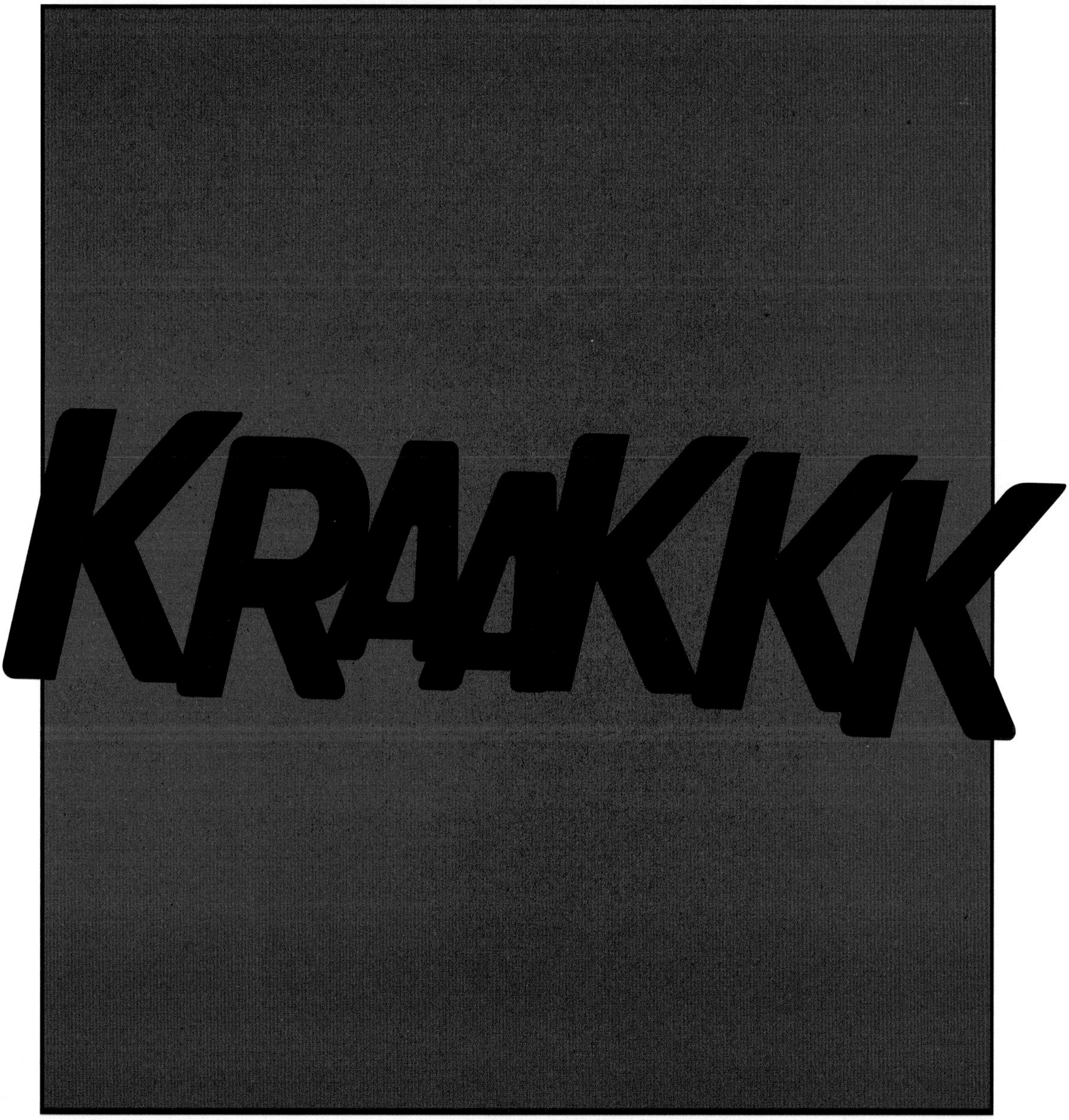
KRAAKKK

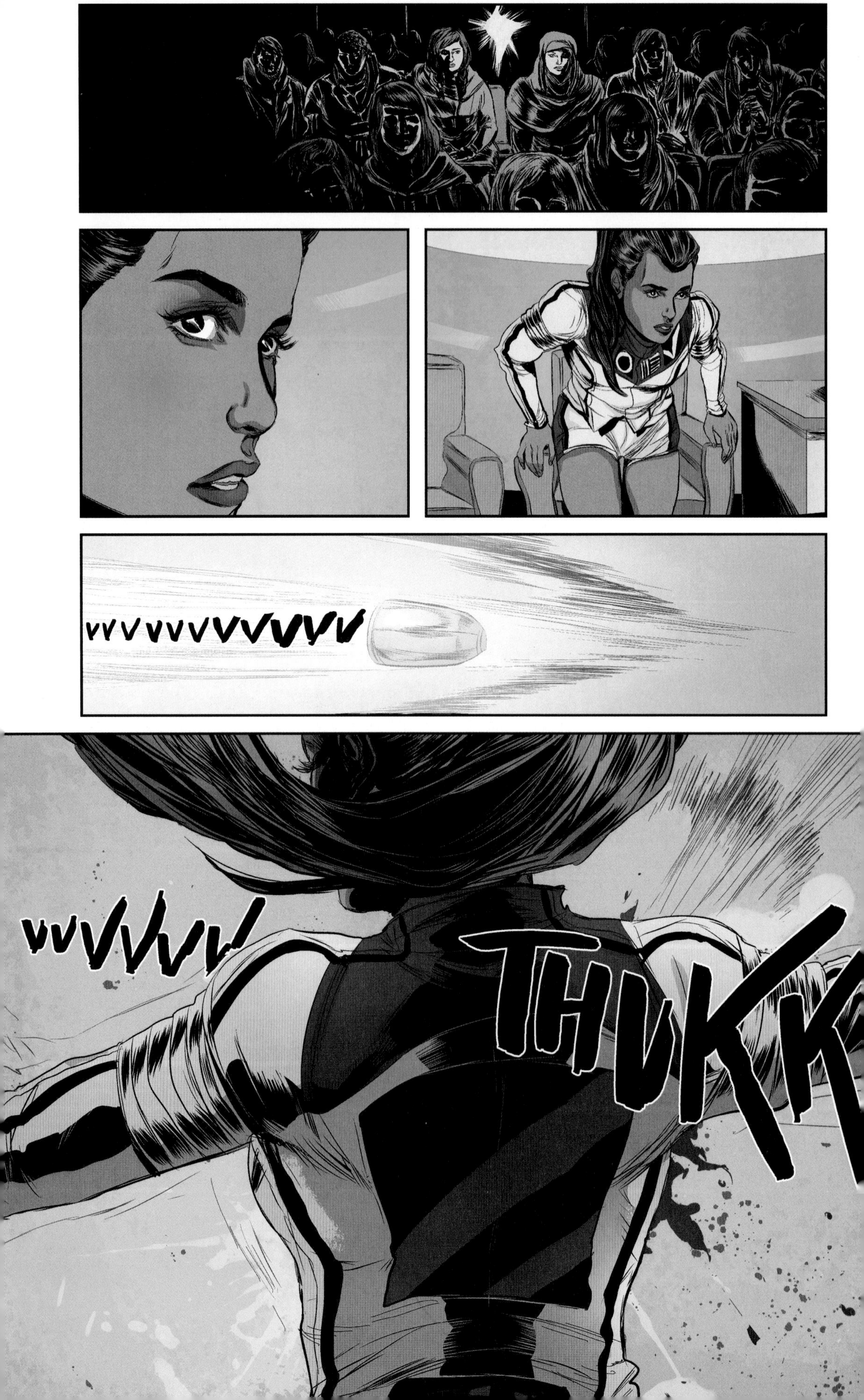
VVVVVVVVVVVVV
VVVVVV
THUKK

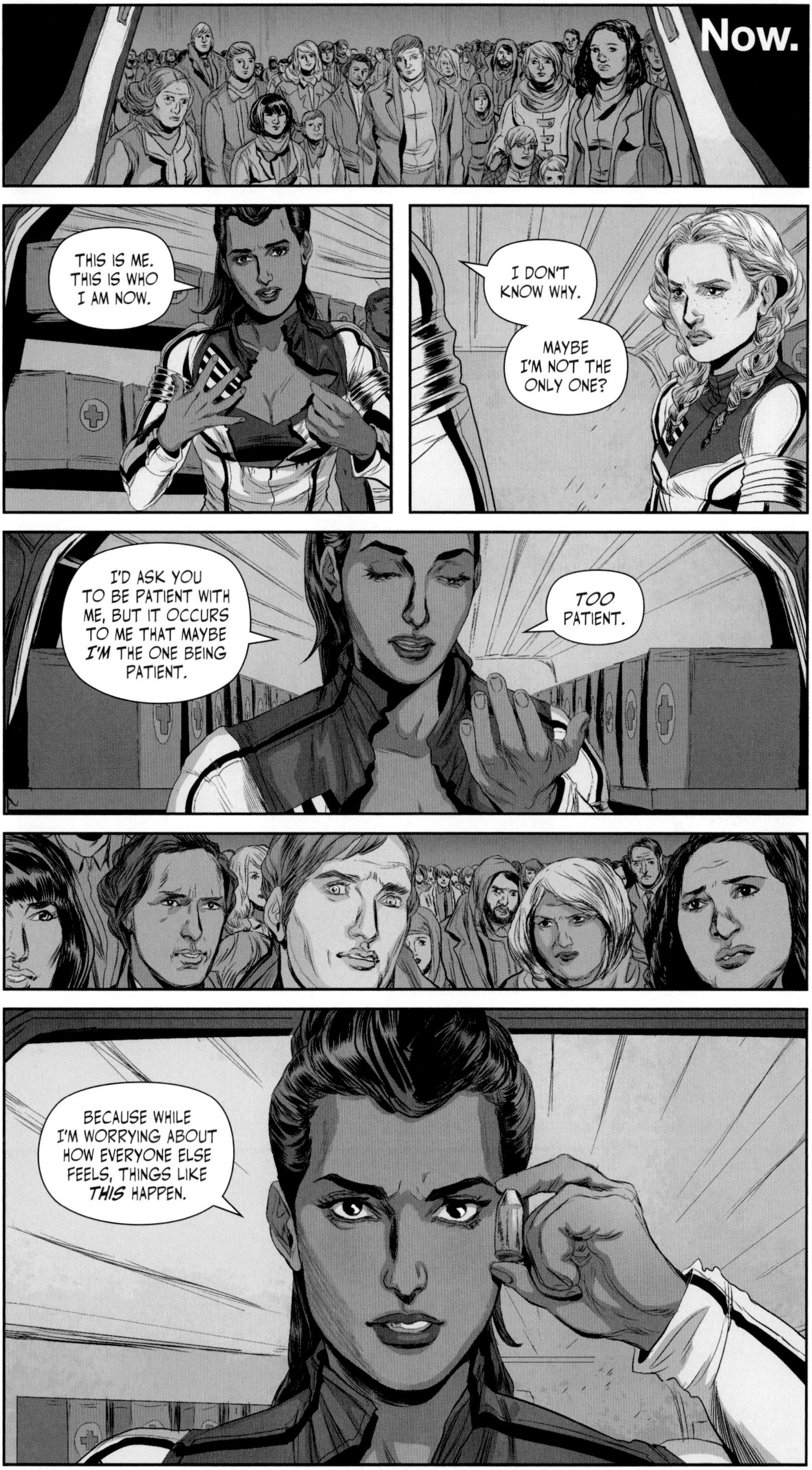
Now.
THIS IS ME. THIS IS WHO I AM NOW.
I DON'T KNOW WHY.
MAYBE I'M NOT THE ONLY ONE?
I'D ASK YOU TO BE PATIENT WITH ME, BUT IT OCCURS TO ME THAT MAYBE *I'M* THE ONE BEING PATIENT.
TOO PATIENT.
BECAUSE WHILE I'M WORRYING ABOUT HOW EVERYONE ELSE FEELS, THINGS LIKE *THIS* HAPPEN.

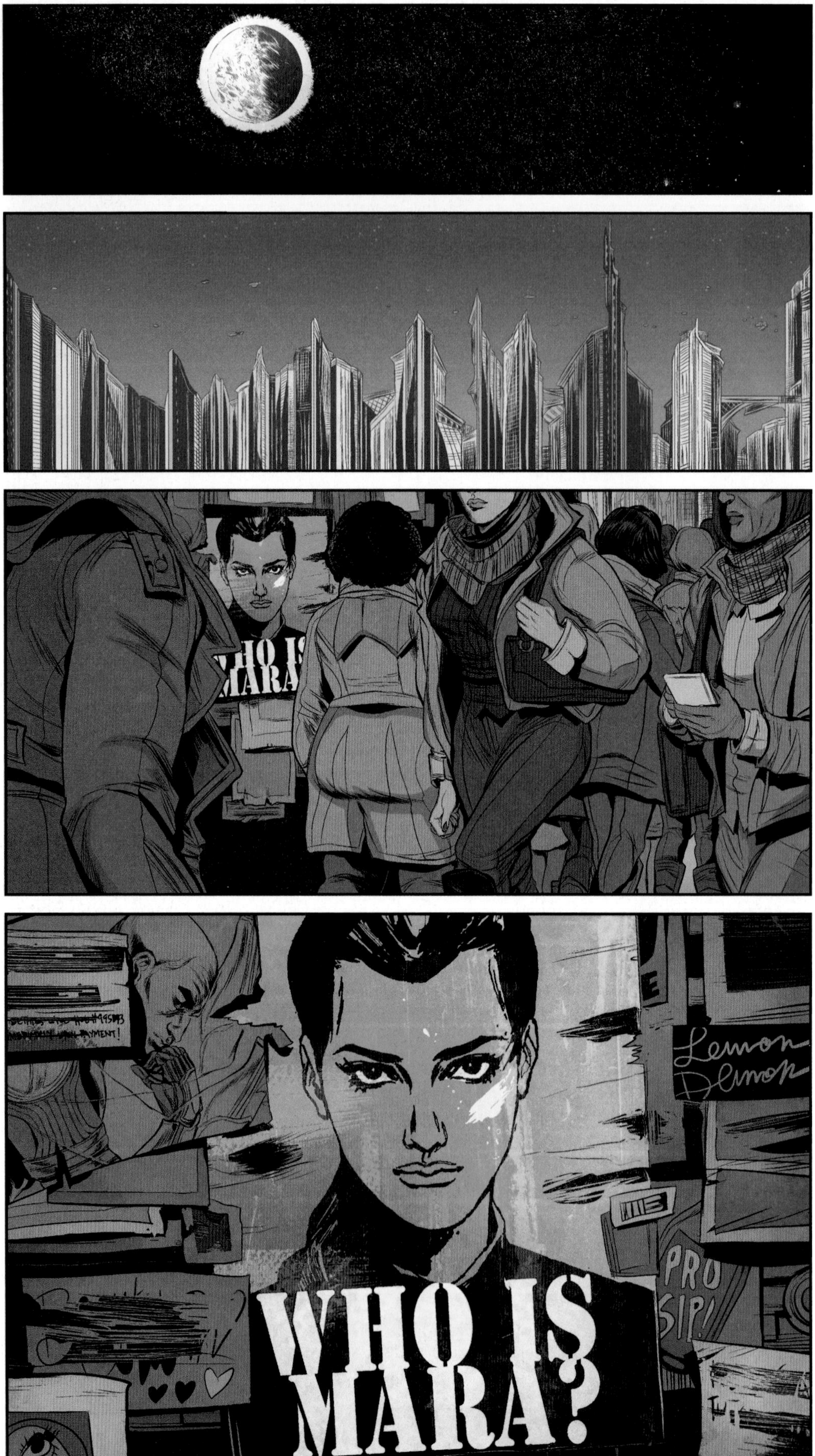
WHO IS MARA?
Lemon Demon
PRO SIP!
WHO IS MARA?

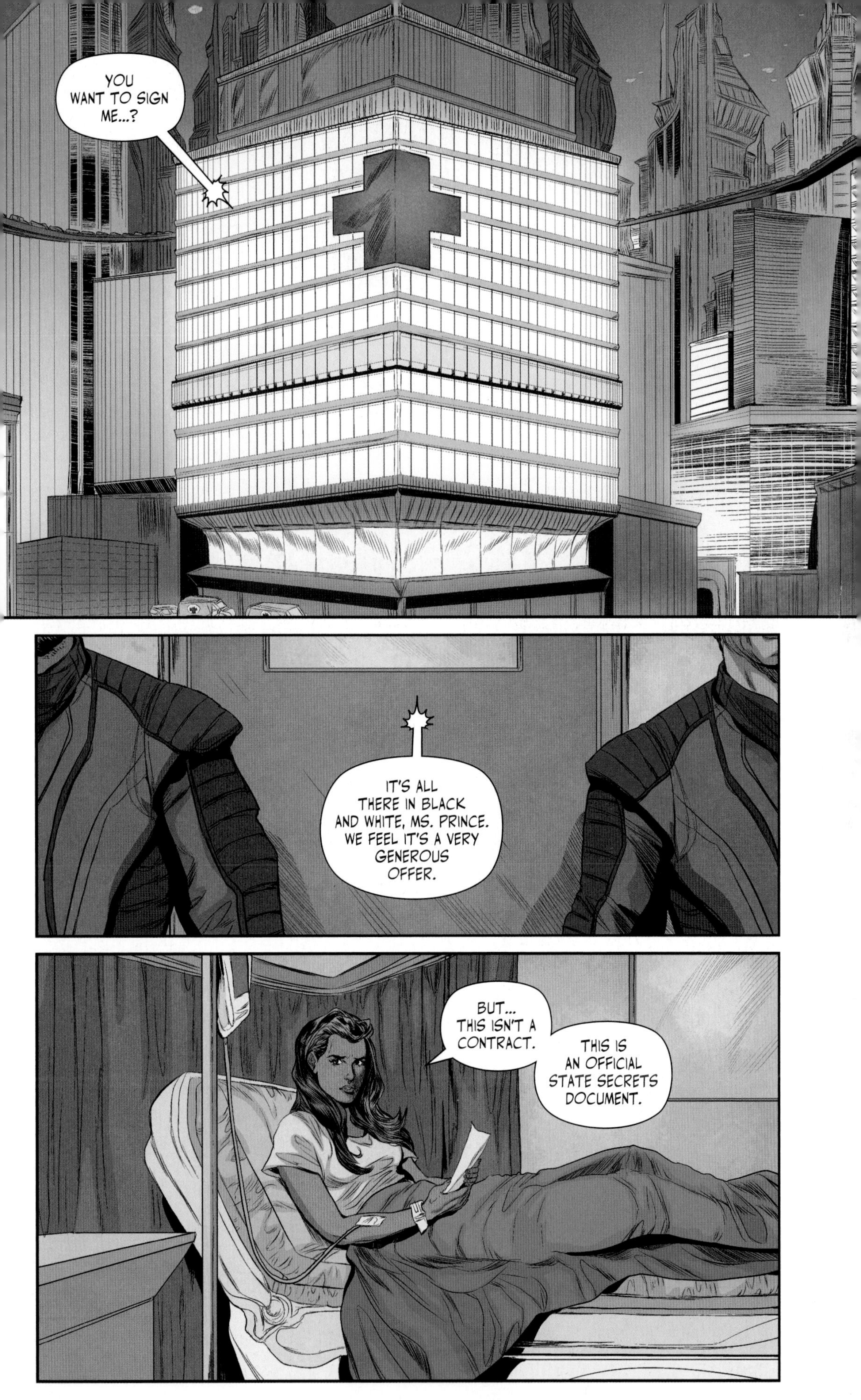
YOU WANT TO SIGN ME...?
IT'S ALL THERE IN BLACK AND WHITE, MS. PRINCE. WE FEEL IT'S A VERY GENEROUS OFFER.
BUT... THIS ISN'T A CONTRACT.
THIS IS AN OFFICIAL STATE SECRETS DOCUMENT.

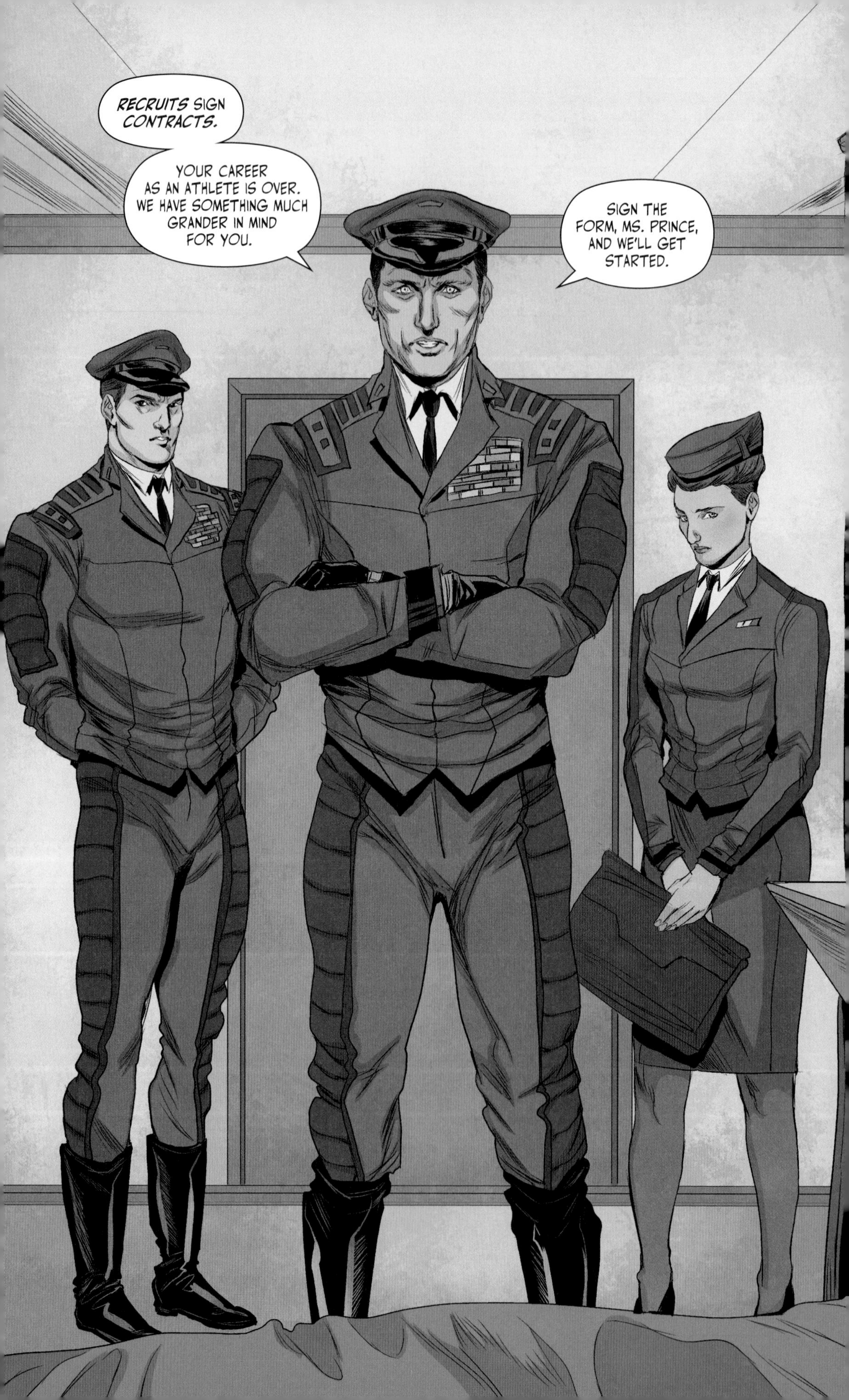
RECRUITS SIGN CONTRACTS.
YOUR CAREER AS AN ATHLETE IS OVER. WE HAVE SOMETHING MUCH GRANDER IN MIND FOR YOU.
SIGN THE FORM, MS. PRINCE, AND WE'LL GET STARTED.

CHAPTER FOUR

SO LET'S BEGIN AGAIN.

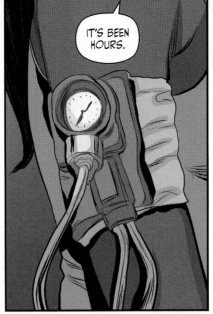

IT'S BEEN HOURS.

SEVEN AND A HALF HOURS, TO BE EXACT. WE'VE HAD A SHIFT CHANGE, WE'VE HAD TO RE-ADMINISTER THE TREATMENTS TWICE, AND I'VE MISSED LUNCH.

AND IN *ALL THAT TIME* YOU'VE NOT ASKED FOR A BITE OF FOOD OR A DROP OF WATER, AND LOOK NONE THE WORSE FOR IT.

YOU ARE AN INTERESTING WOMAN, MS. PRINCE.

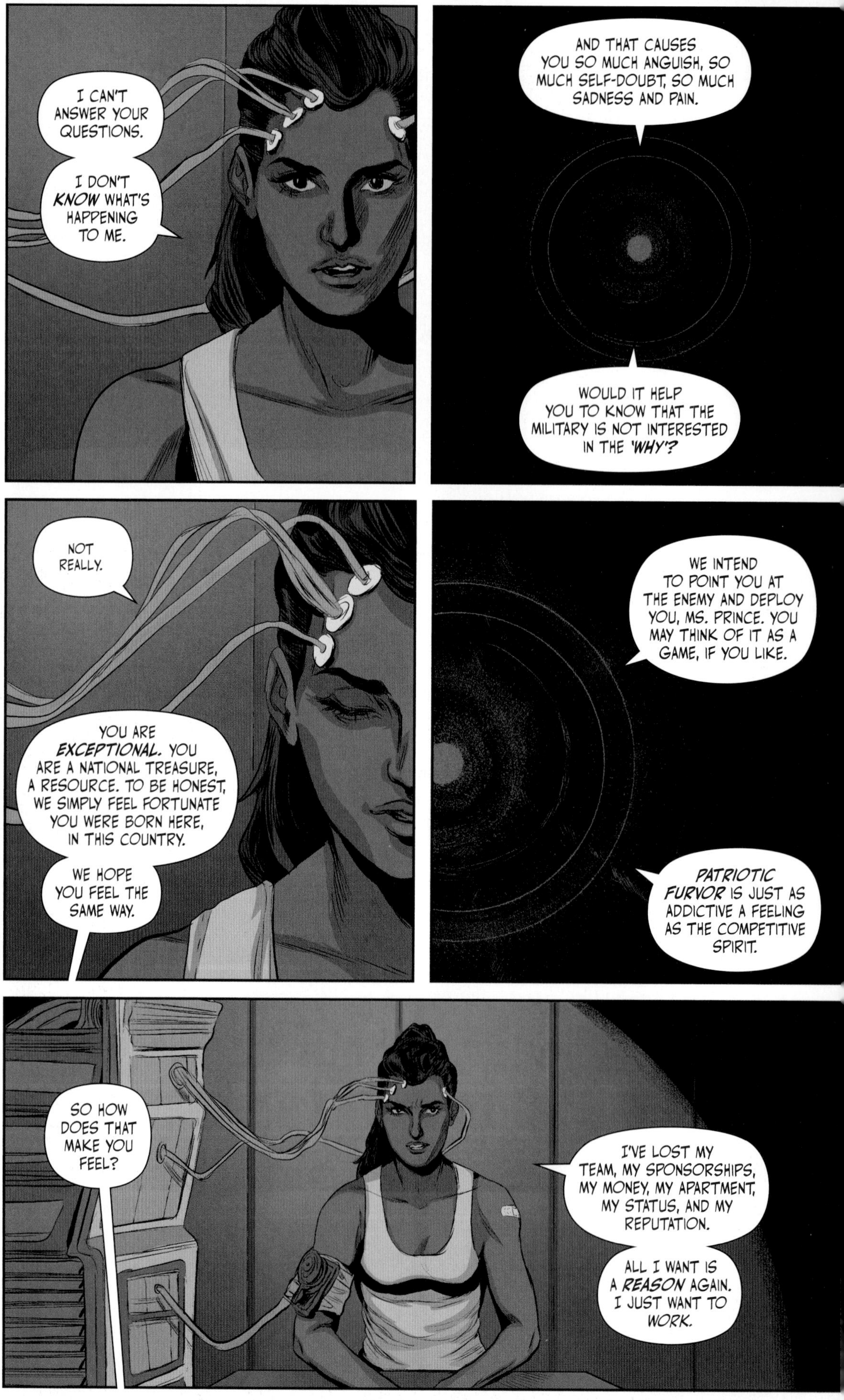
I CAN'T ANSWER YOUR QUESTIONS.
I DON'T *KNOW* WHAT'S HAPPENING TO ME.
AND THAT CAUSES YOU SO MUCH ANGUISH, SO MUCH SELF-DOUBT, SO MUCH SADNESS AND PAIN.
WOULD IT HELP YOU TO KNOW THAT THE MILITARY IS NOT INTERESTED IN THE *'WHY'*?
NOT REALLY.
WE INTEND TO POINT YOU AT THE ENEMY AND DEPLOY YOU, MS. PRINCE. YOU MAY THINK OF IT AS A GAME, IF YOU LIKE.
YOU ARE *EXCEPTIONAL.* YOU ARE A NATIONAL TREASURE, A RESOURCE. TO BE HONEST, WE SIMPLY FEEL FORTUNATE YOU WERE BORN HERE, IN THIS COUNTRY.
WE HOPE YOU FEEL THE SAME WAY.
PATRIOTIC FURVOR IS JUST AS ADDICTIVE A FEELING AS THE COMPETITIVE SPIRIT.
SO HOW DOES THAT MAKE YOU FEEL?
I'VE LOST MY TEAM, MY SPONSORSHIPS, MY MONEY, MY APARTMENT, MY STATUS, AND MY REPUTATION.
ALL I WANT IS A *REASON* AGAIN. I JUST WANT TO *WORK.*

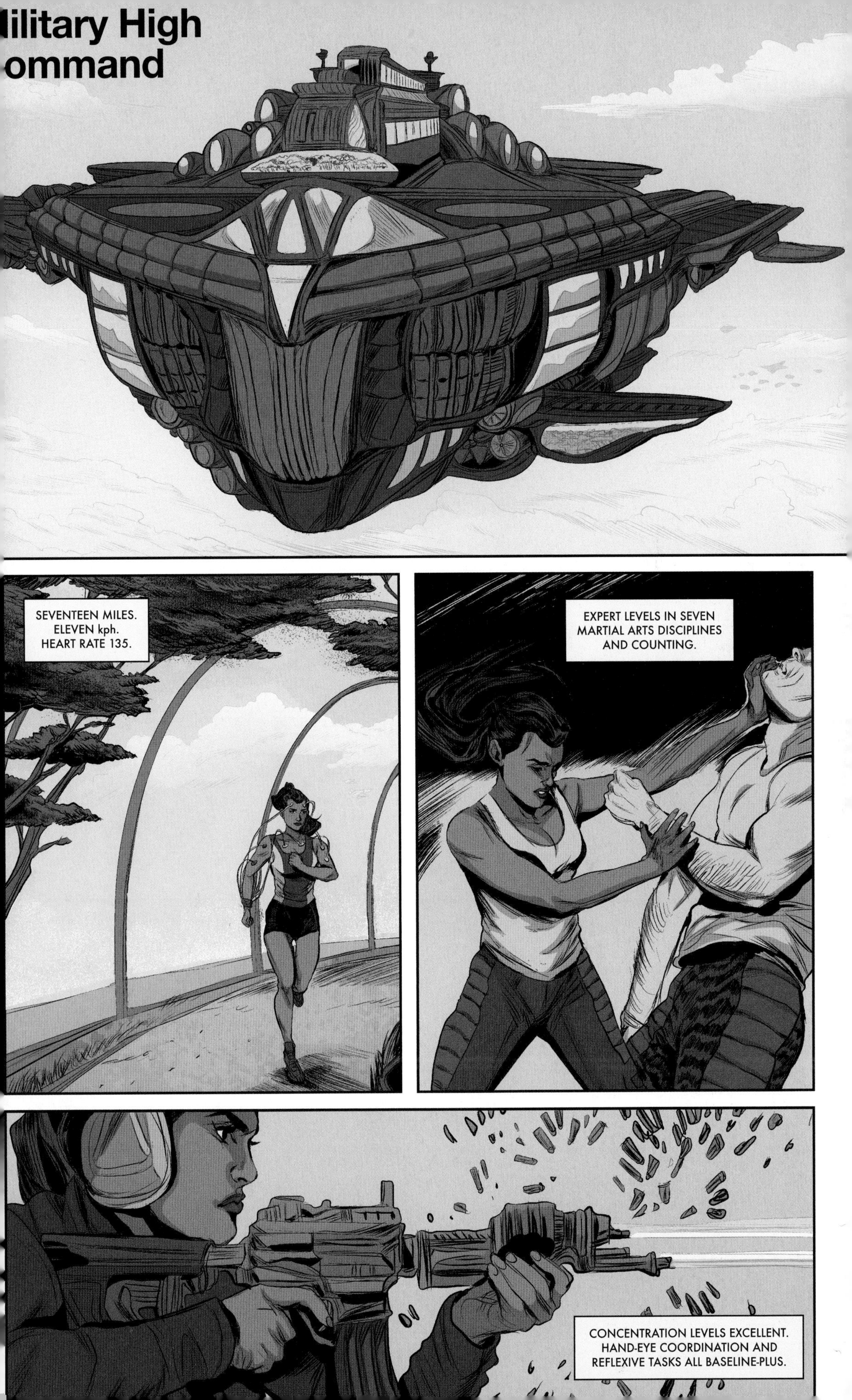
ilitary High
ommand
SEVENTEEN MILES.
ELEVEN kph.
HEART RATE 135.
EXPERT LEVELS IN SEVEN MARTIAL ARTS DISCIPLINES AND COUNTING.
CONCENTRATION LEVELS EXCELLENT. HAND-EYE COORDINATION AND REFLEXIVE TASKS ALL BASELINE-PLUS.

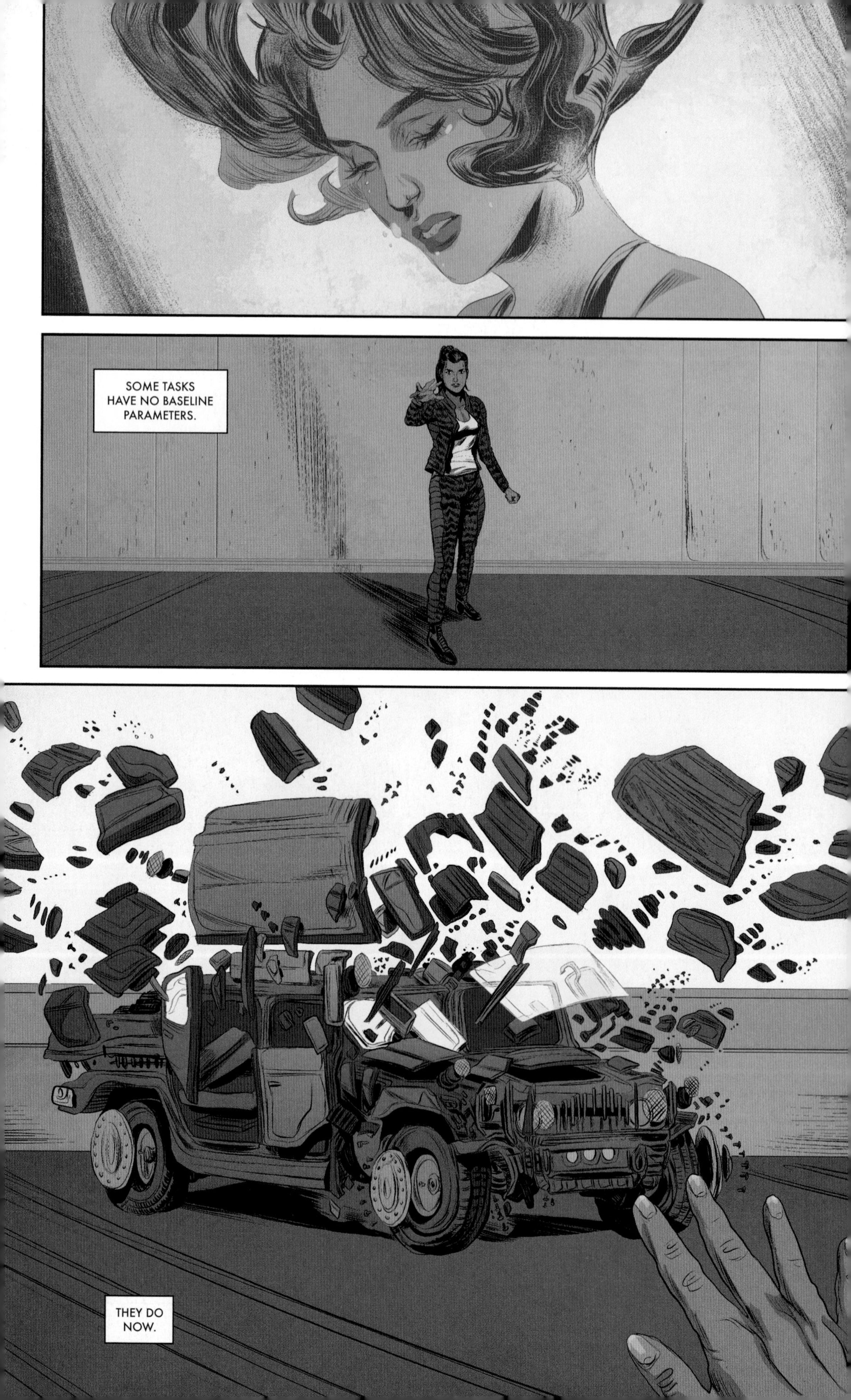
SOME TASKS HAVE NO BASELINE PARAMETERS.
THEY DO NOW.

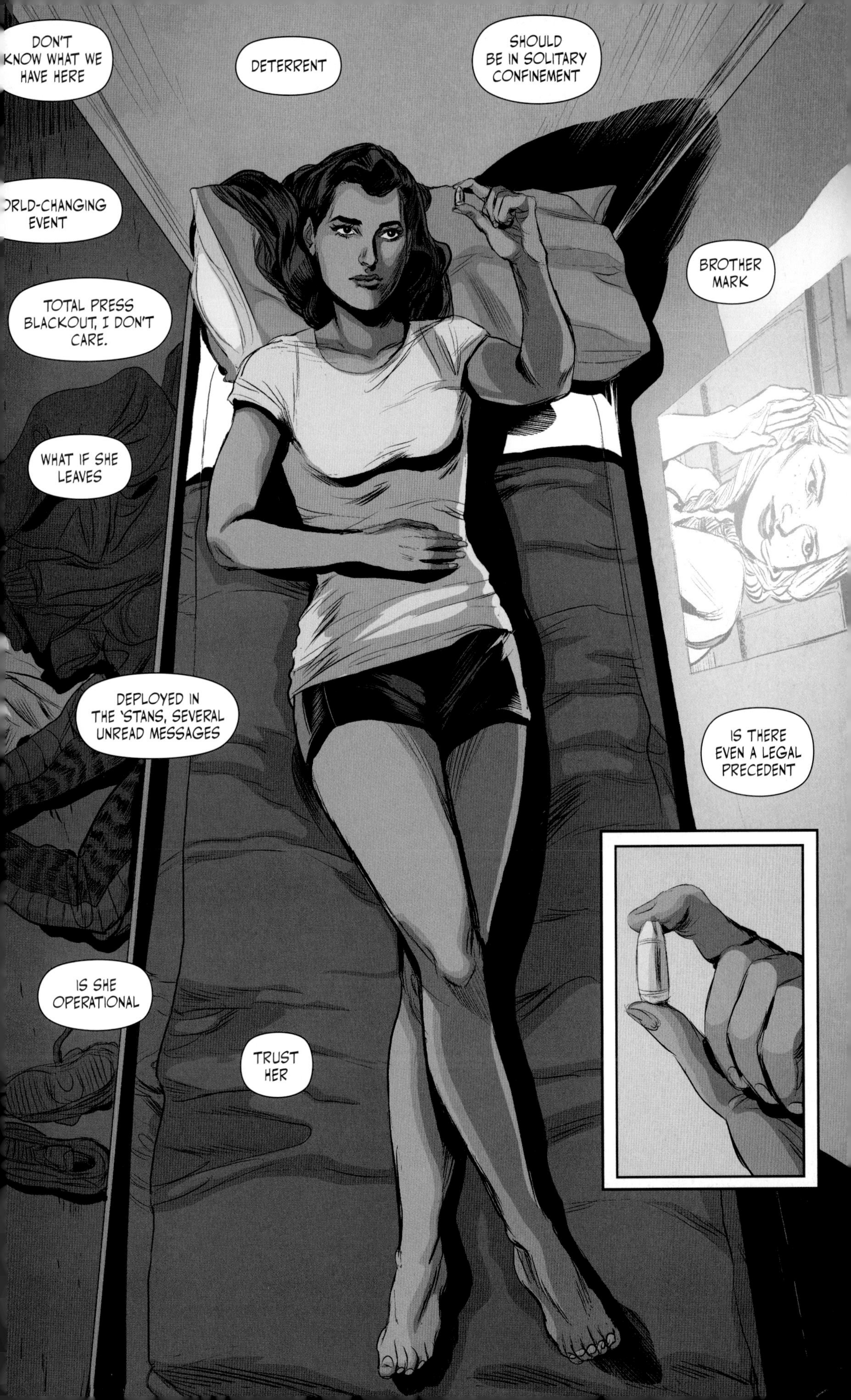
DON'T KNOW WHAT WE HAVE HERE
DETERRENT
SHOULD BE IN SOLITARY CONFINEMENT
ORLD-CHANGING EVENT
BROTHER MARK
TOTAL PRESS BLACKOUT, I DON'T CARE.
WHAT IF SHE LEAVES
DEPLOYED IN THE 'STANS, SEVERAL UNREAD MESSAGES
IS THERE EVEN A LEGAL PRECEDENT
IS SHE OPERATIONAL
TRUST HER

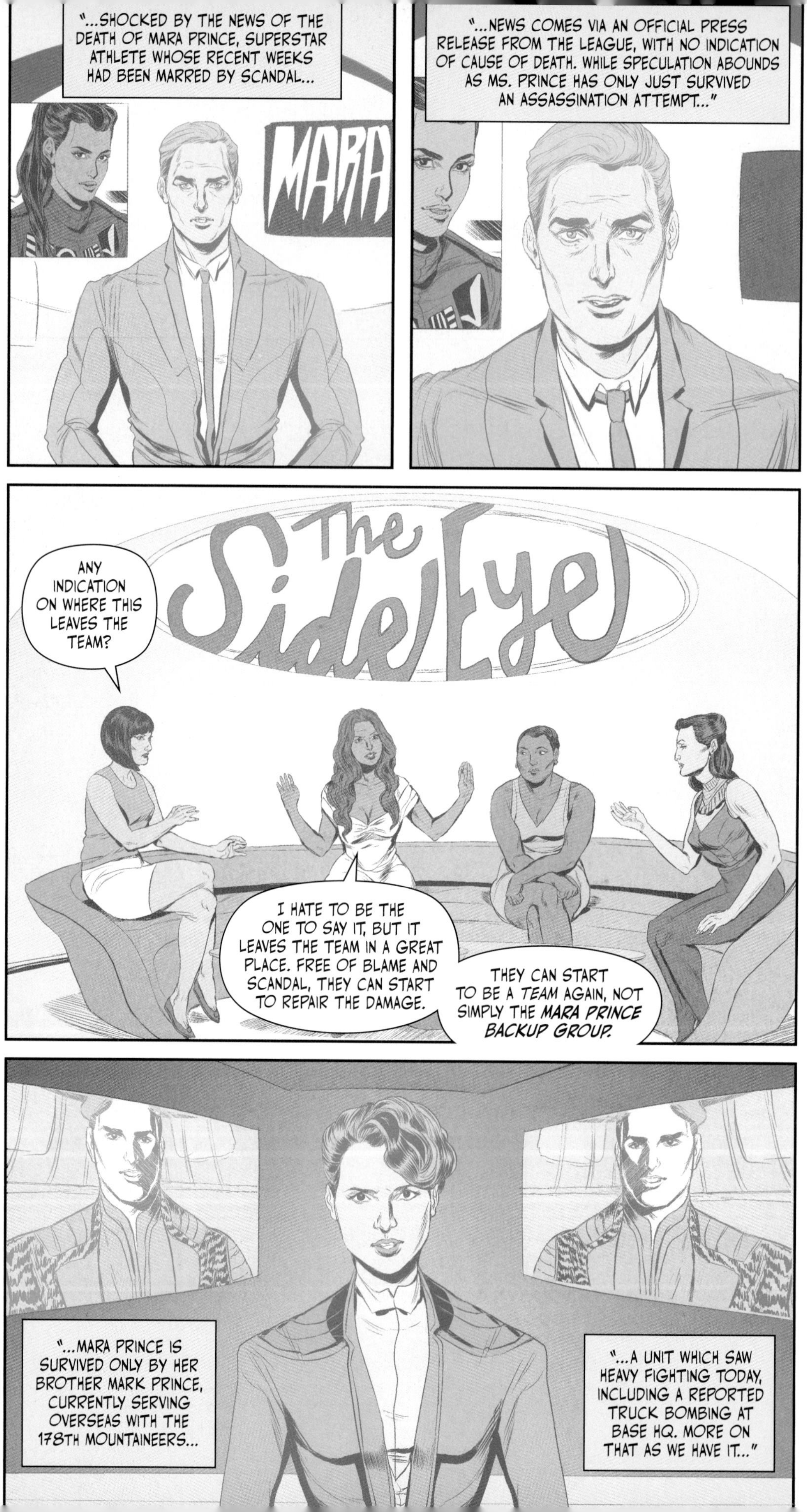
"...SHOCKED BY THE NEWS OF THE DEATH OF MARA PRINCE, SUPERSTAR ATHLETE WHOSE RECENT WEEKS HAD BEEN MARRED BY SCANDAL...
MARA
"...NEWS COMES VIA AN OFFICIAL PRESS RELEASE FROM THE LEAGUE, WITH NO INDICATION OF CAUSE OF DEATH. WHILE SPECULATION ABOUNDS AS MS. PRINCE HAS ONLY JUST SURVIVED AN ASSASSINATION ATTEMPT..."
The Side Eye
ANY INDICATION ON WHERE THIS LEAVES THE TEAM?
I HATE TO BE THE ONE TO SAY IT, BUT IT LEAVES THE TEAM IN A GREAT PLACE. FREE OF BLAME AND SCANDAL, THEY CAN START TO REPAIR THE DAMAGE.
THEY CAN START TO BE A *TEAM* AGAIN, NOT SIMPLY THE *MARA PRINCE BACKUP GROUP.*
"...MARA PRINCE IS SURVIVED ONLY BY HER BROTHER MARK PRINCE, CURRENTLY SERVING OVERSEAS WITH THE 178TH MOUNTAINEERS...
"...A UNIT WHICH SAW HEAVY FIGHTING TODAY, INCLUDING A REPORTED TRUCK BOMBING AT BASE HQ. MORE ON THAT AS WE HAVE IT..."

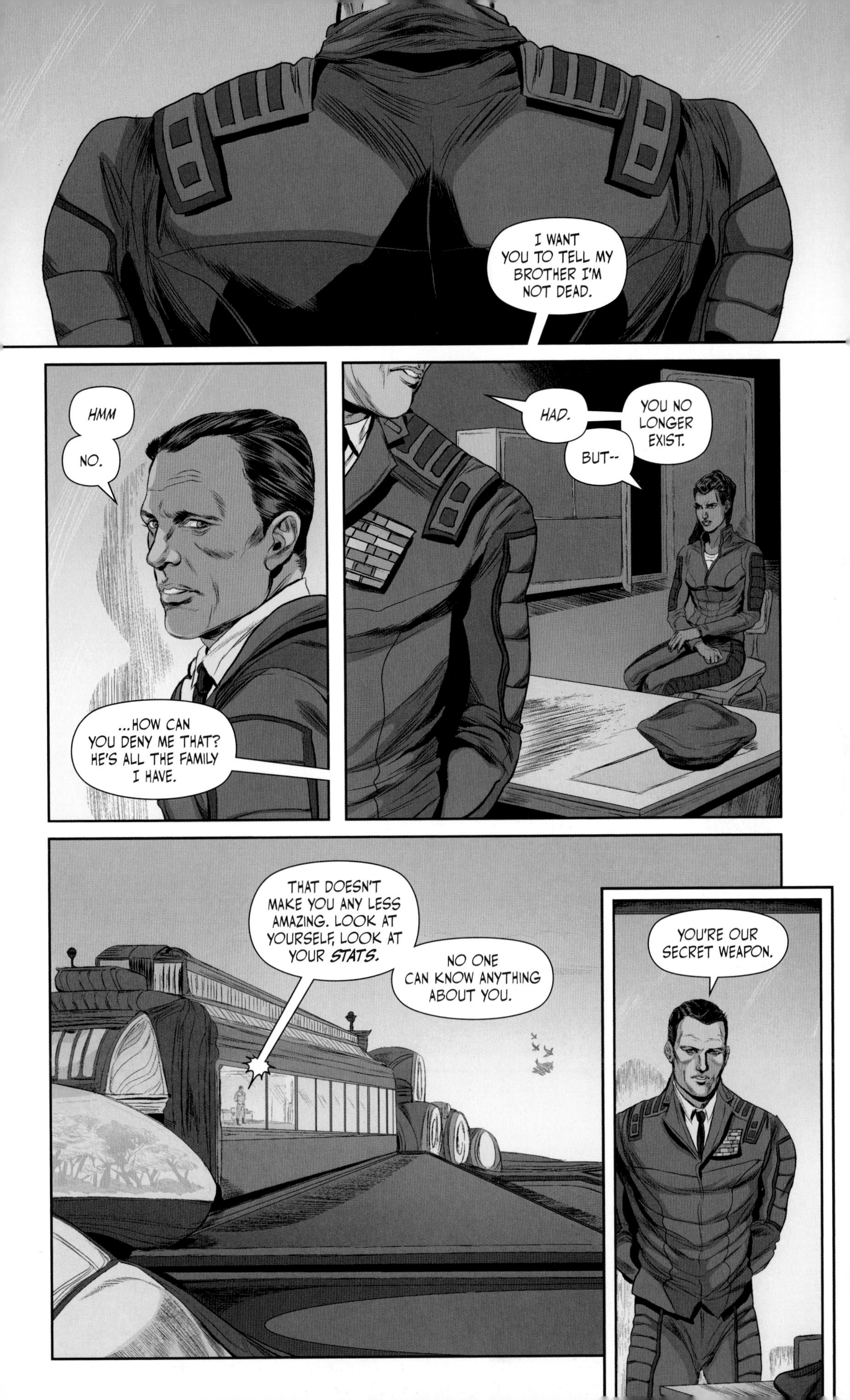
I WANT YOU TO TELL MY BROTHER I'M NOT DEAD.
HMM
NO.
...HOW CAN YOU DENY ME THAT? HE'S ALL THE FAMILY I HAVE.
HAD.
YOU NO LONGER EXIST.
BUT--
THAT DOESN'T MAKE YOU ANY LESS AMAZING. LOOK AT YOURSELF, LOOK AT YOUR *STATS.*
NO ONE CAN KNOW ANYTHING ABOUT YOU.
YOU'RE OUR SECRET WEAPON.

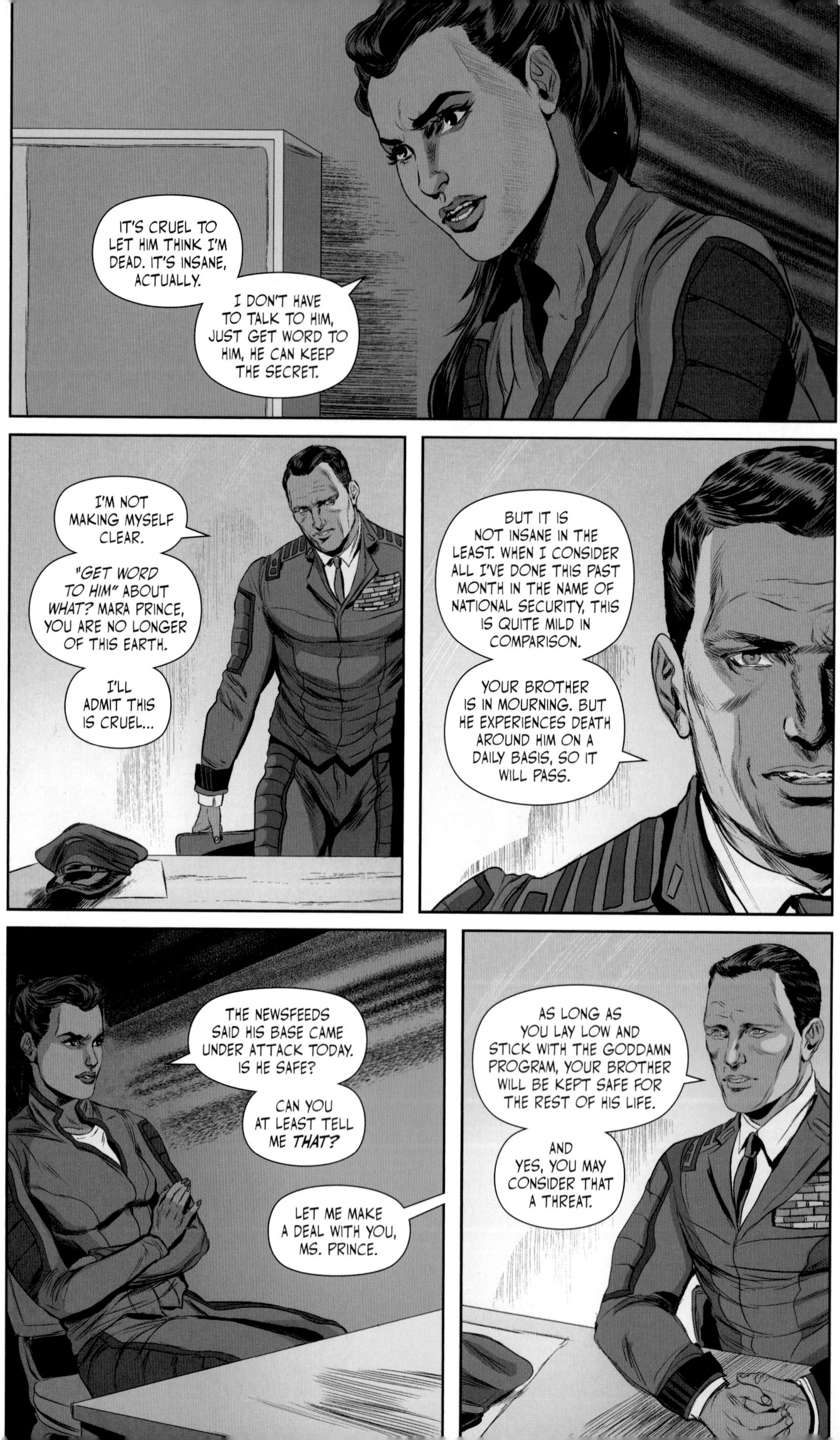
IT'S CRUEL TO LET HIM THINK I'M DEAD. IT'S INSANE, ACTUALLY.
I DON'T HAVE TO TALK TO HIM, JUST GET WORD TO HIM, HE CAN KEEP THE SECRET.
I'M NOT MAKING MYSELF CLEAR.
"GET WORD TO HIM" ABOUT WHAT? MARA PRINCE, YOU ARE NO LONGER OF THIS EARTH.
I'LL ADMIT THIS IS CRUEL...
BUT IT IS NOT INSANE IN THE LEAST. WHEN I CONSIDER ALL I'VE DONE THIS PAST MONTH IN THE NAME OF NATIONAL SECURITY, THIS IS QUITE MILD IN COMPARISON.
YOUR BROTHER IS IN MOURNING. BUT HE EXPERIENCES DEATH AROUND HIM ON A DAILY BASIS, SO IT WILL PASS.
THE NEWSFEEDS SAID HIS BASE CAME UNDER ATTACK TODAY. IS HE SAFE?
CAN YOU AT LEAST TELL ME *THAT?*
LET ME MAKE A DEAL WITH YOU, MS. PRINCE.
AS LONG AS YOU LAY LOW AND STICK WITH THE GODDAMN PROGRAM, YOUR BROTHER WILL BE KEPT SAFE FOR THE REST OF HIS LIFE.
AND YES, YOU MAY CONSIDER THAT A THREAT.

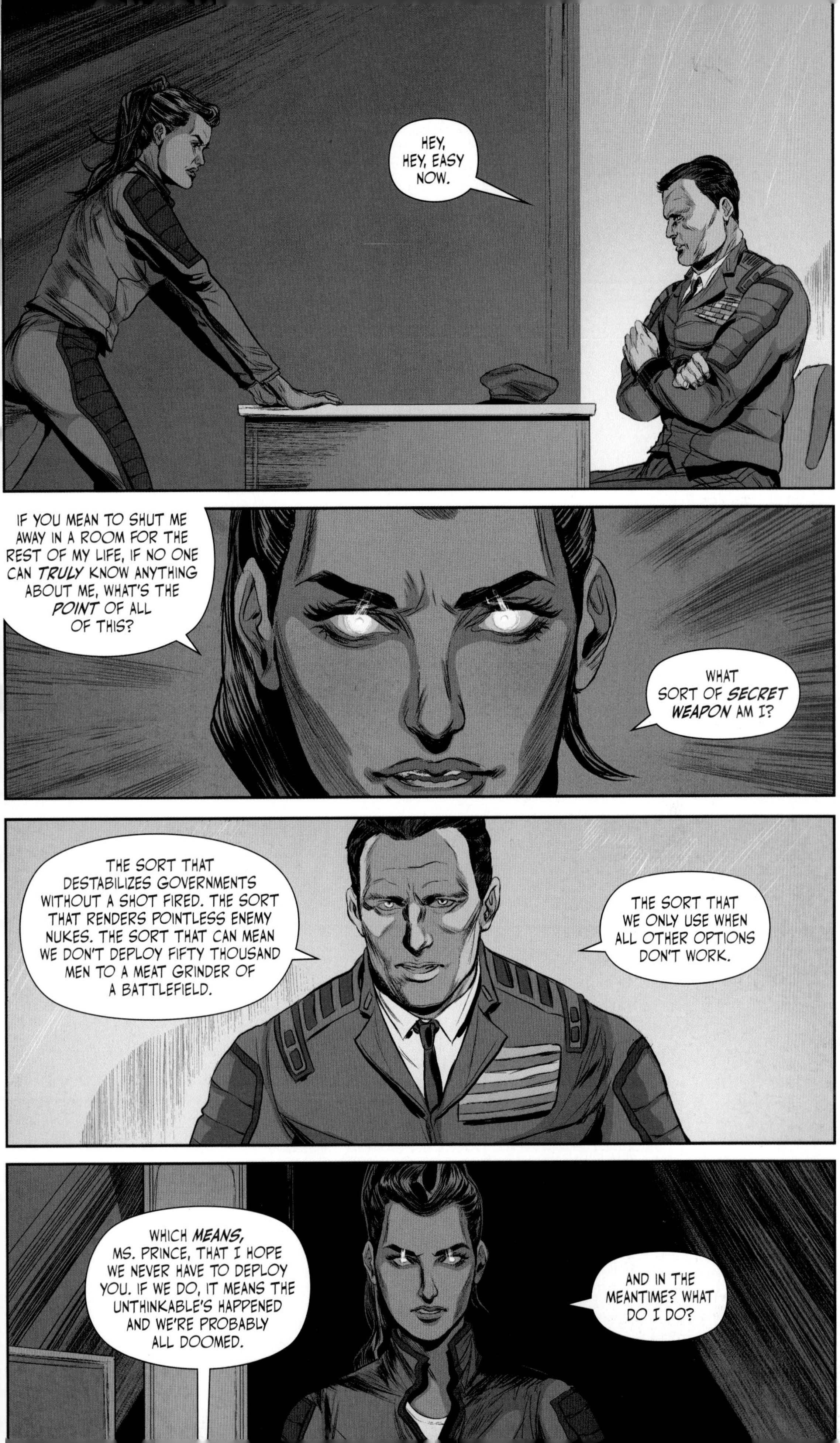
HEY, HEY, EASY NOW.
IF YOU MEAN TO SHUT ME AWAY IN A ROOM FOR THE REST OF MY LIFE, IF NO ONE CAN *TRULY* KNOW ANYTHING ABOUT ME, WHAT'S THE *POINT* OF ALL OF THIS?
WHAT SORT OF *SECRET WEAPON* AM I?
THE SORT THAT DESTABILIZES GOVERNMENTS WITHOUT A SHOT FIRED. THE SORT THAT RENDERS POINTLESS ENEMY NUKES. THE SORT THAT CAN MEAN WE DON'T DEPLOY FIFTY THOUSAND MEN TO A MEAT GRINDER OF A BATTLEFIELD.
THE SORT THAT WE ONLY USE WHEN ALL OTHER OPTIONS DON'T WORK.
WHICH *MEANS,* MS. PRINCE, THAT I HOPE WE NEVER HAVE TO DEPLOY YOU. IF WE DO, IT MEANS THE UNTHINKABLE'S HAPPENED AND WE'RE PROBABLY ALL DOOMED.
AND IN THE MEANTIME? WHAT DO I DO?

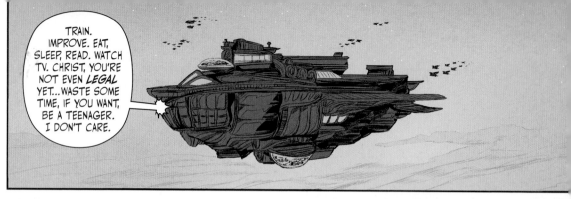

TRAIN. IMPROVE. EAT, SLEEP, READ. WATCH TV. CHRIST, YOU'RE NOT EVEN *LEGAL* YET...WASTE SOME TIME, IF YOU WANT, BE A TEENAGER. I DON'T CARE.

YOUR BROTHER'S UNIT IS RELOCATING. SO WE'LL PULL HIM OUT, ASSIGN HIM SOME SPECIAL TRAINING. WE'LL ADVANCE HIM IN RANK, KEEP HIM OFF THE FRONT LINES.

ON MY HONOR, YOU PLAY BALL, FORGIVE THE PHRASE, AND HE STAYS ALIVE.

I *DO* TAKE THAT AS A THREAT, COMMANDER.

AS YOU LIKE.

DISMISSED.

YES SIR.

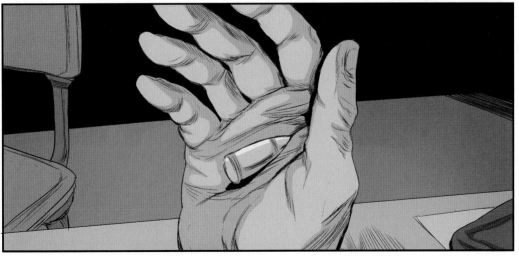

IT TOOK HER NINETY MINUTES TO ESCAPE.

TWENTY OF THOSE WERE SPENT FINDING OUT THE LAST KNOWN LOCATION OF HER BROTHER'S PLATOON.

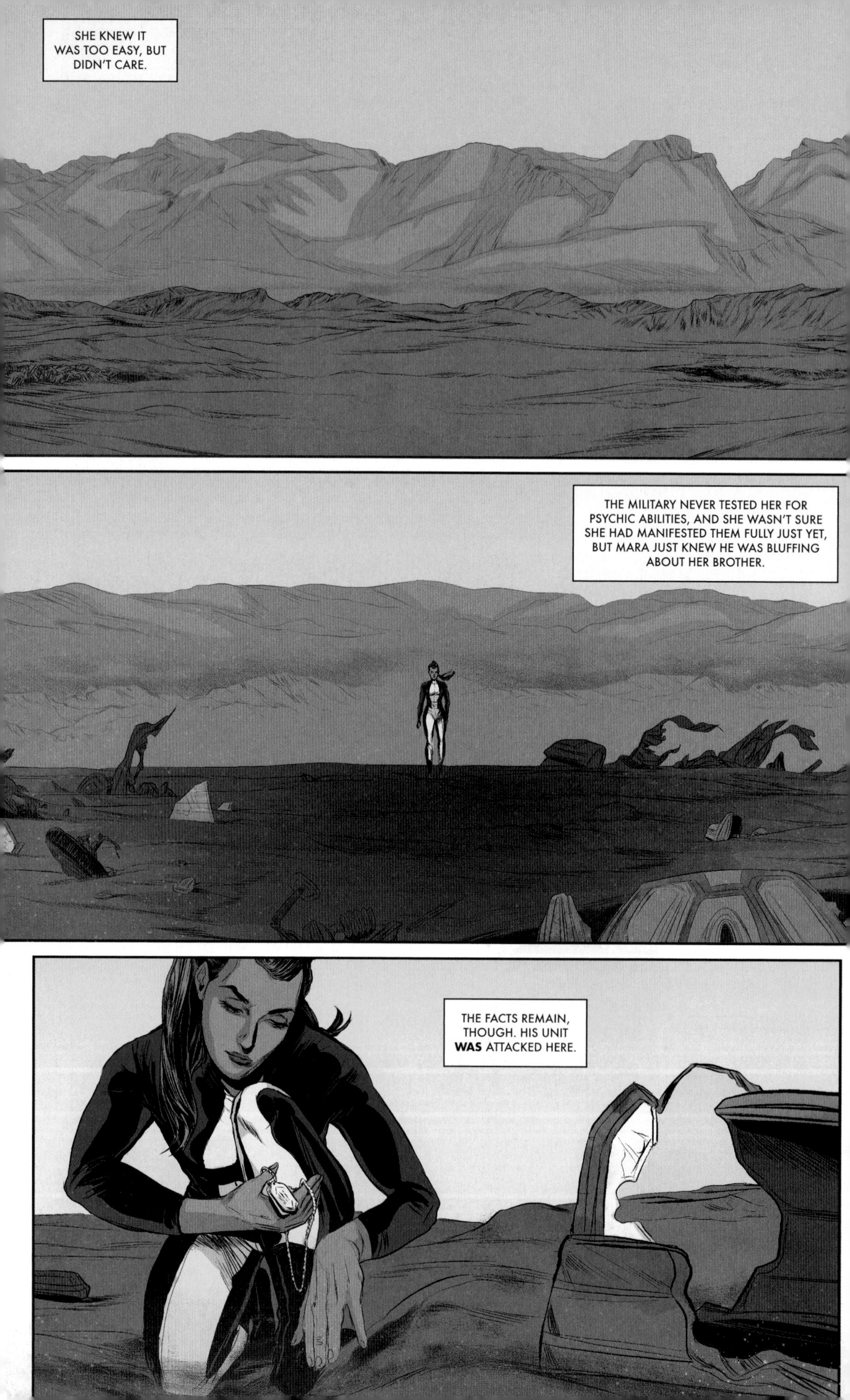
SHE KNEW IT WAS TOO EASY, BUT DIDN'T CARE.
THE MILITARY NEVER TESTED HER FOR PSYCHIC ABILITIES, AND SHE WASN'T SURE SHE HAD MANIFESTED THEM FULLY JUST YET, BUT MARA JUST KNEW HE WAS BLUFFING ABOUT HER BROTHER.
THE FACTS REMAIN, THOUGH. HIS UNIT **WAS** ATTACKED HERE.

AND THEY PULLED OUT.

BUT TO WHERE?

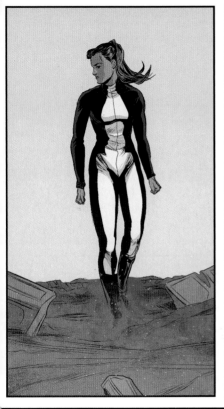

THE WHINE OF WEAPONS COMING ONLINE.

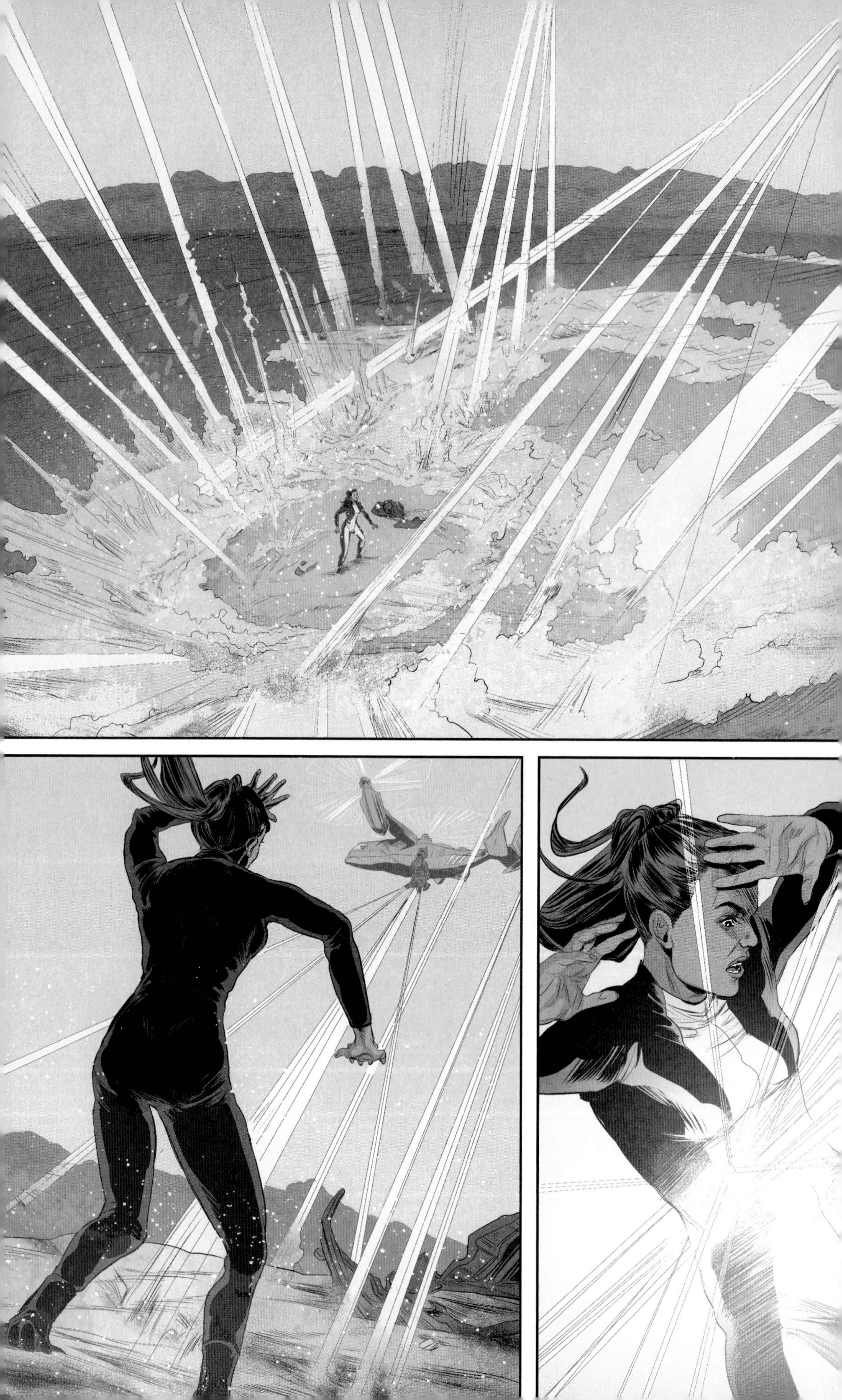

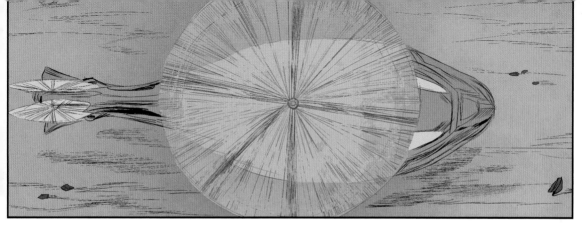

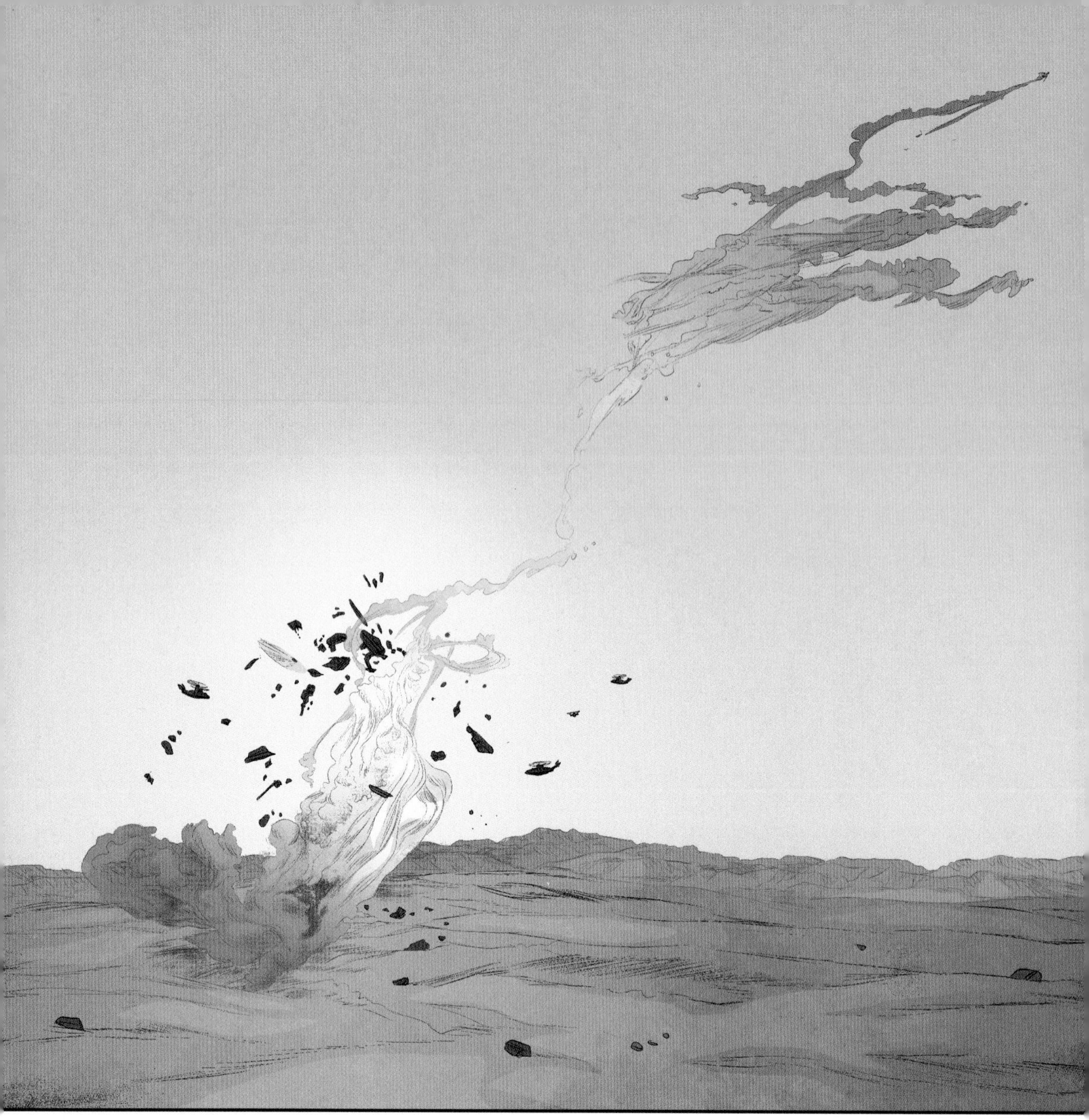

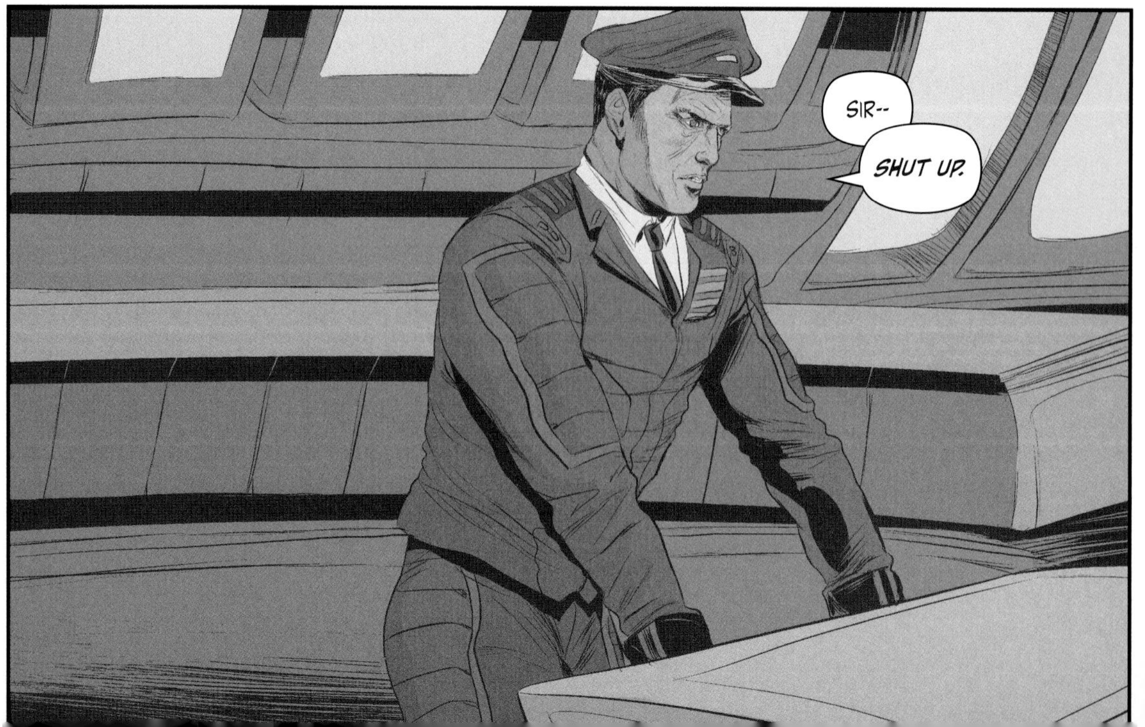
SIR--
SHUT UP.

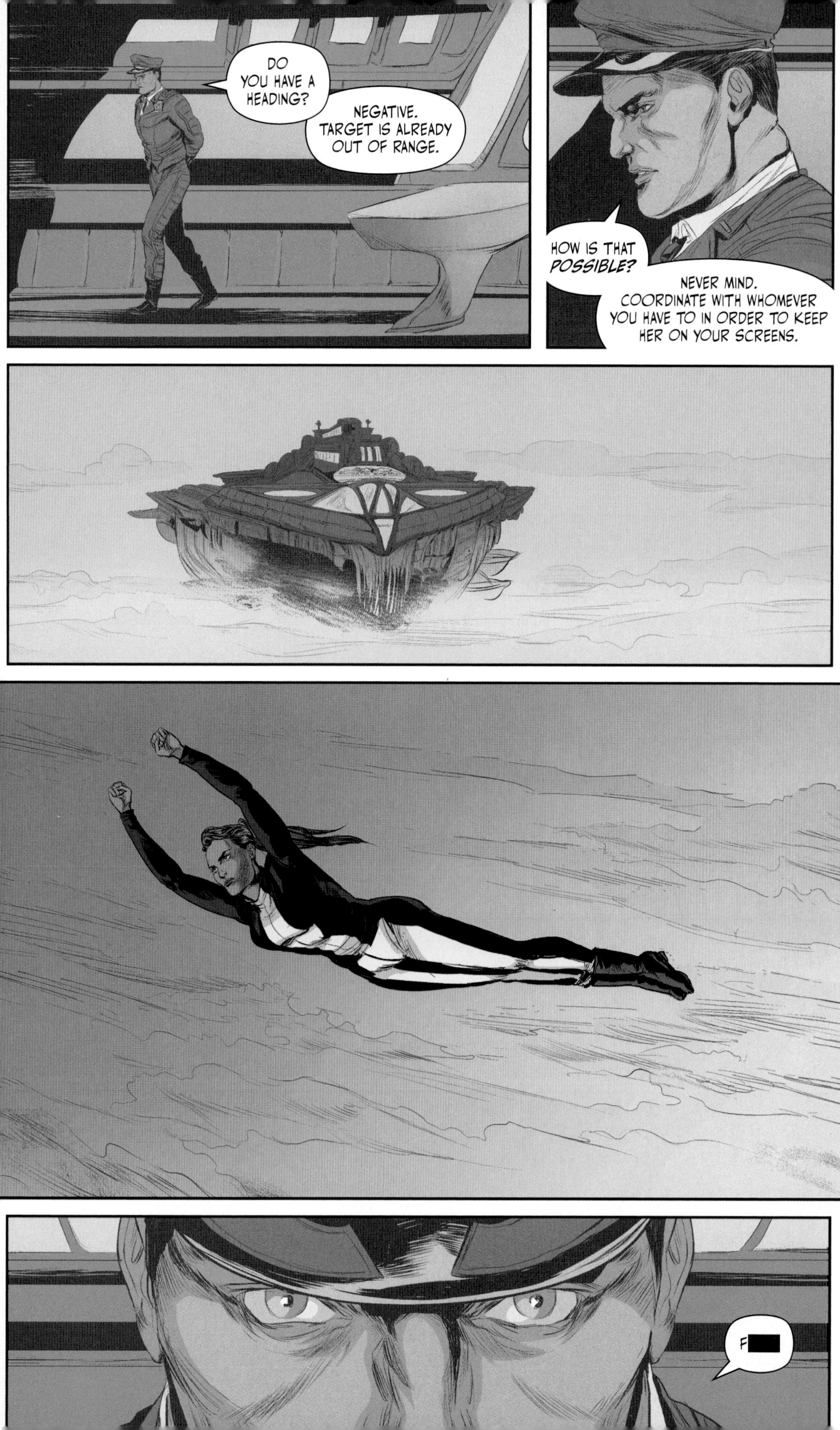
DO YOU HAVE A HEADING?
NEGATIVE. TARGET IS ALREADY OUT OF RANGE.
HOW IS THAT *POSSIBLE?*
NEVER MIND. COORDINATE WITH WHOMEVER YOU HAVE TO IN ORDER TO KEEP HER ON YOUR SCREENS.
F[redacted]

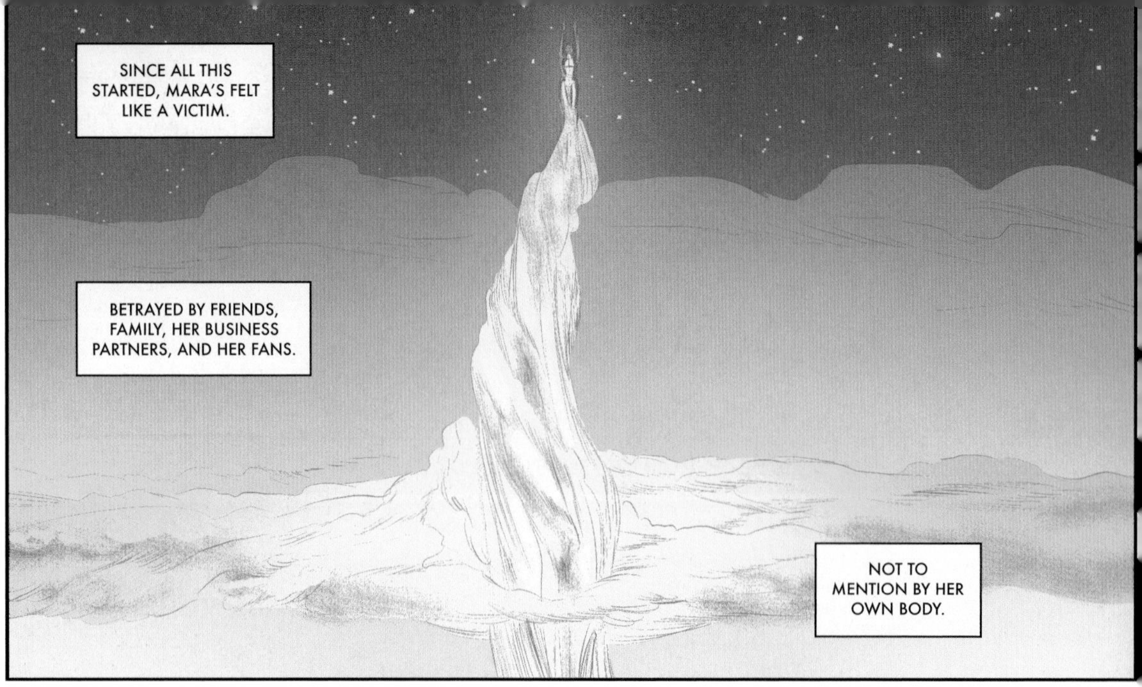
SINCE ALL THIS STARTED, MARA'S FELT LIKE A VICTIM.
BETRAYED BY FRIENDS, FAMILY, HER BUSINESS PARTNERS, AND HER FANS.
NOT TO MENTION BY HER OWN BODY.

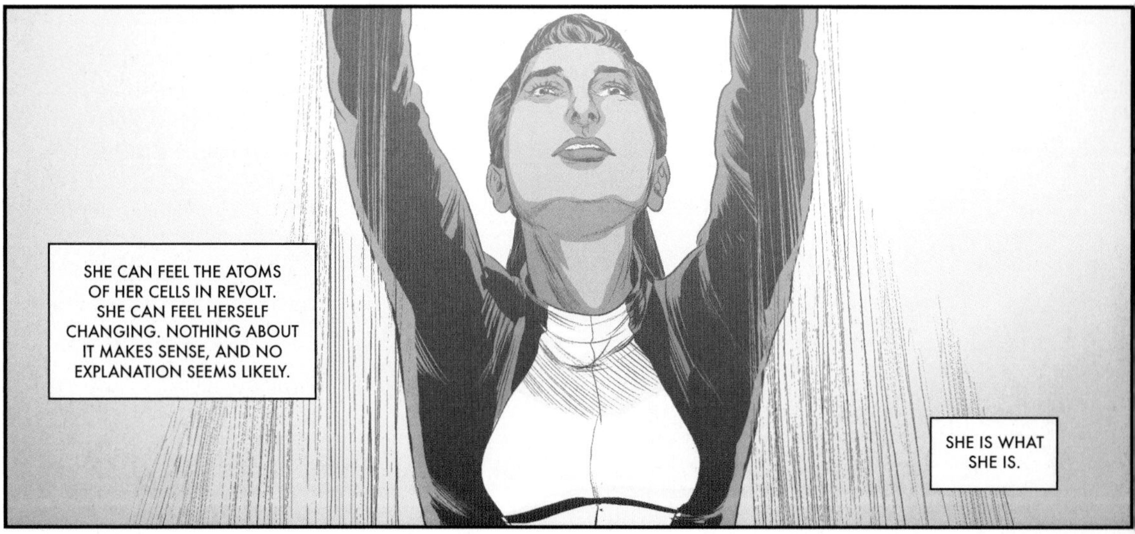
SHE CAN FEEL THE ATOMS OF HER CELLS IN REVOLT. SHE CAN FEEL HERSELF CHANGING. NOTHING ABOUT IT MAKES SENSE, AND NO EXPLANATION SEEMS LIKELY.
SHE IS WHAT SHE IS.

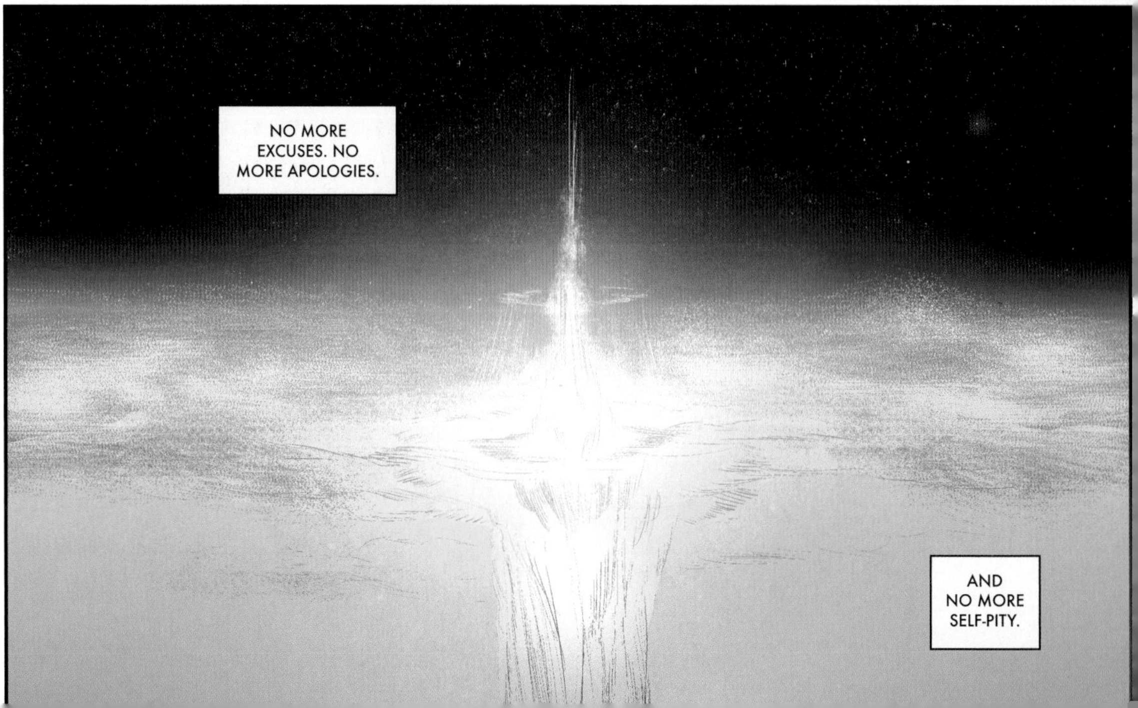
NO MORE EXCUSES. NO MORE APOLOGIES.
AND NO MORE SELF-PITY.

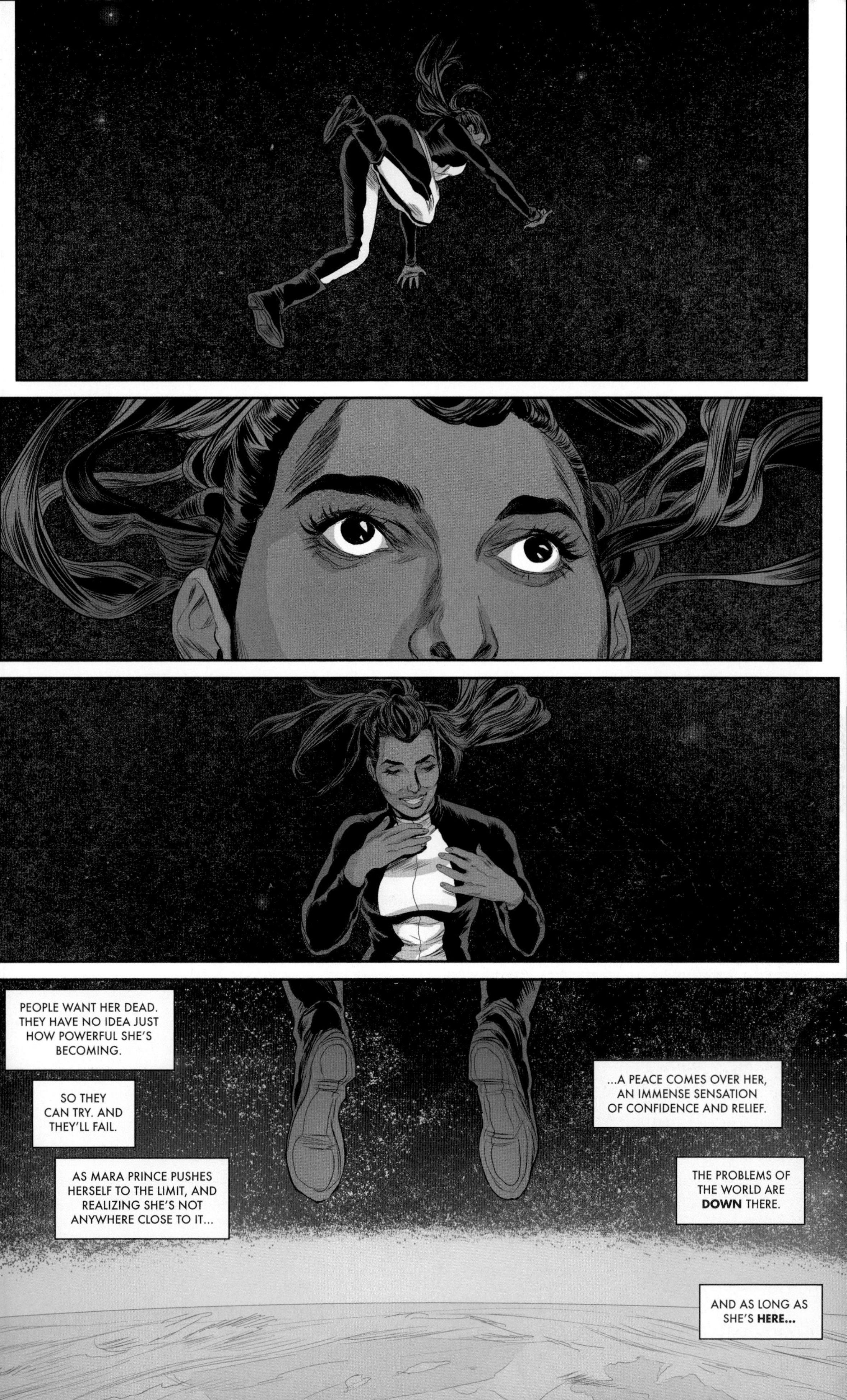
PEOPLE WANT HER DEAD. THEY HAVE NO IDEA JUST HOW POWERFUL SHE'S BECOMING.
SO THEY CAN TRY. AND THEY'LL FAIL.
AS MARA PRINCE PUSHES HERSELF TO THE LIMIT, AND REALIZING SHE'S NOT ANYWHERE CLOSE TO IT...
...A PEACE COMES OVER HER, AN IMMENSE SENSATION OF CONFIDENCE AND RELIEF.
THE PROBLEMS OF THE WORLD ARE **DOWN** THERE.
AND AS LONG AS SHE'S **HERE...**

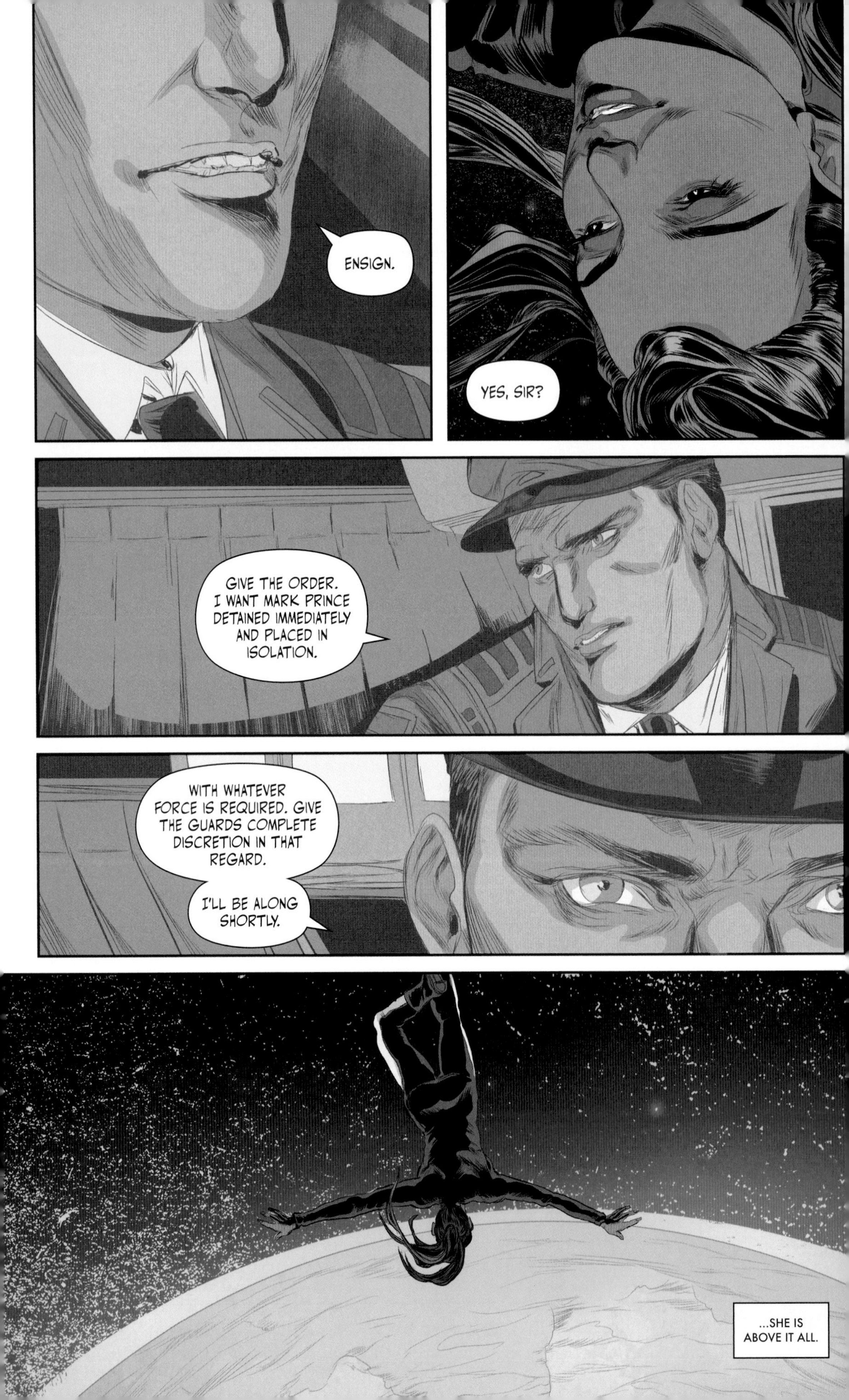
ENSIGN.
YES, SIR?
GIVE THE ORDER. I WANT MARK PRINCE DETAINED IMMEDIATELY AND PLACED IN ISOLATION.
WITH WHATEVER FORCE IS REQUIRED. GIVE THE GUARDS COMPLETE DISCRETION IN THAT REGARD.
I'LL BE ALONG SHORTLY.
...SHE IS ABOVE IT ALL.

CHAPTER FIVE

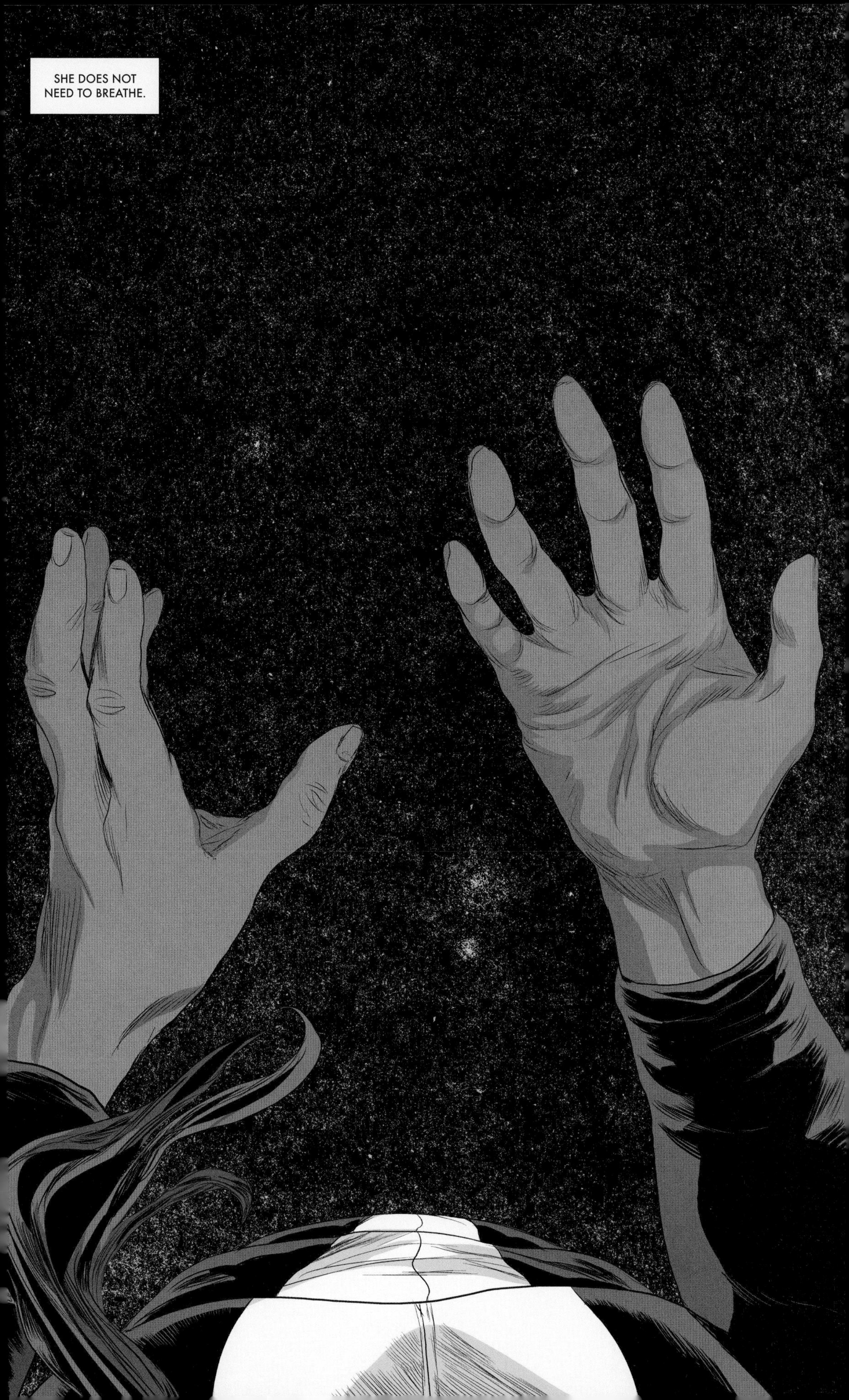
SHE DOES NOT
NEED TO BREATHE.

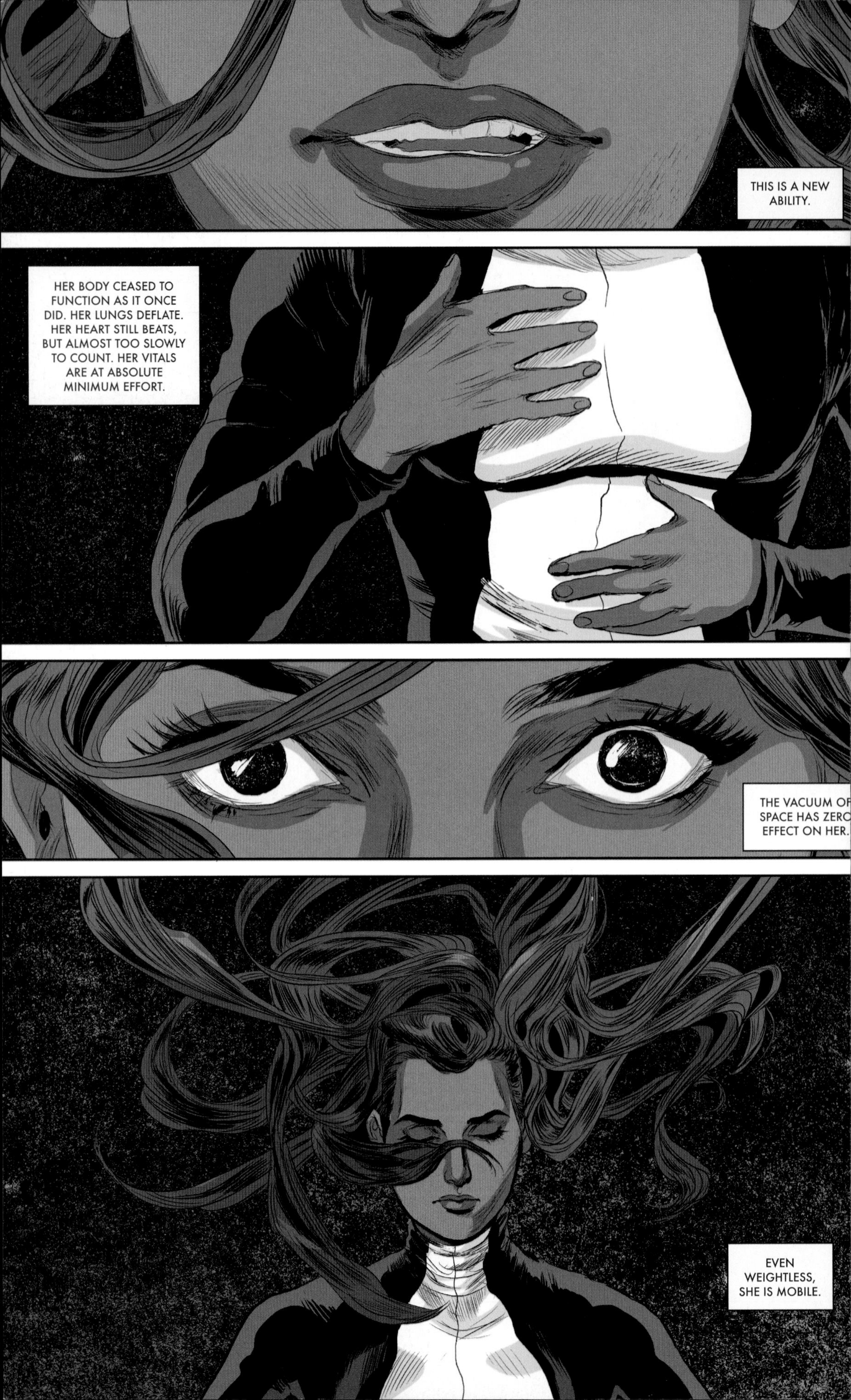

THIS IS A NEW ABILITY.
HER BODY CEASED TO FUNCTION AS IT ONCE DID. HER LUNGS DEFLATE. HER HEART STILL BEATS, BUT ALMOST TOO SLOWLY TO COUNT. HER VITALS ARE AT ABSOLUTE MINIMUM EFFORT.
THE VACUUM OF SPACE HAS ZERO EFFECT ON HER.
EVEN WEIGHTLESS, SHE IS MOBILE.

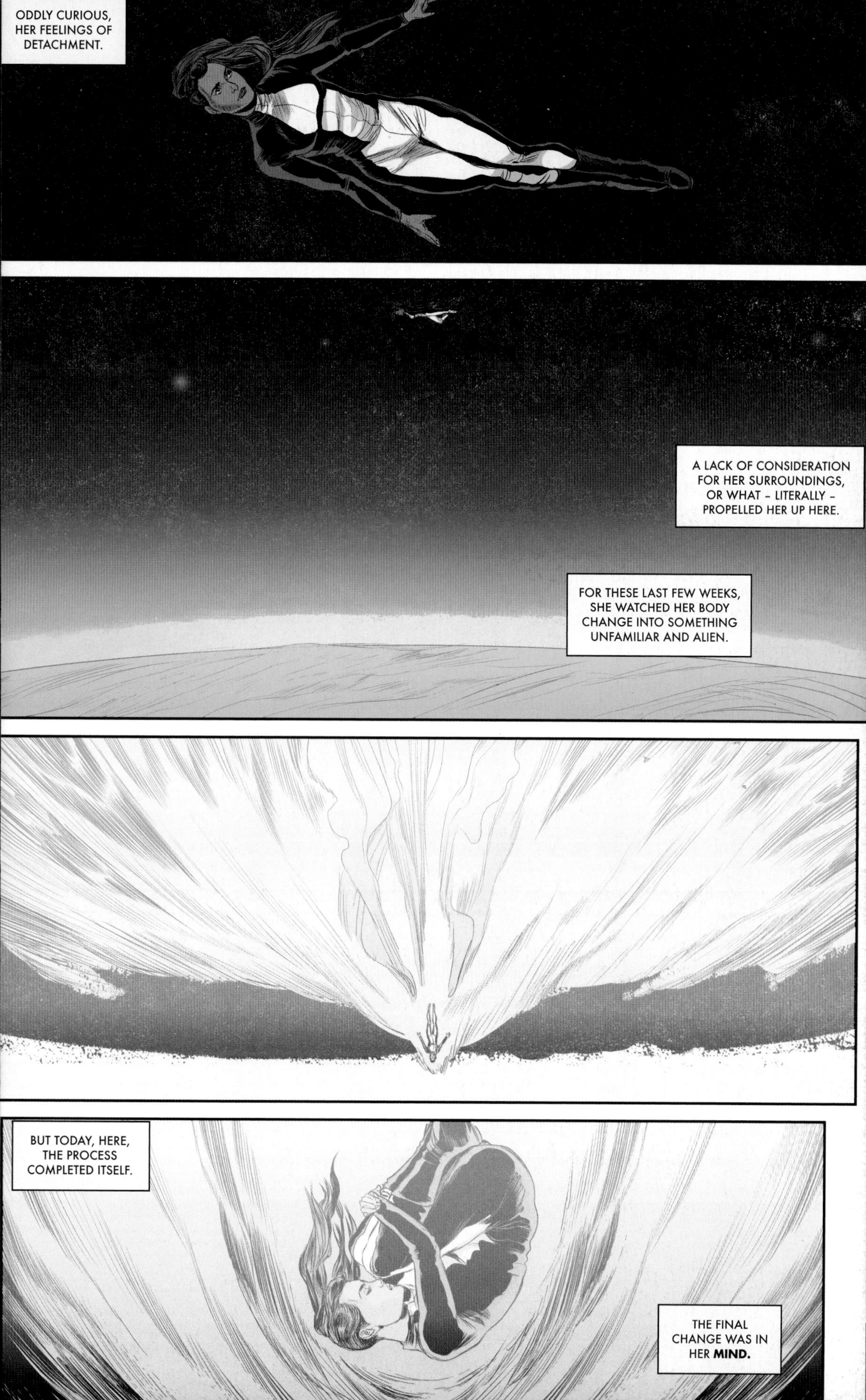
ODDLY CURIOUS, HER FEELINGS OF DETACHMENT.
A LACK OF CONSIDERATION FOR HER SURROUNDINGS, OR WHAT – LITERALLY – PROPELLED HER UP HERE.
FOR THESE LAST FEW WEEKS, SHE WATCHED HER BODY CHANGE INTO SOMETHING UNFAMILIAR AND ALIEN.
BUT TODAY, HERE, THE PROCESS COMPLETED ITSELF.
THE FINAL CHANGE WAS IN HER **MIND.**

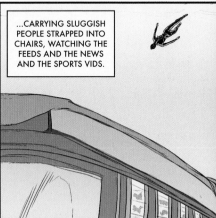

THE MASSIVE AIRBORNE PEOPLE MOVERS, SLOW-DRONING ACROSS CONTINENTS...

...CARRYING SLUGGISH PEOPLE STRAPPED INTO CHAIRS, WATCHING THE FEEDS AND THE NEWS AND THE SPORTS VIDS.

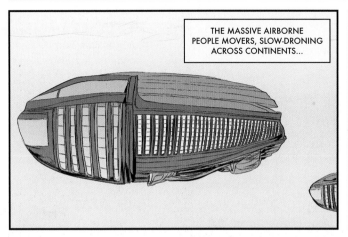

ONLY DREAMING OF BEING BETTER.

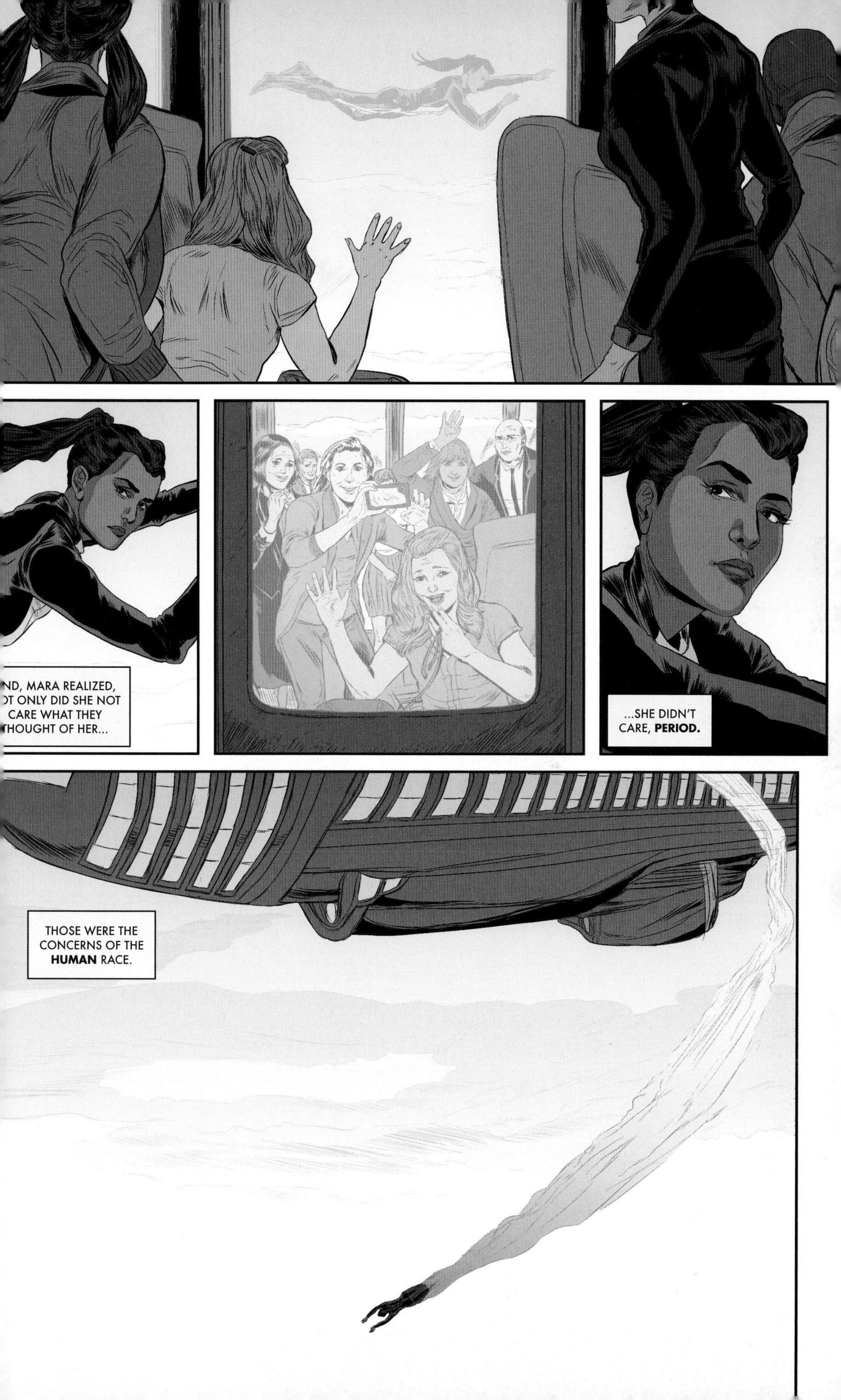
ND, MARA REALIZED,
OT ONLY DID SHE NOT
CARE WHAT THEY
HOUGHT OF HER...
...SHE DIDN'T
CARE, **PERIOD.**
THOSE WERE THE
CONCERNS OF THE
HUMAN RACE.

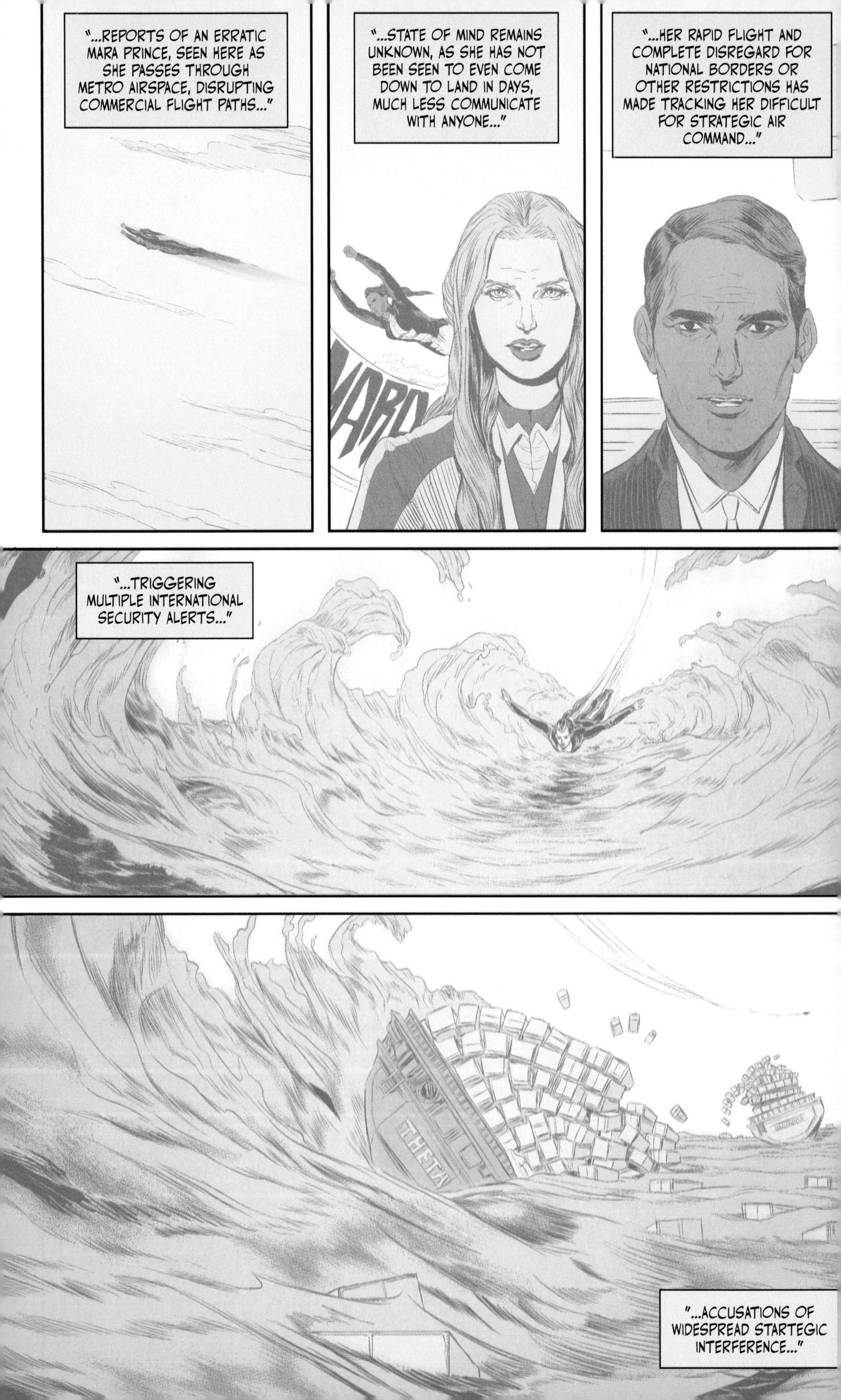
"...REPORTS OF AN ERRATIC MARA PRINCE, SEEN HERE AS SHE PASSES THROUGH METRO AIRSPACE, DISRUPTING COMMERCIAL FLIGHT PATHS..."
"...STATE OF MIND REMAINS UNKNOWN, AS SHE HAS NOT BEEN SEEN TO EVEN COME DOWN TO LAND IN DAYS, MUCH LESS COMMUNICATE WITH ANYONE..."
"...HER RAPID FLIGHT AND COMPLETE DISREGARD FOR NATIONAL BORDERS OR OTHER RESTRICTIONS HAS MADE TRACKING HER DIFFICULT FOR STRATEGIC AIR COMMAND..."
"...TRIGGERING MULTIPLE INTERNATIONAL SECURITY ALERTS..."
THETA
"...ACCUSATIONS OF WIDESPREAD STARTEGIC INTERFERENCE..."

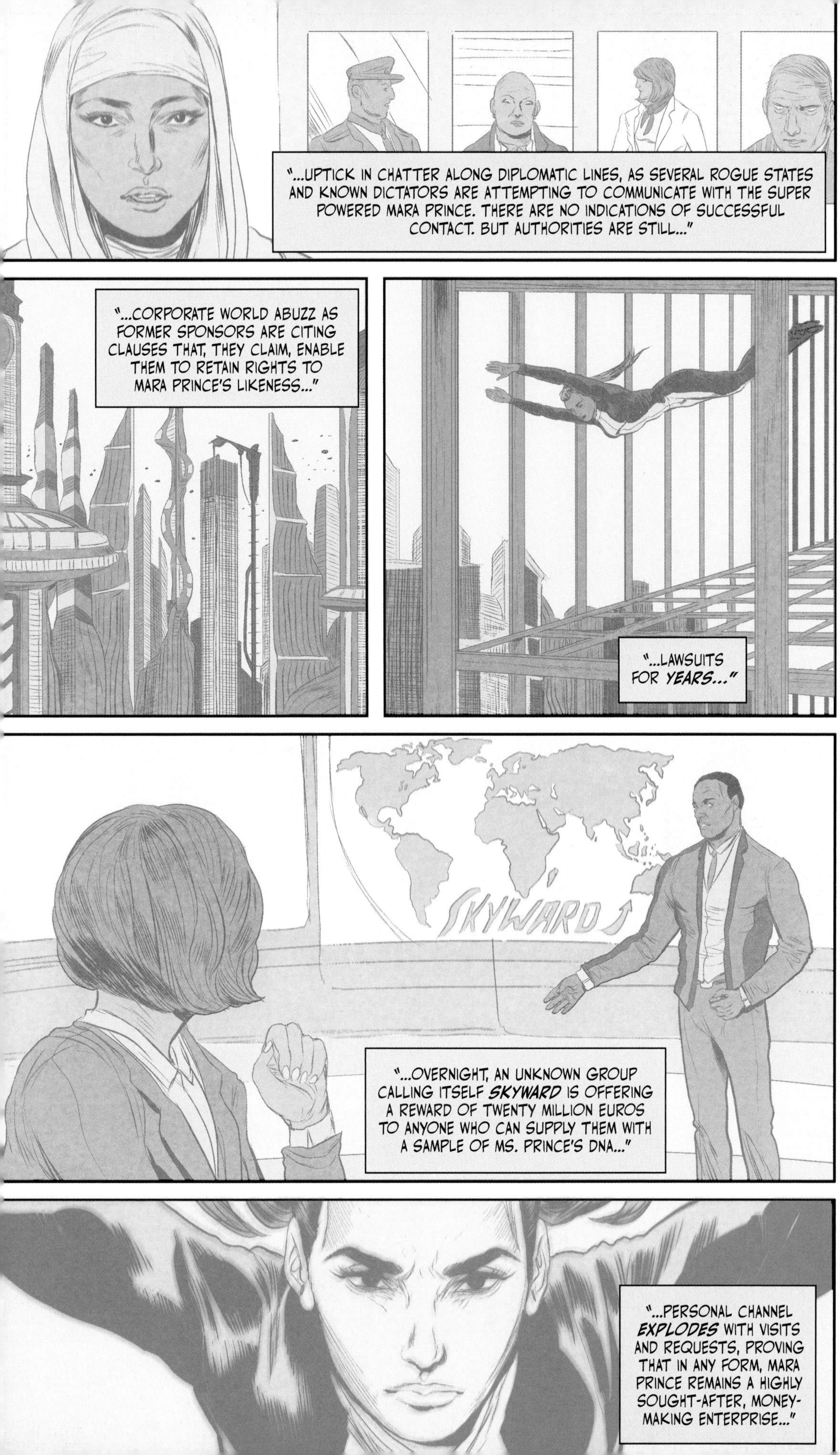
"...UPTICK IN CHATTER ALONG DIPLOMATIC LINES, AS SEVERAL ROGUE STATES AND KNOWN DICTATORS ARE ATTEMPTING TO COMMUNICATE WITH THE SUPER POWERED MARA PRINCE. THERE ARE NO INDICATIONS OF SUCCESSFUL CONTACT. BUT AUTHORITIES ARE STILL..."
"...CORPORATE WORLD ABUZZ AS FORMER SPONSORS ARE CITING CLAUSES THAT, THEY CLAIM, ENABLE THEM TO RETAIN RIGHTS TO MARA PRINCE'S LIKENESS..."
"...LAWSUITS FOR *YEARS...*"
SKYWARD
"...OVERNIGHT, AN UNKNOWN GROUP CALLING ITSELF *SKYWARD* IS OFFERING A REWARD OF TWENTY MILLION EUROS TO ANYONE WHO CAN SUPPLY THEM WITH A SAMPLE OF MS. PRINCE'S DNA..."
"...PERSONAL CHANNEL *EXPLODES* WITH VISITS AND REQUESTS, PROVING THAT IN ANY FORM, MARA PRINCE REMAINS A HIGHLY SOUGHT-AFTER, MONEY-MAKING ENTERPRISE..."

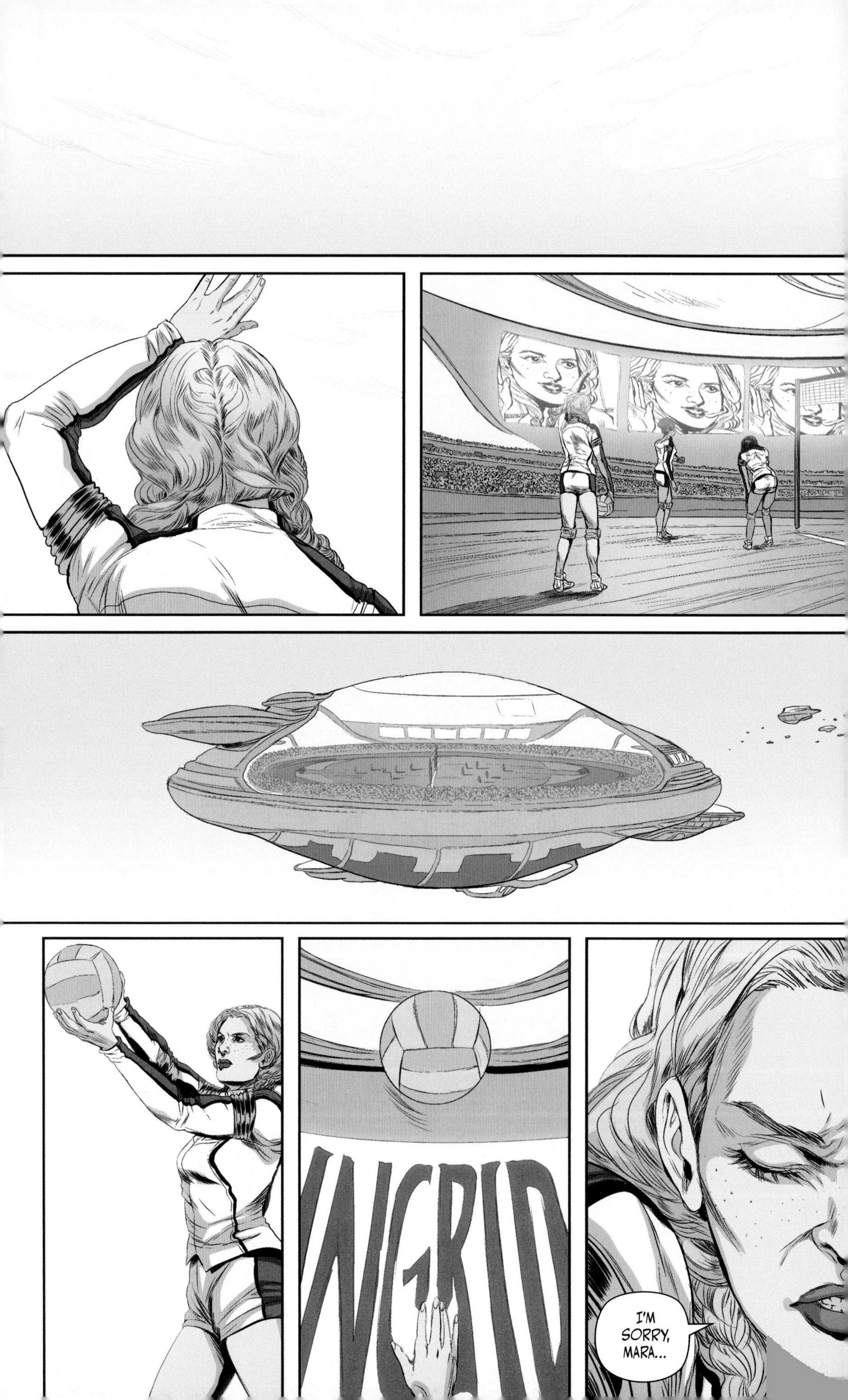

INGRID
I'M SORRY, MARA...

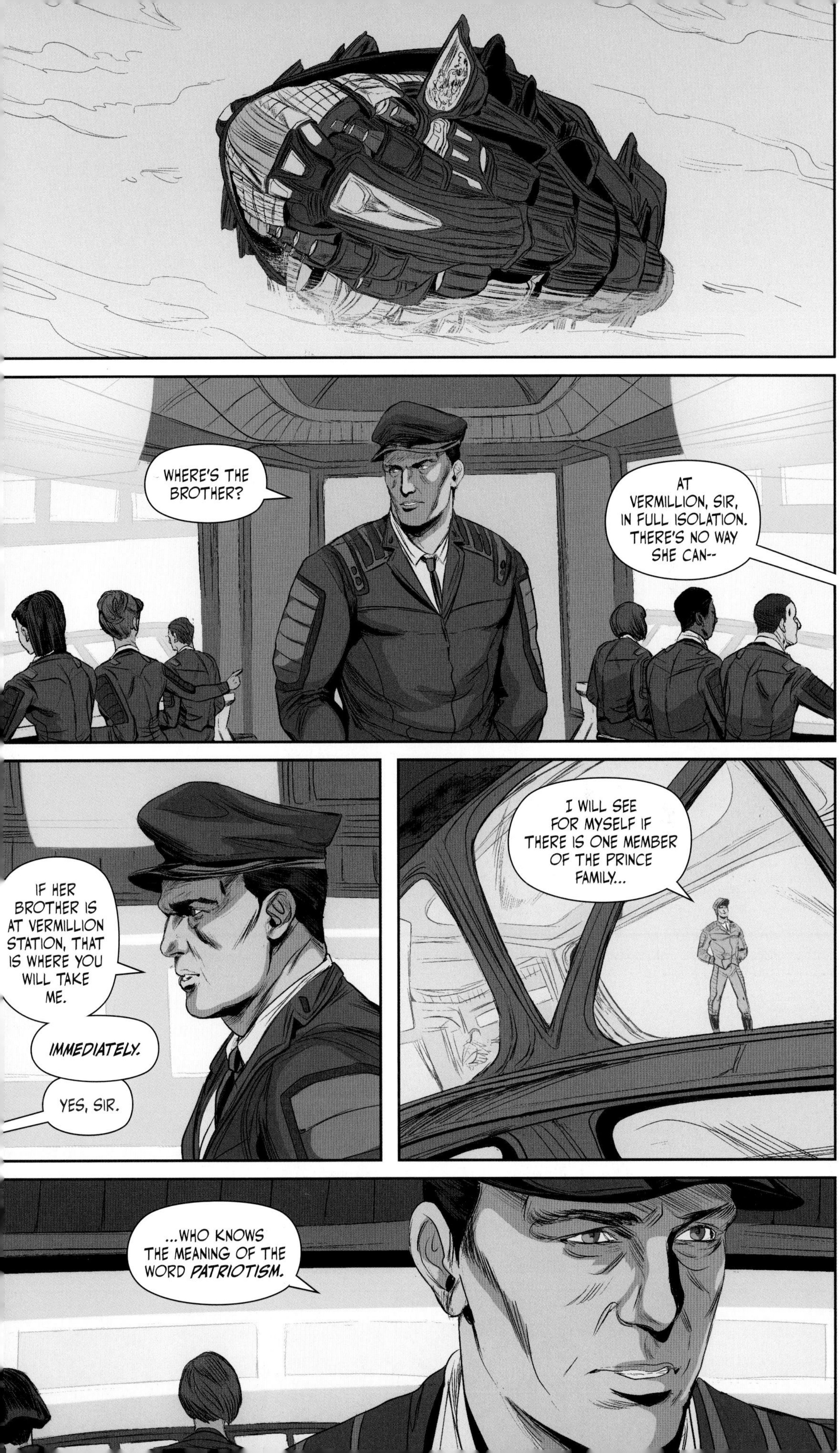
WHERE'S THE BROTHER?
AT VERMILLION, SIR, IN FULL ISOLATION. THERE'S NO WAY SHE CAN--
IF HER BROTHER IS AT VERMILLION STATION, THAT IS WHERE YOU WILL TAKE ME.
IMMEDIATELY.
YES, SIR.
I WILL SEE FOR MYSELF IF THERE IS ONE MEMBER OF THE PRINCE FAMILY...
...WHO KNOWS THE MEANING OF THE WORD PATRIOTISM.

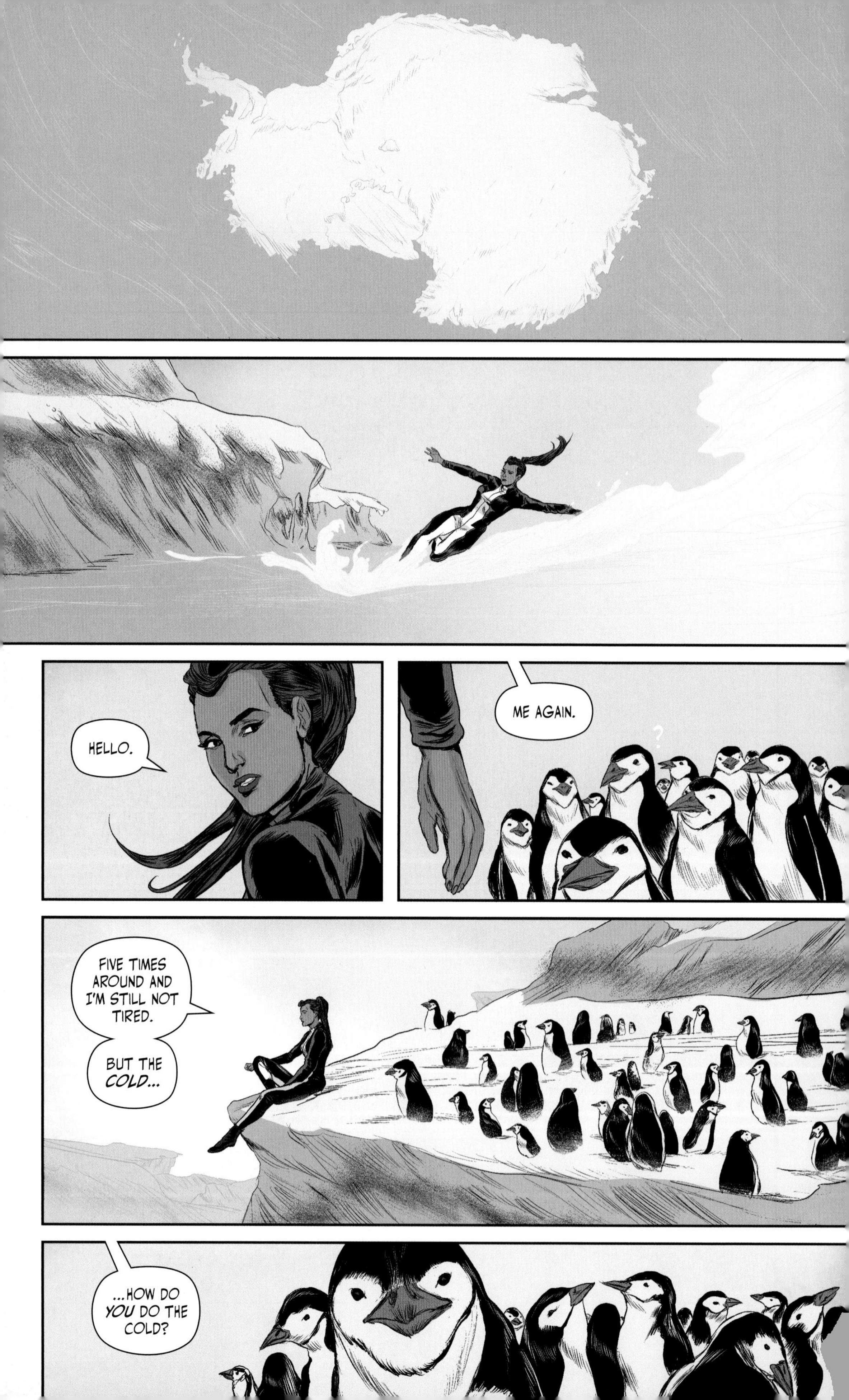
HELLO.
ME AGAIN.
?
FIVE TIMES AROUND AND I'M STILL NOT TIRED.
BUT THE *COLD*...
...HOW DO *YOU* DO THE COLD?

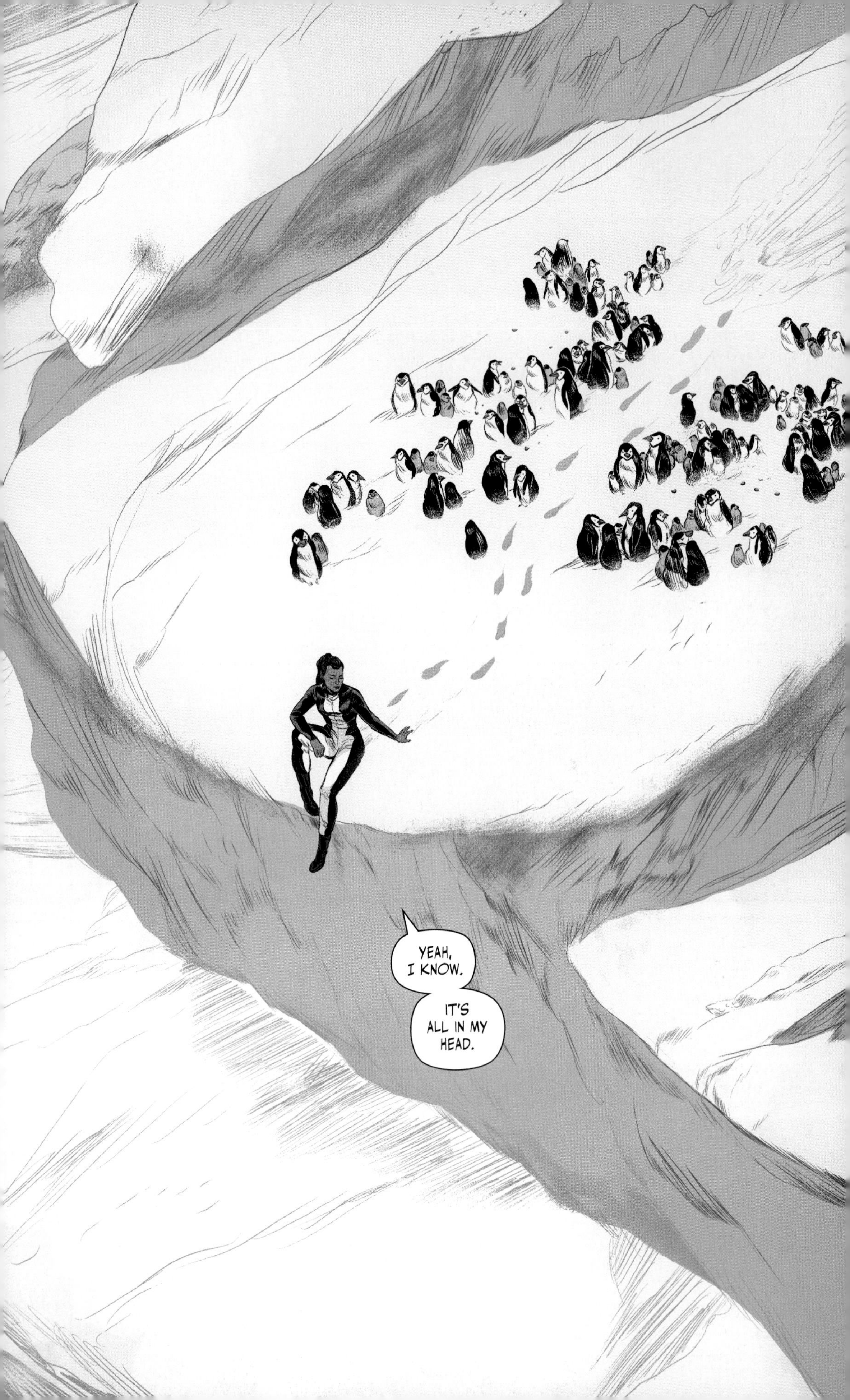
YEAH, I KNOW.
IT'S ALL IN MY HEAD.

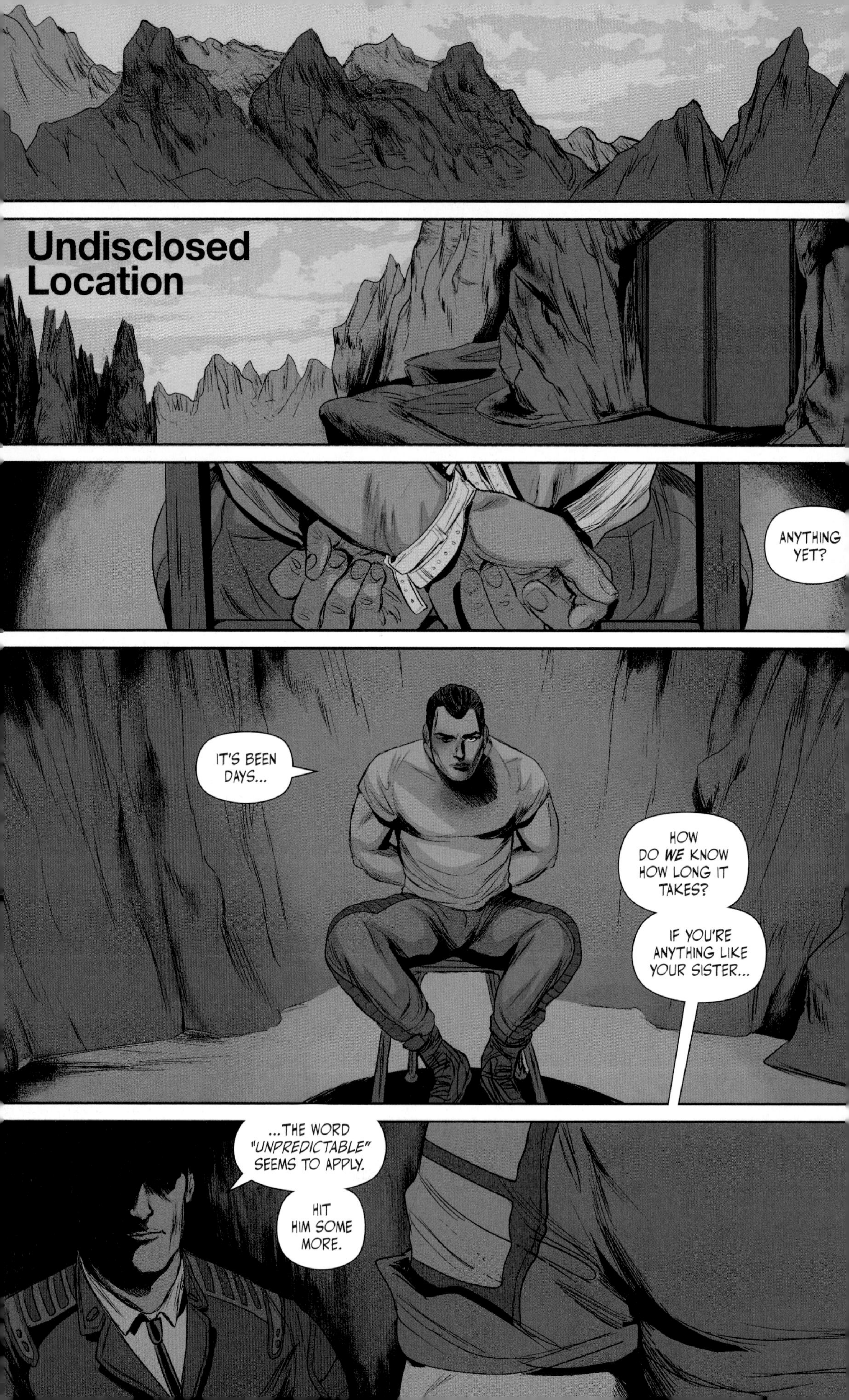
Undisclosed Location
ANYTHING YET?
IT'S BEEN DAYS...
HOW DO WE KNOW HOW LONG IT TAKES?
IF YOU'RE ANYTHING LIKE YOUR SISTER...
...THE WORD "UNPREDICTABLE" SEEMS TO APPLY.
HIT HIM SOME MORE.

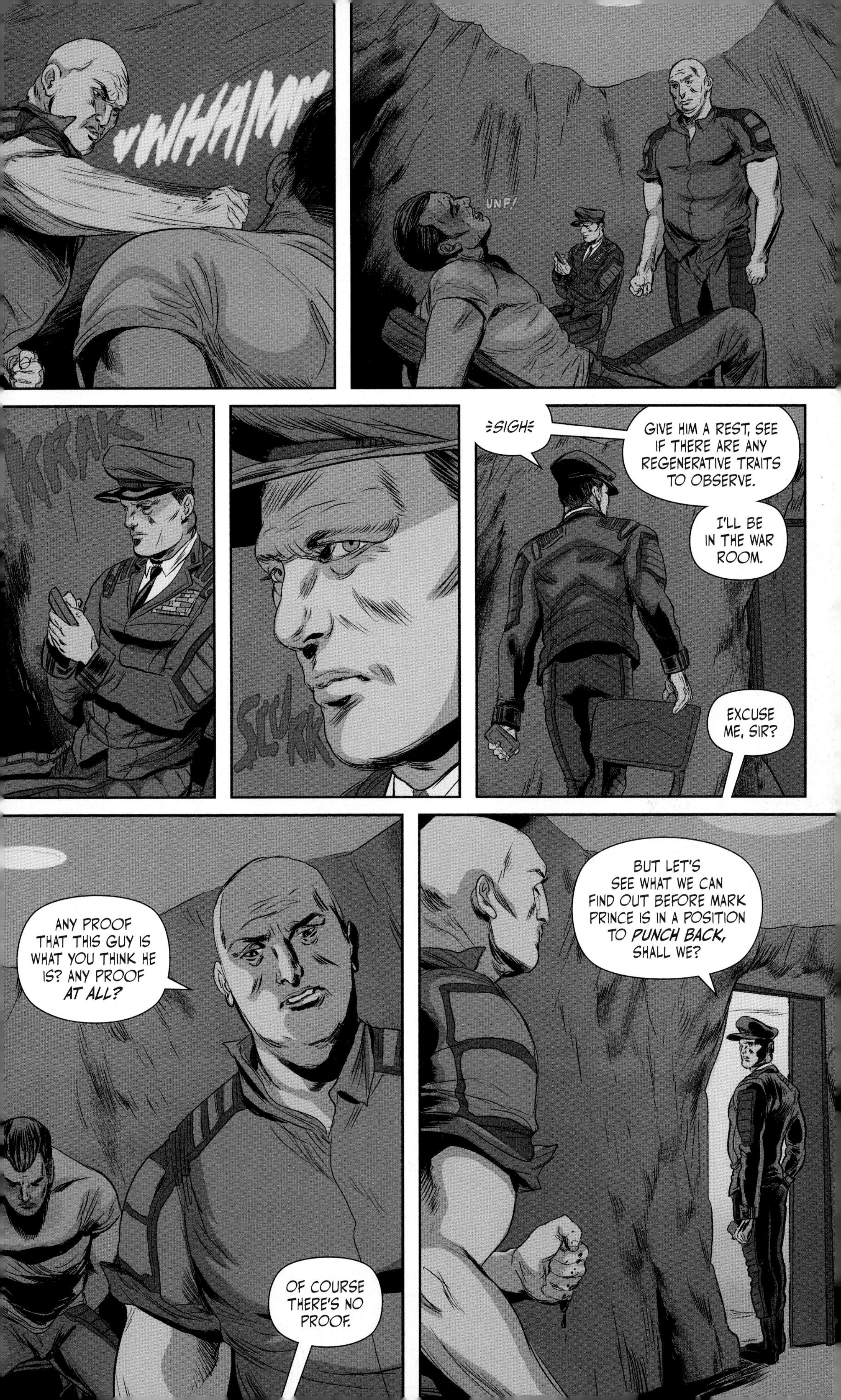
WHAM
UNF!
KRAK
SCLUKK
SIGH
GIVE HIM A REST, SEE IF THERE ARE ANY REGENERATIVE TRAITS TO OBSERVE.
I'LL BE IN THE WAR ROOM.
EXCUSE ME, SIR?
ANY PROOF THAT THIS GUY IS WHAT YOU THINK HE IS? ANY PROOF AT ALL?
OF COURSE THERE'S NO PROOF.
BUT LET'S SEE WHAT WE CAN FIND OUT BEFORE MARK PRINCE IS IN A POSITION TO PUNCH BACK, SHALL WE?

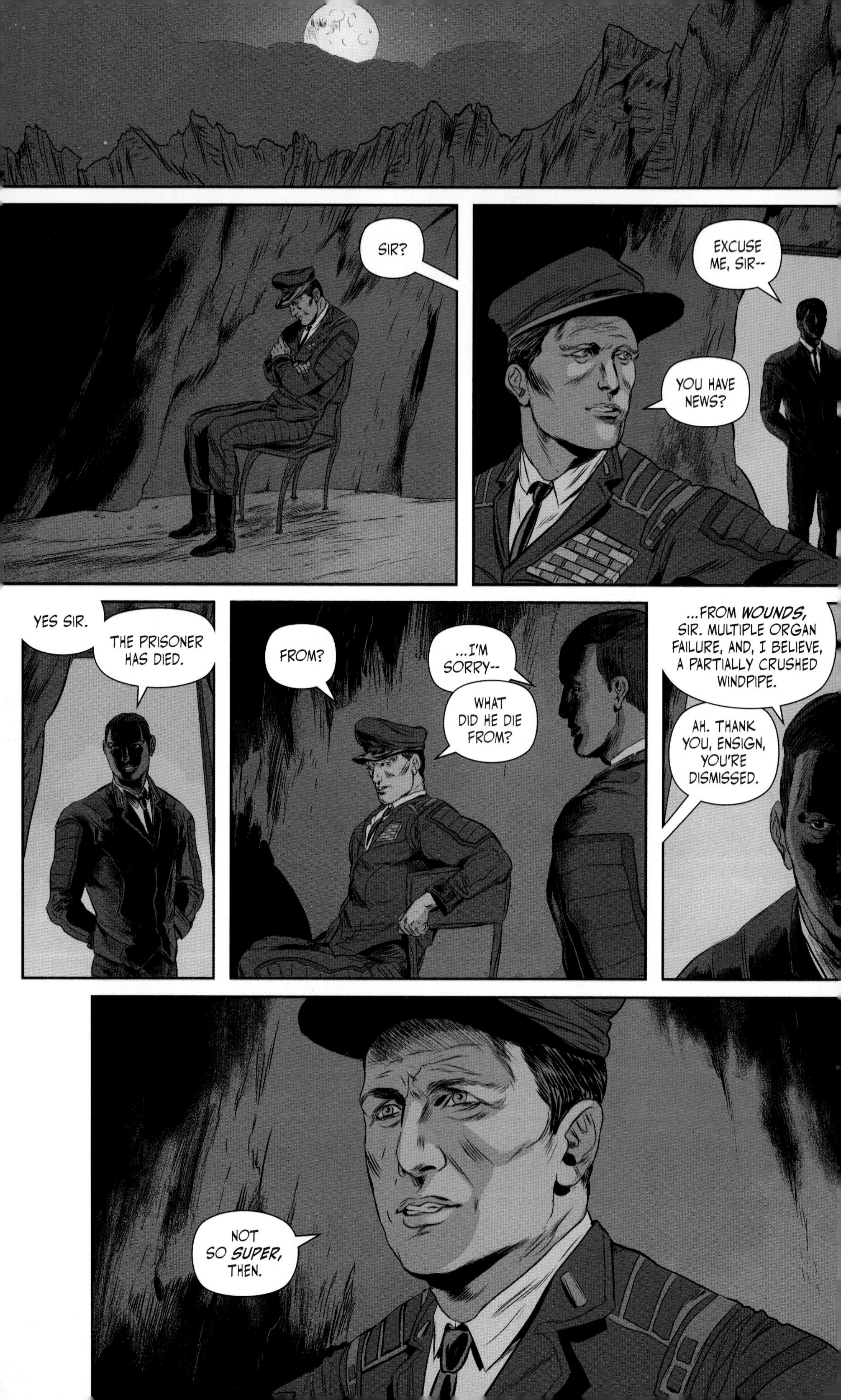
SIR?
EXCUSE ME, SIR--
YOU HAVE NEWS?
YES SIR.
THE PRISONER HAS DIED.
FROM?
...I'M SORRY--
WHAT DID HE DIE FROM?
...FROM WOUNDS, SIR. MULTIPLE ORGAN FAILURE, AND, I BELIEVE, A PARTIALLY CRUSHED WINDPIPE.
AH. THANK YOU, ENSIGN, YOU'RE DISMISSED.
NOT SO SUPER, THEN.

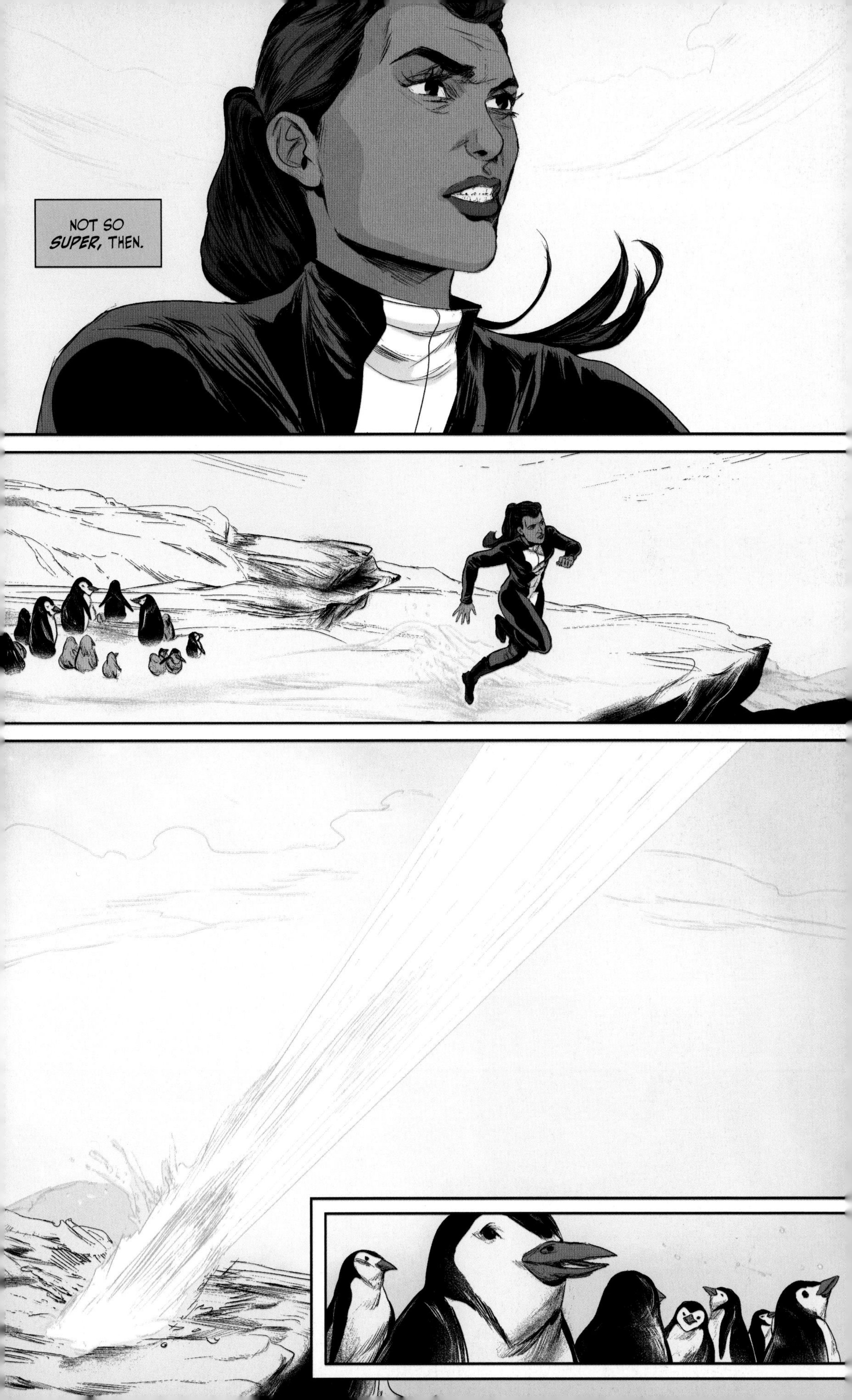
NOT SO SUPER, THEN.

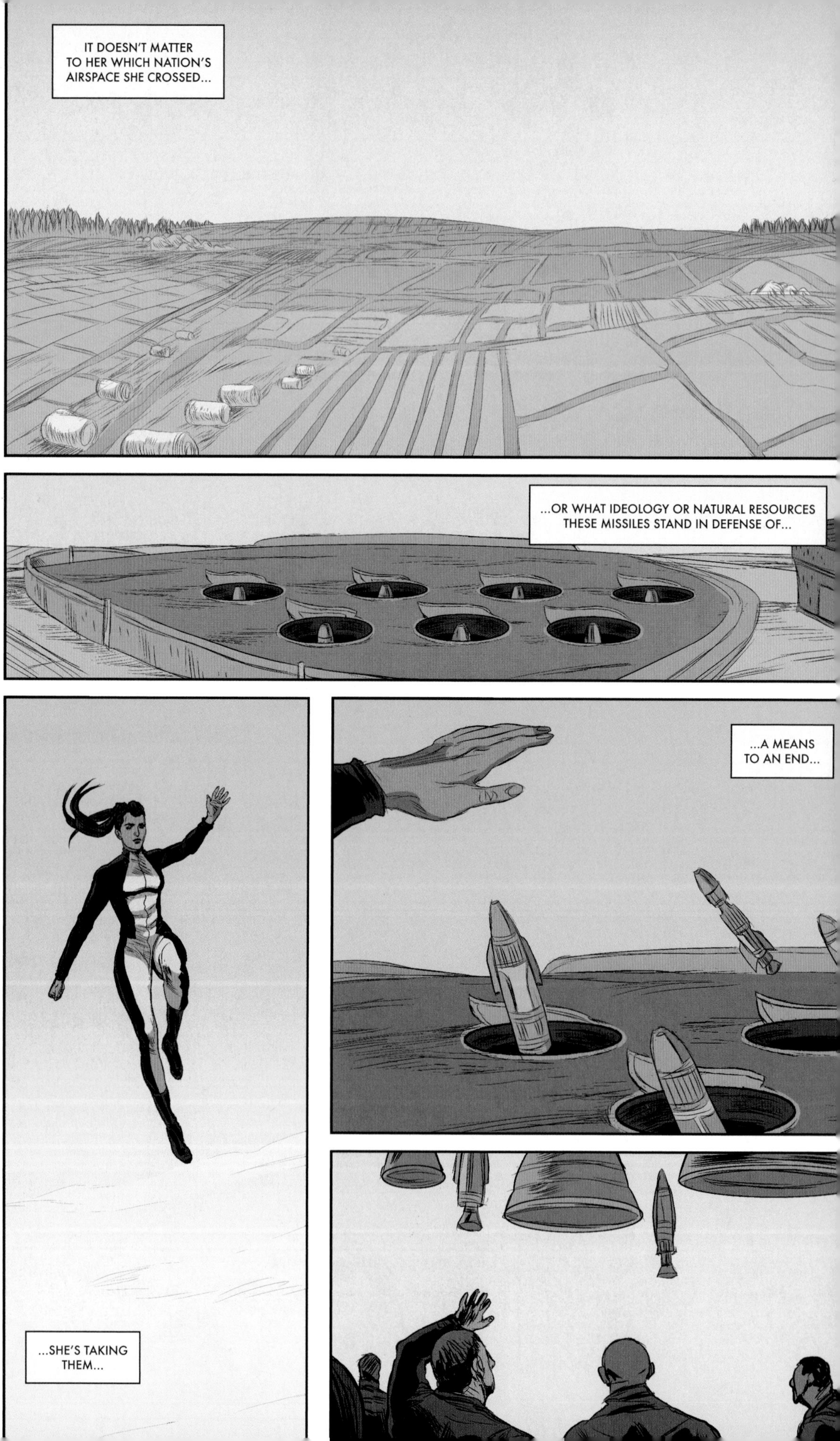
IT DOESN'T MATTER TO HER WHICH NATION'S AIRSPACE SHE CROSSED...
...OR WHAT IDEOLOGY OR NATURAL RESOURCES THESE MISSILES STAND IN DEFENSE OF...
...SHE'S TAKING THEM...
...A MEANS TO AN END...

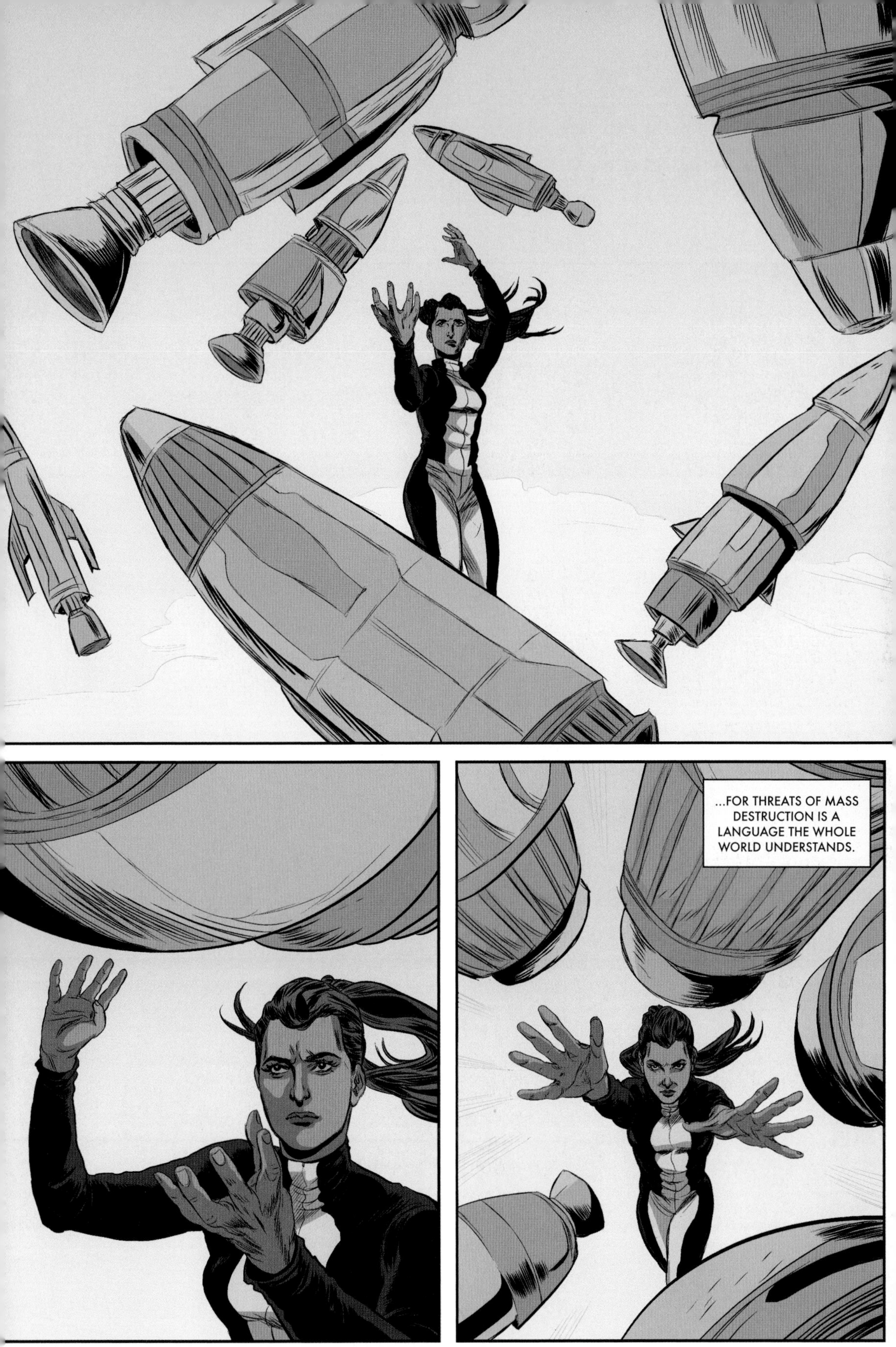
...FOR THREATS OF MASS DESTRUCTION IS A LANGUAGE THE WHOLE WORLD UNDERSTANDS.

THIS IS MARA PRINCE.

TODAY MY BROTHER MARK PRINCE WAS KILLED BY MILITARY INTERROGATORS. THEY WANTED TO SEE IF HE WAS LIKE ME. THEY WANTED TO SEE IF WHATEVER IS HAPPENING TO ME WAS HAPPENING TO HIM ALSO.

BECAUSE I WOULDN'T GIVE THEM WHAT THEY WANTED: MY BODY, MY SOUL, AND MY FREEDOM.

MARK, A PROFESSIONAL BATTLEFIELD SOLDIER... HE GAVE THE MILITARY ALL THOSE THINGS AND MORE. BUT IT WASN'T ENOUGH.

AND NOW THIS WORLD HAS TAKEN ALMOST EVERYTHING FROM ME IT CAN.

THERE IS *ONE THING* LEFT, AND I'M *OFFERING* IT UP FREELY.

MY CITIZENSHIP AS A MEMBER OF THE HUMAN RACE.

I NO LONGER WANT IT. IT'S MEANINGLESS TO ME.

THE THING IS, DESPITE EVERYTHING THAT'S HAPPENED TO ME, ONE THING'S BEEN CONSTANT: I WAS *NEVER* A THREAT TO *ANYONE.*

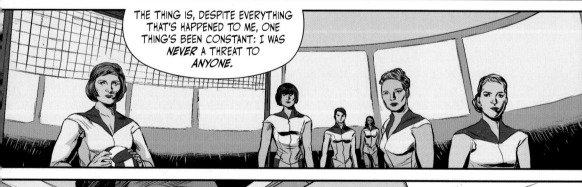

BUT YOU TREATED ME LIKE I WAS.

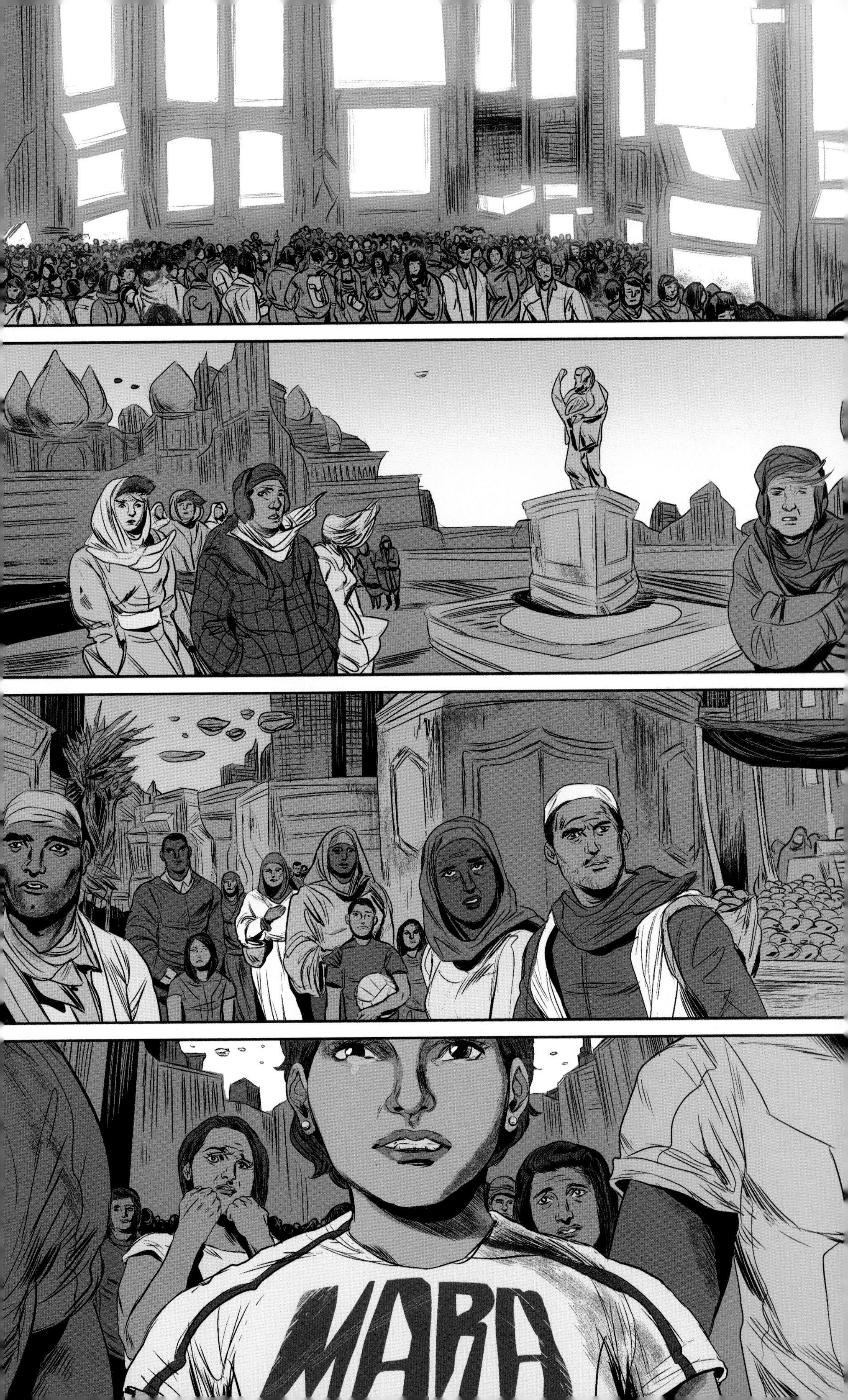
MARA

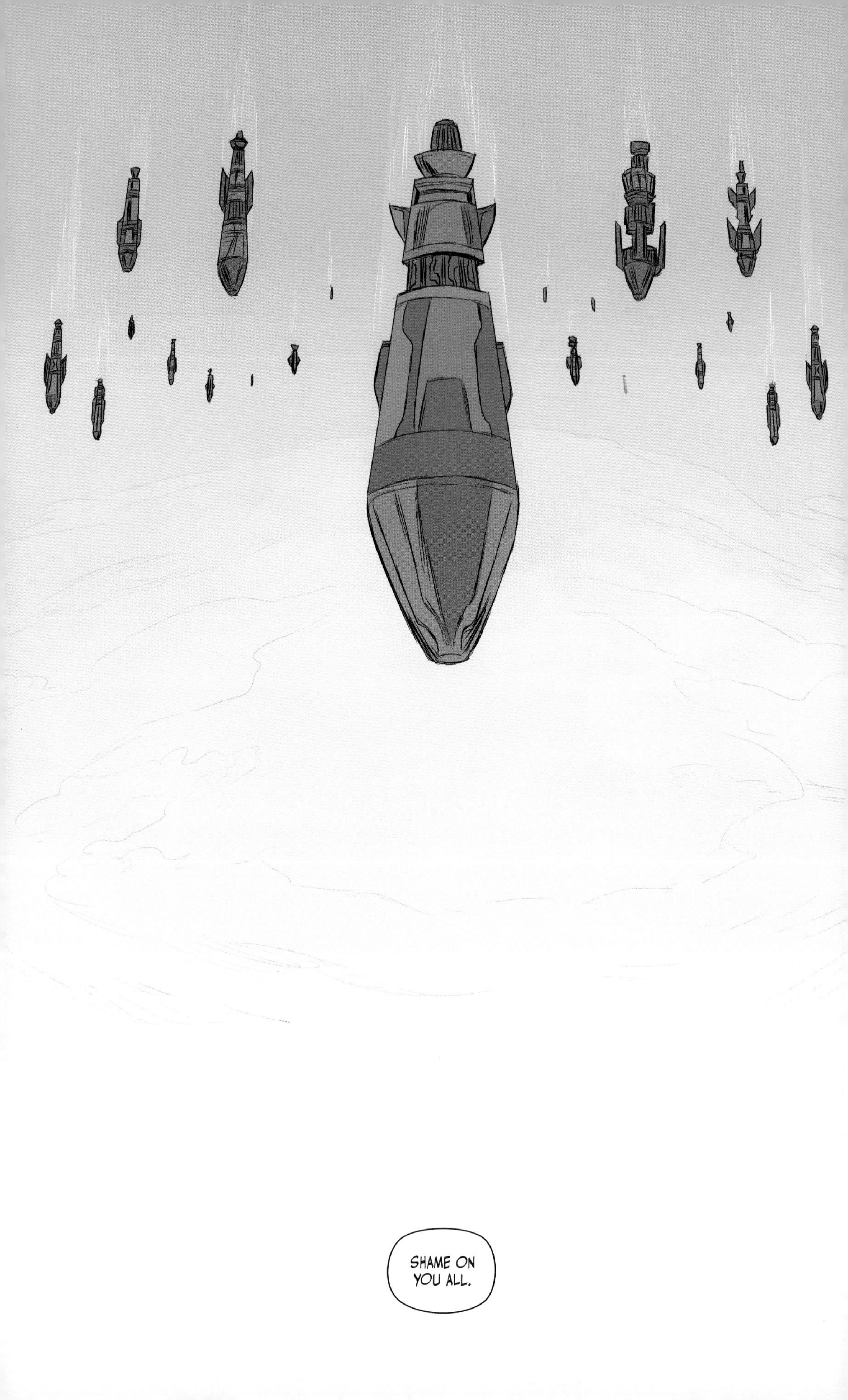
SHAME ON
YOU ALL.

CHAPTER SIX

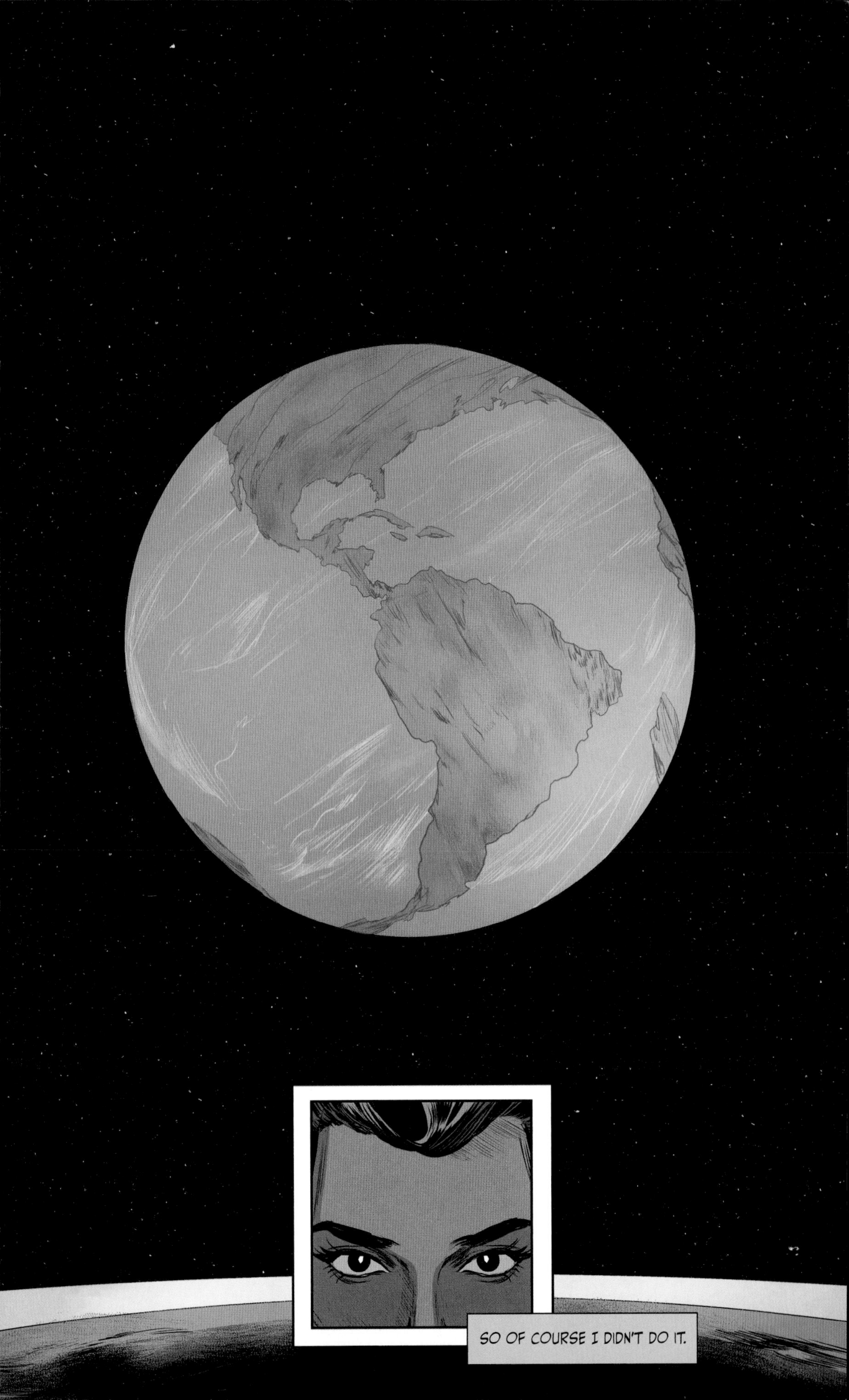
SO OF COURSE I DIDN'T DO IT.

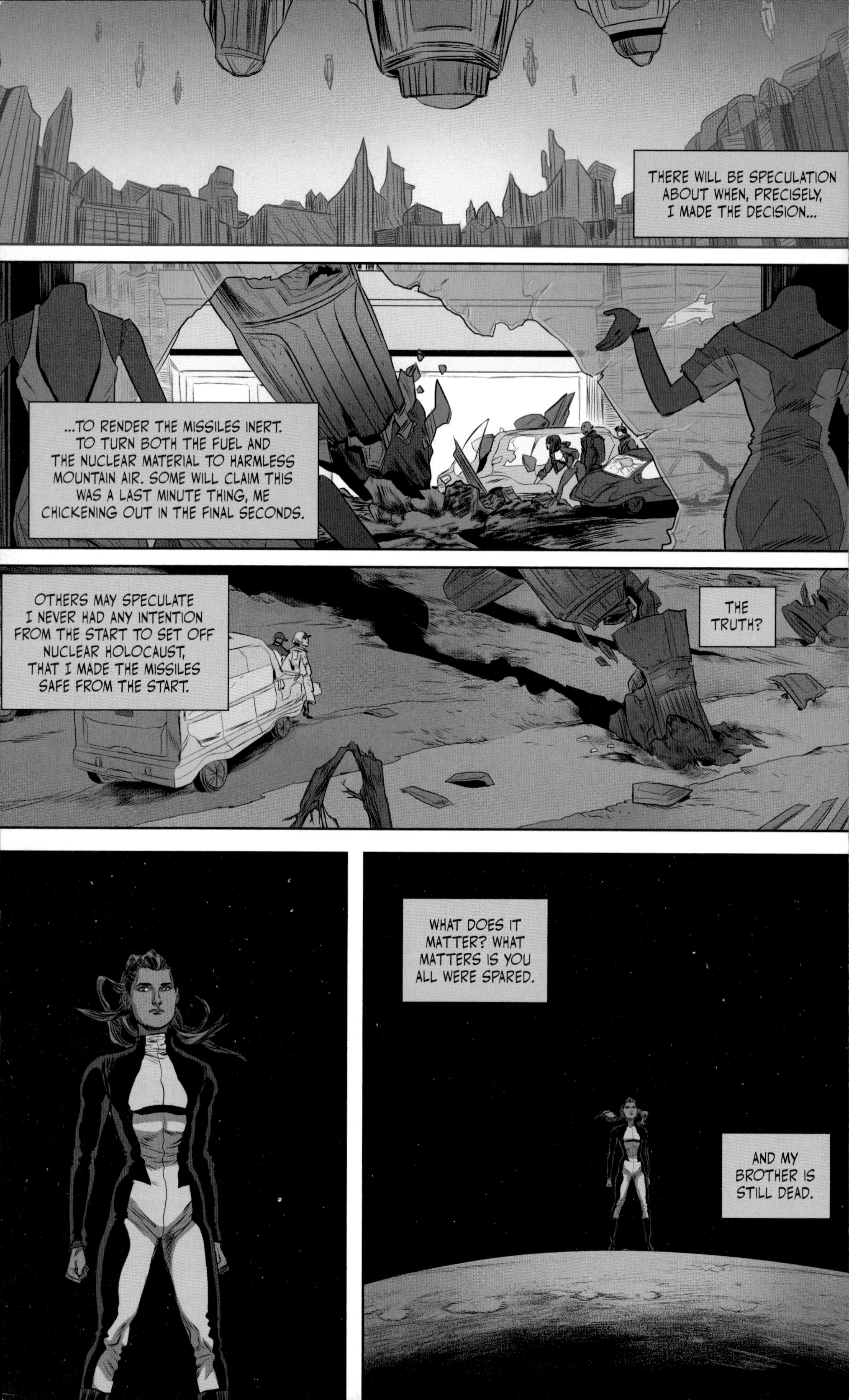
THERE WILL BE SPECULATION ABOUT WHEN, PRECISELY, I MADE THE DECISION...
...TO RENDER THE MISSILES INERT. TO TURN BOTH THE FUEL AND THE NUCLEAR MATERIAL TO HARMLESS MOUNTAIN AIR. SOME WILL CLAIM THIS WAS A LAST MINUTE THING, ME CHICKENING OUT IN THE FINAL SECONDS.
OTHERS MAY SPECULATE I NEVER HAD ANY INTENTION FROM THE START TO SET OFF NUCLEAR HOLOCAUST, THAT I MADE THE MISSILES SAFE FROM THE START.
THE TRUTH?
WHAT DOES IT MATTER? WHAT MATTERS IS YOU ALL WERE SPARED.
AND MY BROTHER IS STILL DEAD.

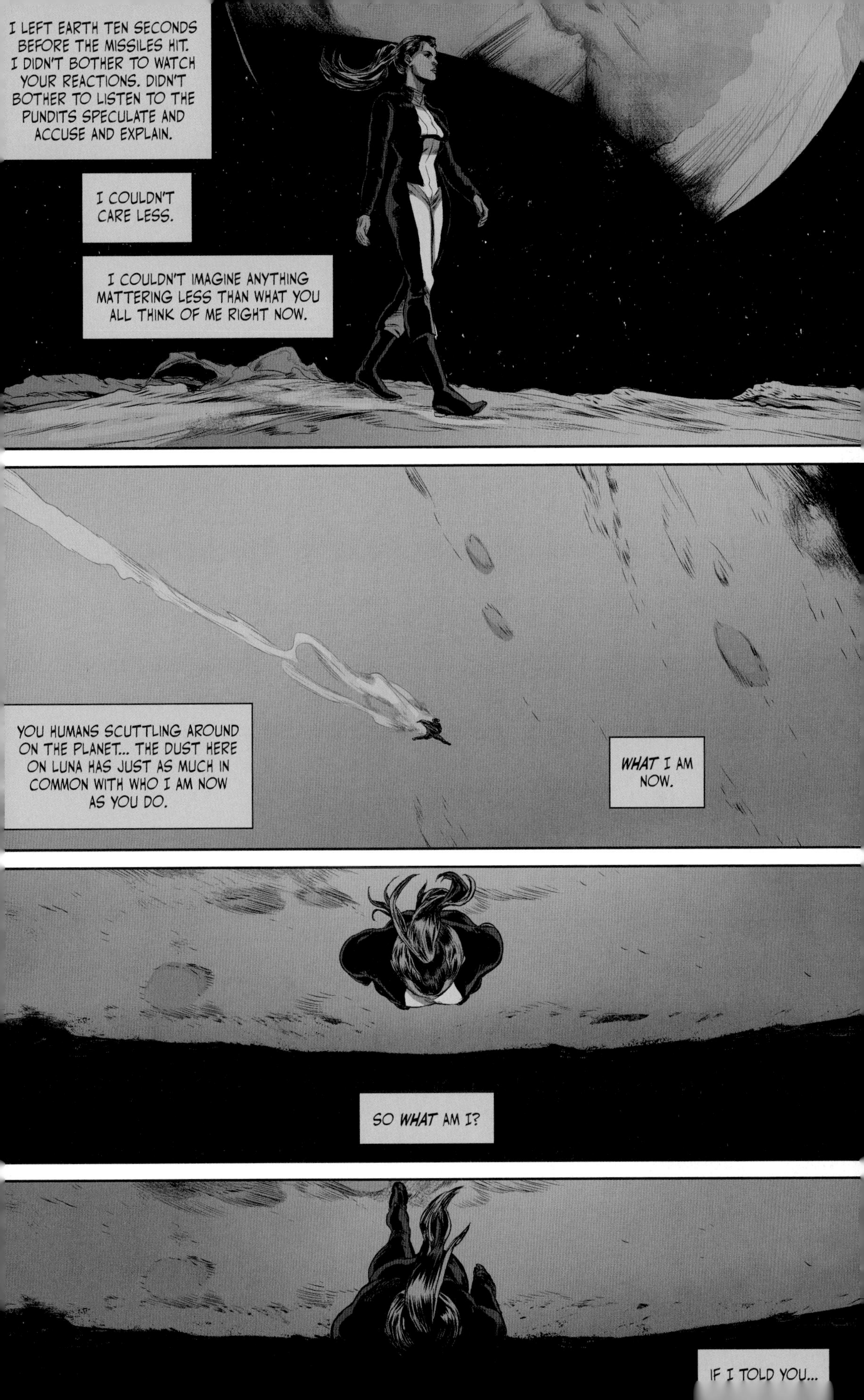
I LEFT EARTH TEN SECONDS BEFORE THE MISSILES HIT. I DIDN'T BOTHER TO WATCH YOUR REACTIONS. DIDN'T BOTHER TO LISTEN TO THE PUNDITS SPECULATE AND ACCUSE AND EXPLAIN.
I COULDN'T CARE LESS.
I COULDN'T IMAGINE ANYTHING MATTERING LESS THAN WHAT YOU ALL THINK OF ME RIGHT NOW.
YOU HUMANS SCUTTLING AROUND ON THE PLANET... THE DUST HERE ON LUNA HAS JUST AS MUCH IN COMMON WITH WHO I AM NOW AS YOU DO.
WHAT I AM NOW.
SO WHAT AM I?
IF I TOLD YOU...

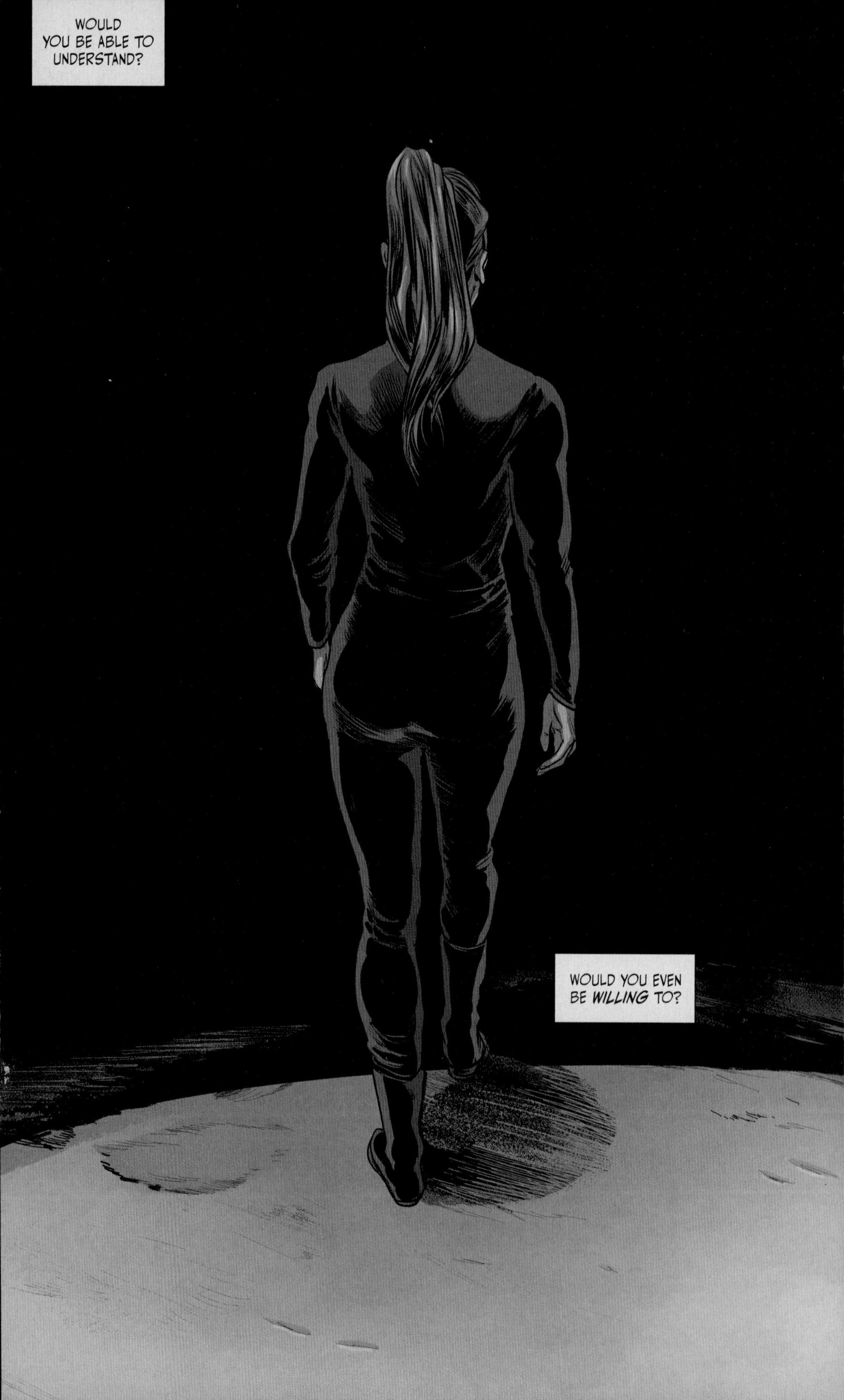
WOULD YOU BE ABLE TO UNDERSTAND?
WOULD YOU EVEN BE *WILLING* TO?

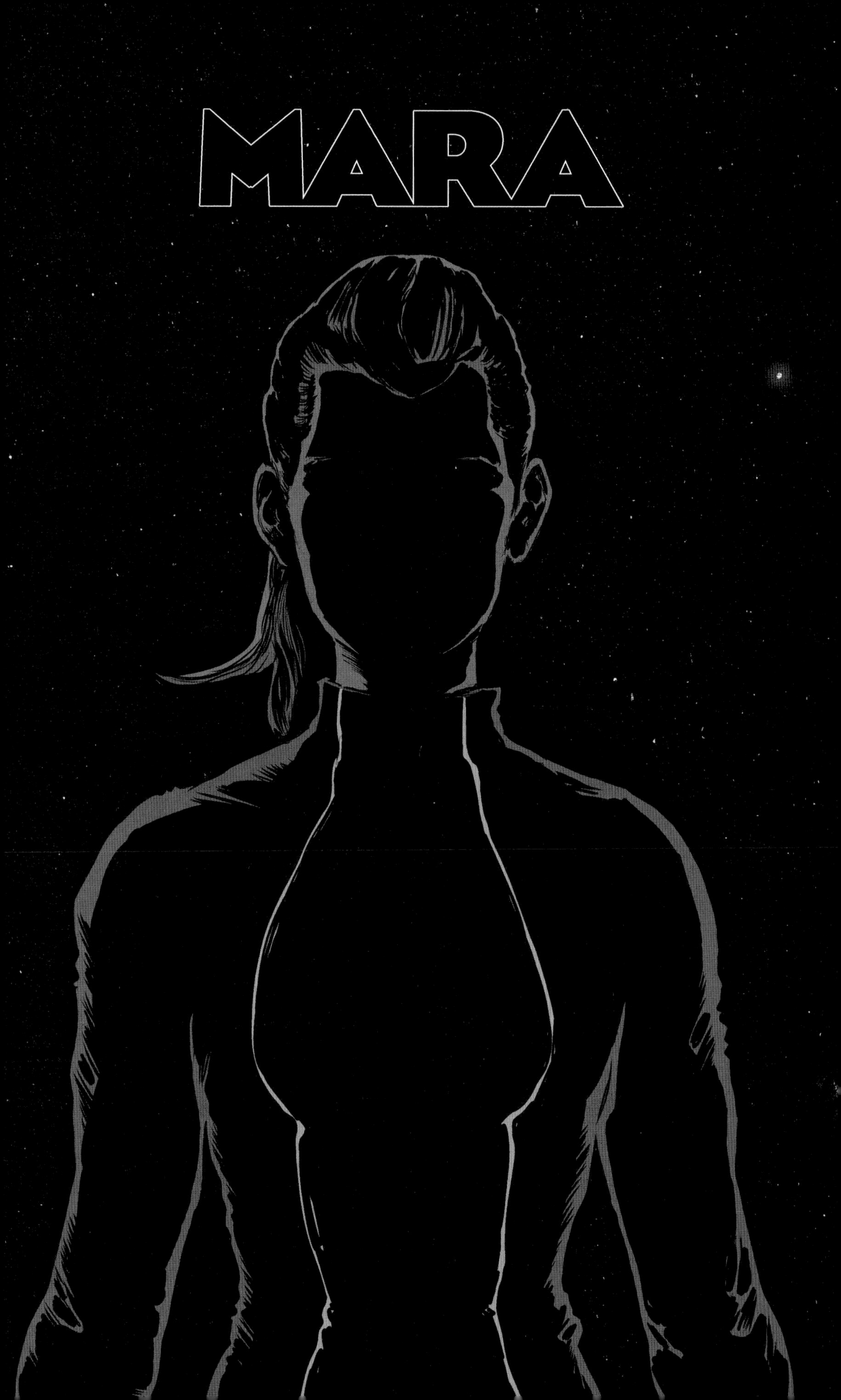
MARA

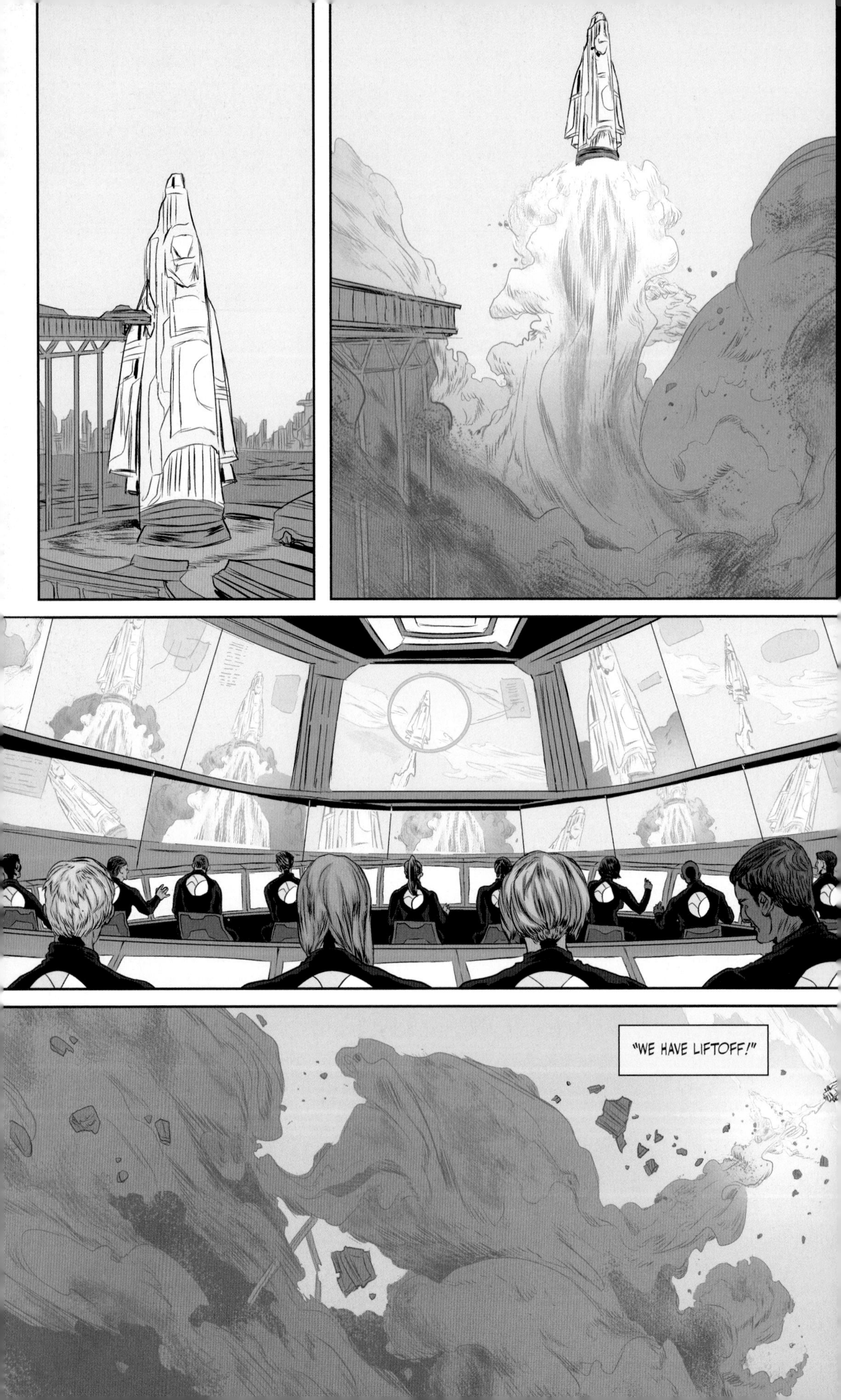
"WE HAVE LIFTOFF!"

"A TRULY MOMENTOUS DAY, AS WE, FOR THE FIRST TIME IN DECADES, AGAIN LOOK TO THE STARS."

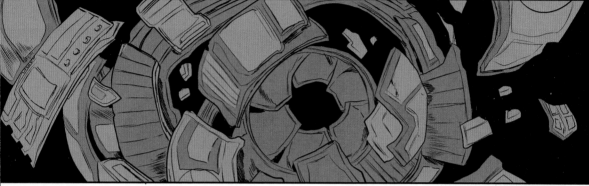

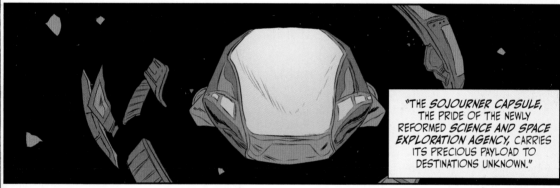

"THE *SOJOURNER CAPSULE*, THE PRIDE OF THE NEWLY REFORMED *SCIENCE AND SPACE EXPLORATION AGENCY*, CARRIES ITS PRECIOUS PAYLOAD TO DESTINATIONS UNKNOWN."

"WHAT IS THAT PAYLOAD?"

"PLANET EARTH'S FIRST CREWED FLIGHT TO DEEP SPACE."

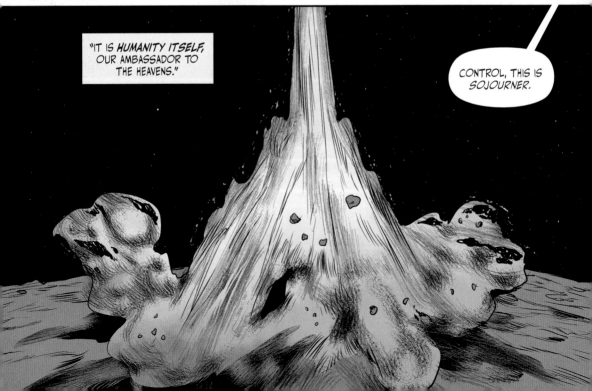

"IT IS *HUMANITY ITSELF,* OUR AMBASSADOR TO THE HEAVENS."

CONTROL, THIS IS *SOJOURNER.*

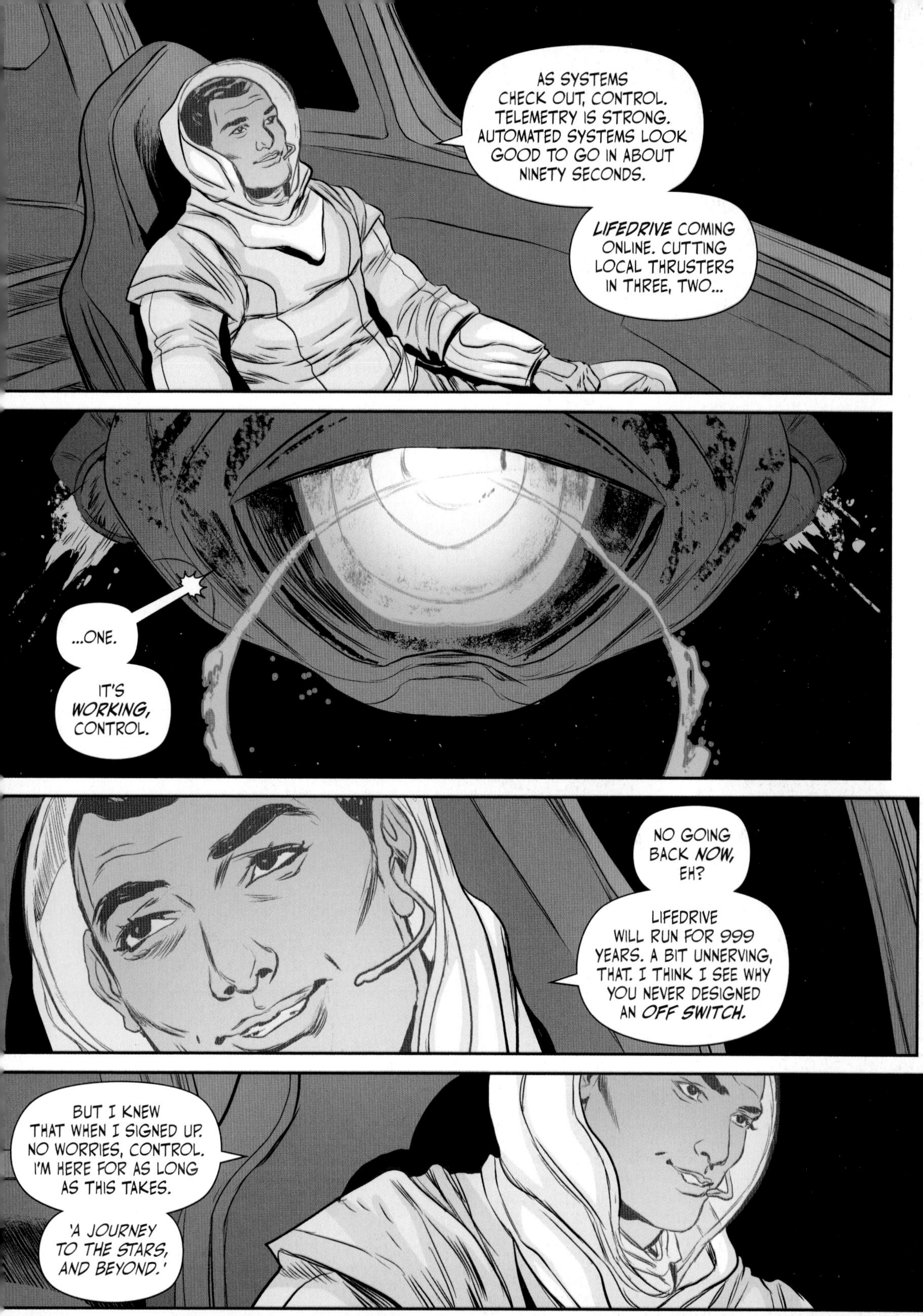
AS SYSTEMS CHECK OUT, CONTROL. TELEMETRY IS STRONG. AUTOMATED SYSTEMS LOOK GOOD TO GO IN ABOUT NINETY SECONDS.
LIFEDRIVE COMING ONLINE. CUTTING LOCAL THRUSTERS IN THREE, TWO...
...ONE.
IT'S WORKING, CONTROL.
NO GOING BACK NOW, EH?
LIFEDRIVE WILL RUN FOR 999 YEARS. A BIT UNNERVING, THAT. I THINK I SEE WHY YOU NEVER DESIGNED AN OFF SWITCH.
BUT I KNEW THAT WHEN I SIGNED UP. NO WORRIES, CONTROL. I'M HERE FOR AS LONG AS THIS TAKES.
'A JOURNEY TO THE STARS, AND BEYOND.'

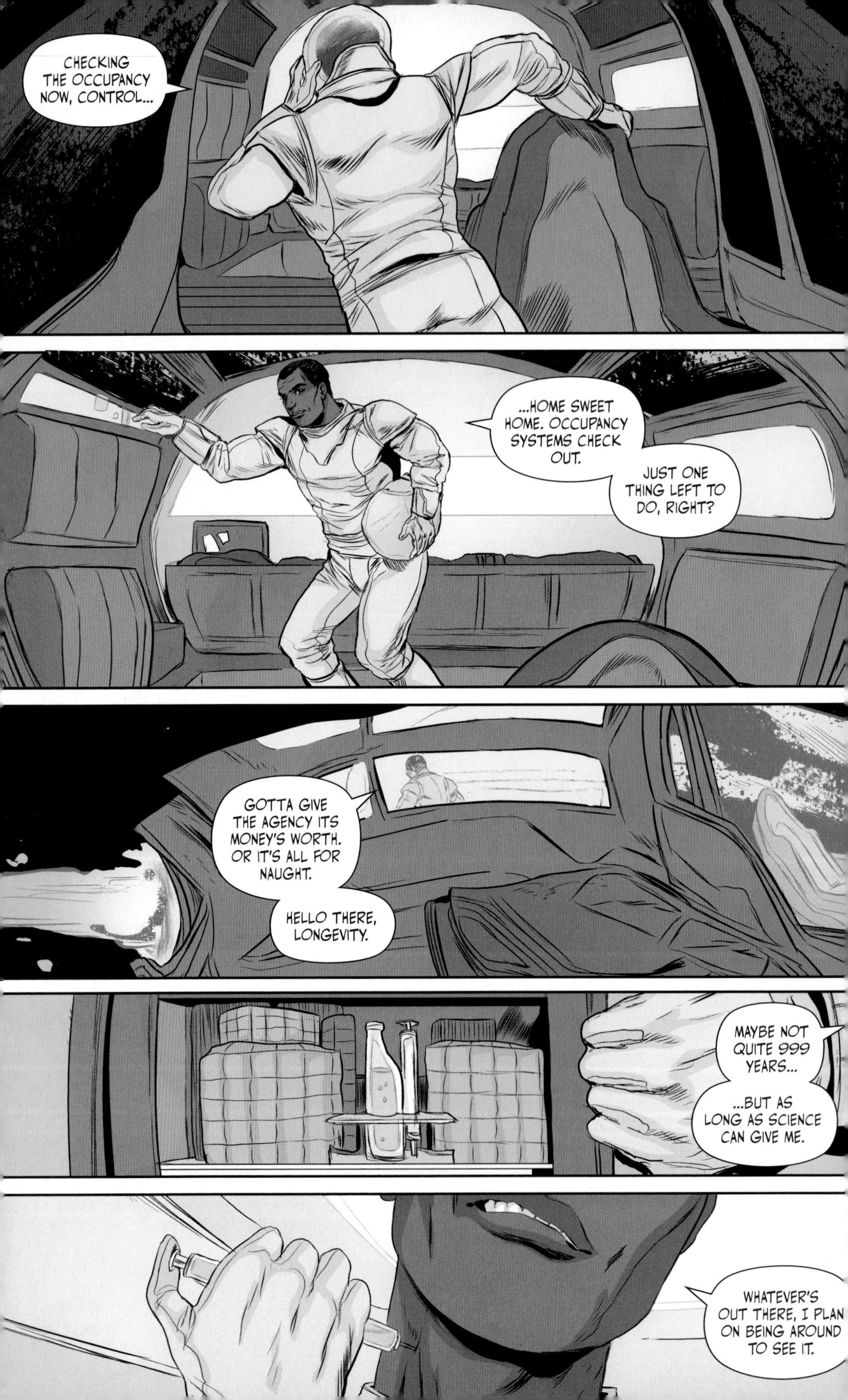
CHECKING THE OCCUPANCY NOW, CONTROL...
...HOME SWEET HOME. OCCUPANCY SYSTEMS CHECK OUT.
JUST ONE THING LEFT TO DO, RIGHT?
GOTTA GIVE THE AGENCY ITS MONEY'S WORTH. OR IT'S ALL FOR NAUGHT.
HELLO THERE, LONGEVITY.
MAYBE NOT QUITE 999 YEARS...
...BUT AS LONG AS SCIENCE CAN GIVE ME.
WHATEVER'S OUT THERE, I PLAN ON BEING AROUND TO SEE IT.

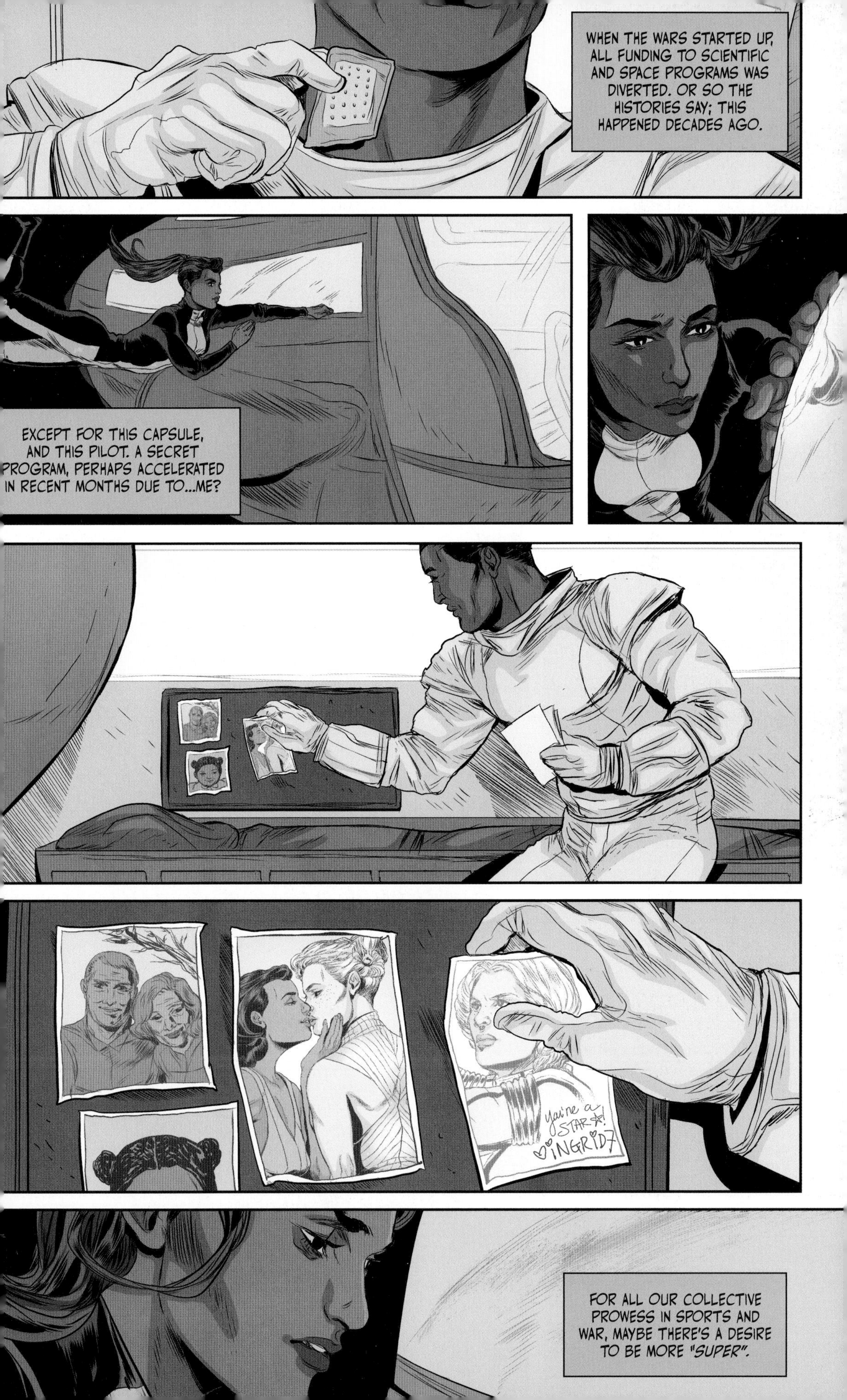
WHEN THE WARS STARTED UP, ALL FUNDING TO SCIENTIFIC AND SPACE PROGRAMS WAS DIVERTED. OR SO THE HISTORIES SAY; THIS HAPPENED DECADES AGO.
EXCEPT FOR THIS CAPSULE, AND THIS PILOT. A SECRET PROGRAM, PERHAPS ACCELERATED IN RECENT MONTHS DUE TO...ME?
you're a STAR!
INGRID7
FOR ALL OUR COLLECTIVE PROWESS IN SPORTS AND WAR, MAYBE THERE'S A DESIRE TO BE MORE "SUPER".

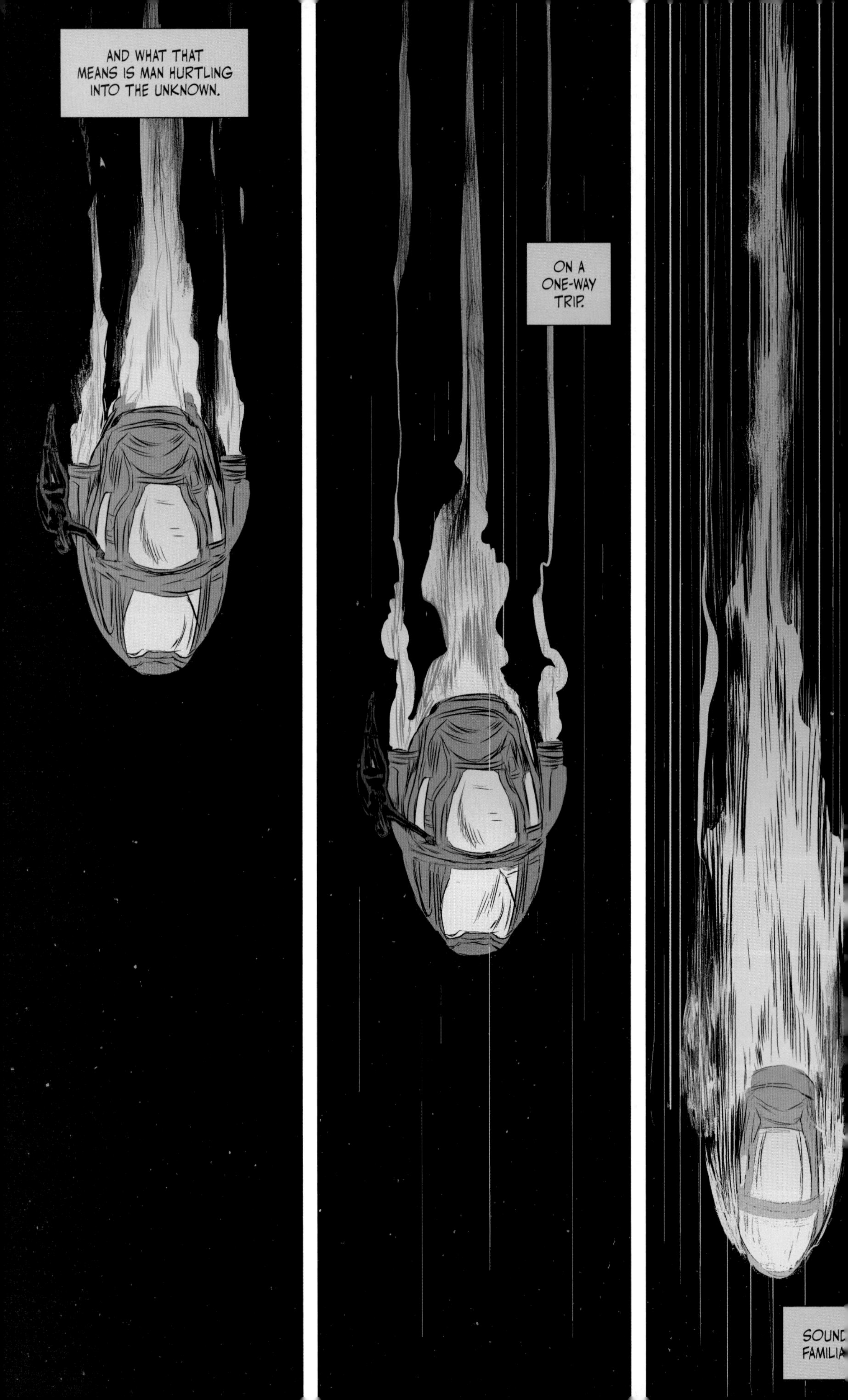

AND WHAT THAT MEANS IS MAN HURTLING INTO THE UNKNOWN.
ON A ONE-WAY TRIP.
SOUND FAMILIA

MY FATHER.

MY MOTHER.

PARENTS FOR ALL OF SIX YEARS, THEIR OBLIGATION TO THE STATE COMPLETE.

I DON'T WANT TO GO.

YOU'LL GO.

YOUR BROTHER DIDN'T CRY.

I'M NOT CRYING!

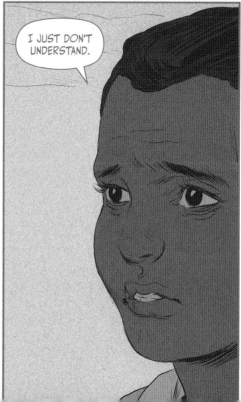

I JUST DON'T UNDERSTAND.

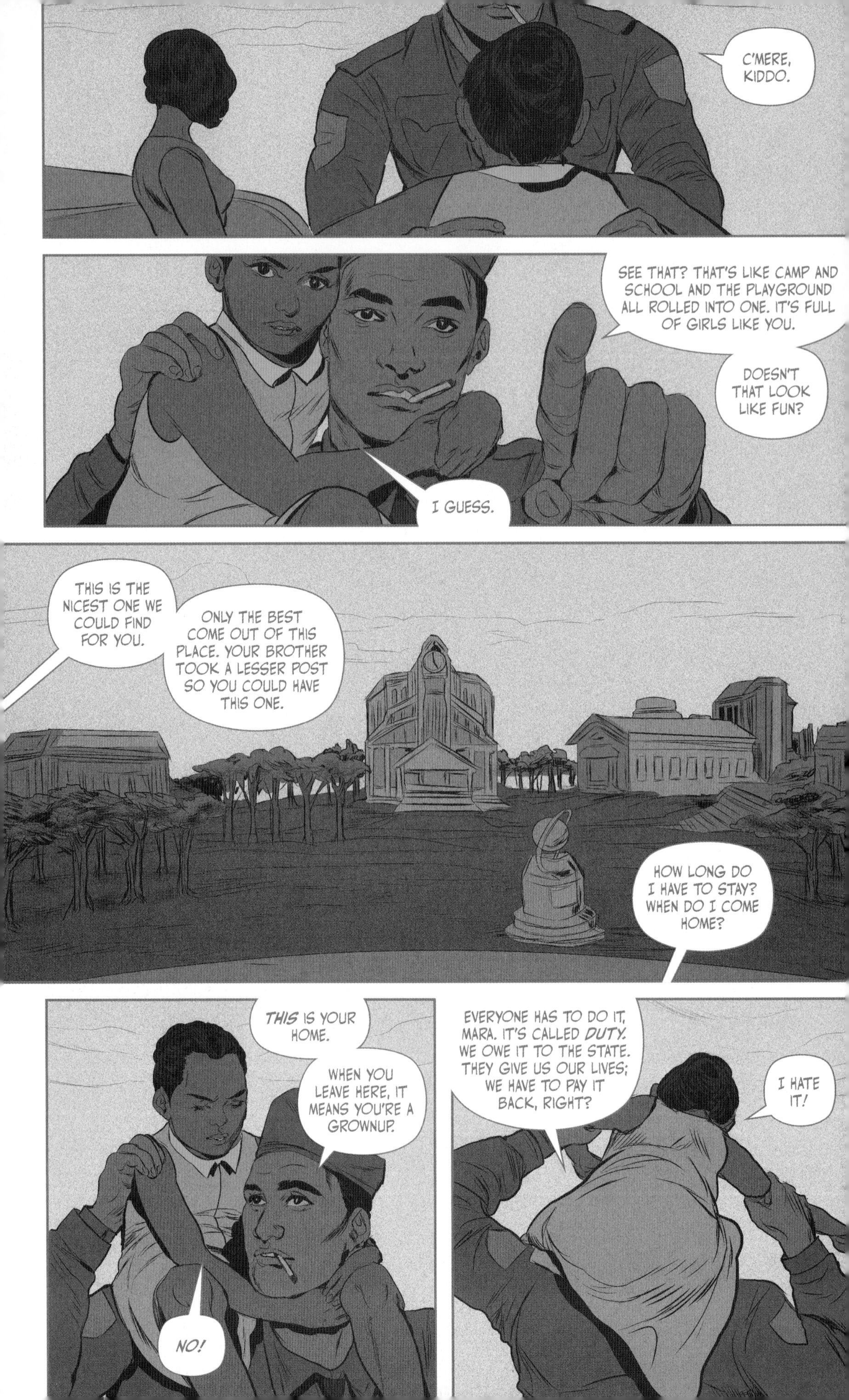
C'MERE, KIDDO.
SEE THAT? THAT'S LIKE CAMP AND SCHOOL AND THE PLAYGROUND ALL ROLLED INTO ONE. IT'S FULL OF GIRLS LIKE YOU.
DOESN'T THAT LOOK LIKE FUN?
I GUESS.
THIS IS THE NICEST ONE WE COULD FIND FOR YOU.
ONLY THE BEST COME OUT OF THIS PLACE. YOUR BROTHER TOOK A LESSER POST SO YOU COULD HAVE THIS ONE.
HOW LONG DO I HAVE TO STAY? WHEN DO I COME HOME?
THIS IS YOUR HOME.
WHEN YOU LEAVE HERE, IT MEANS YOU'RE A GROWNUP.
NO!
EVERYONE HAS TO DO IT, MARA. IT'S CALLED *DUTY.* WE OWE IT TO THE STATE. THEY GIVE US OUR LIVES; WE HAVE TO PAY IT BACK, RIGHT?
I HATE IT!

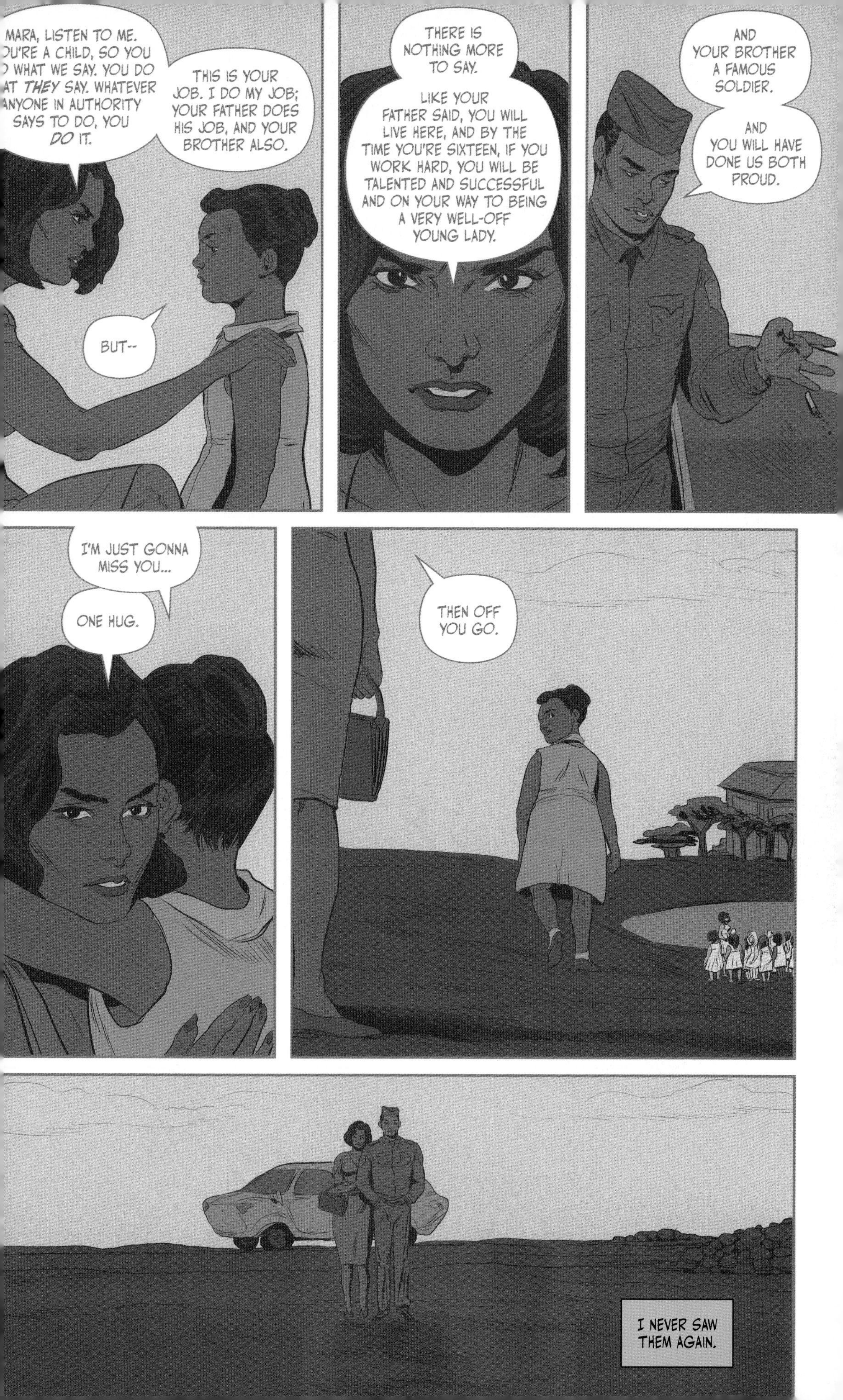
MARA, LISTEN TO ME. OU'RE A CHILD, SO YOU WHAT WE SAY. YOU DO AT *THEY* SAY. WHATEVER ANYONE IN AUTHORITY SAYS TO DO, YOU *DO* IT.
THIS IS YOUR JOB. I DO MY JOB; YOUR FATHER DOES HIS JOB, AND YOUR BROTHER ALSO.
BUT--
THERE IS NOTHING MORE TO SAY.
LIKE YOUR FATHER SAID, YOU WILL LIVE HERE, AND BY THE TIME YOU'RE SIXTEEN, IF YOU WORK HARD, YOU WILL BE TALENTED AND SUCCESSFUL AND ON YOUR WAY TO BEING A VERY WELL-OFF YOUNG LADY.
AND YOUR BROTHER A FAMOUS SOLDIER.
AND YOU WILL HAVE DONE US BOTH PROUD.
I'M JUST GONNA MISS YOU...
ONE HUG.
THEN OFF YOU GO.
I NEVER SAW THEM AGAIN.

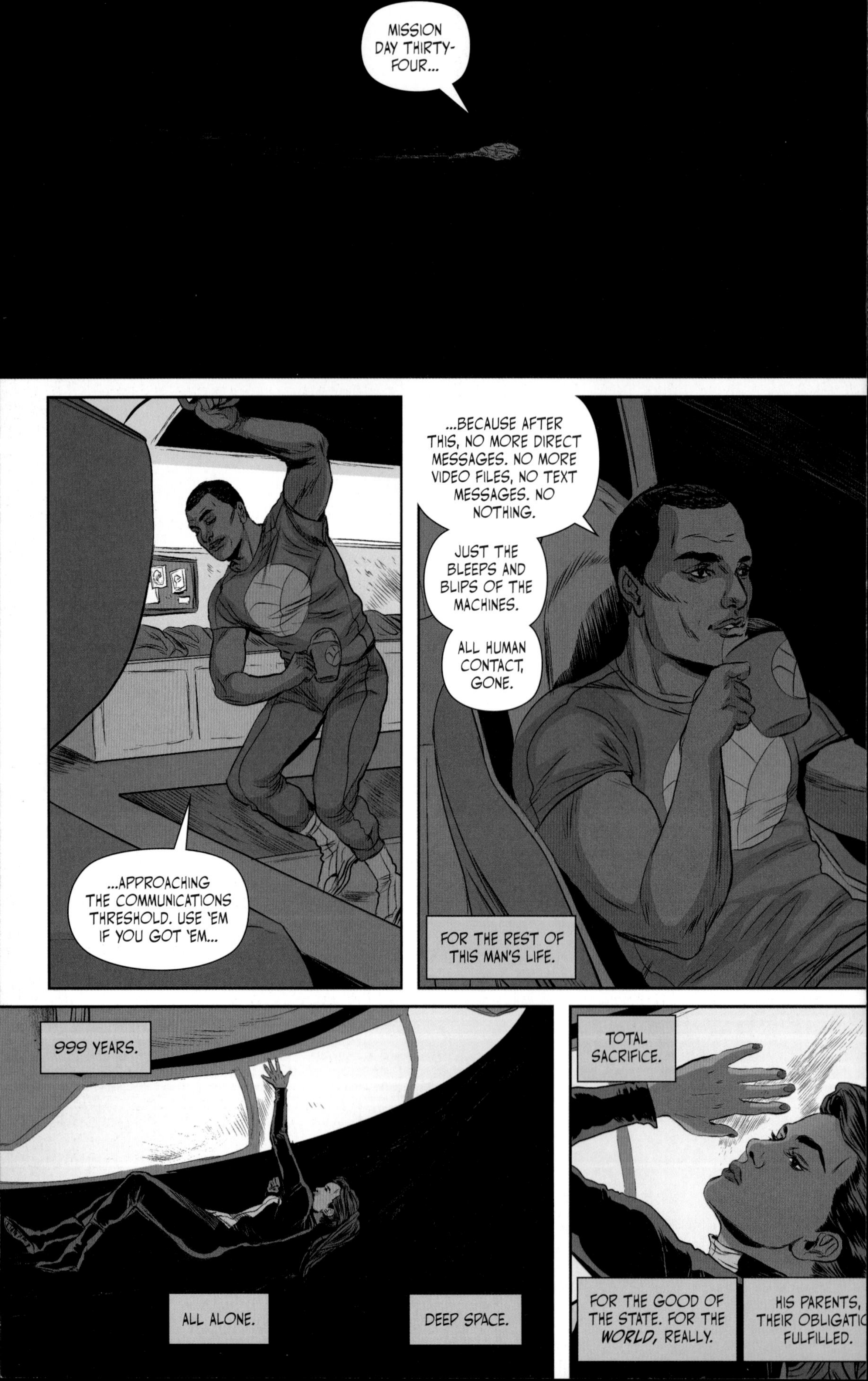
MISSION DAY THIRTY-FOUR...
...APPROACHING THE COMMUNICATIONS THRESHOLD. USE 'EM IF YOU GOT 'EM...
...BECAUSE AFTER THIS, NO MORE DIRECT MESSAGES. NO MORE VIDEO FILES, NO TEXT MESSAGES. NO NOTHING.
JUST THE BLEEPS AND BLIPS OF THE MACHINES.
ALL HUMAN CONTACT, GONE.
FOR THE REST OF THIS MAN'S LIFE.
999 YEARS.
ALL ALONE.
DEEP SPACE.
TOTAL SACRIFICE.
FOR THE GOOD OF THE STATE. FOR THE *WORLD*, REALLY.
HIS PARENTS, THEIR OBLIGATIC FULFILLED.

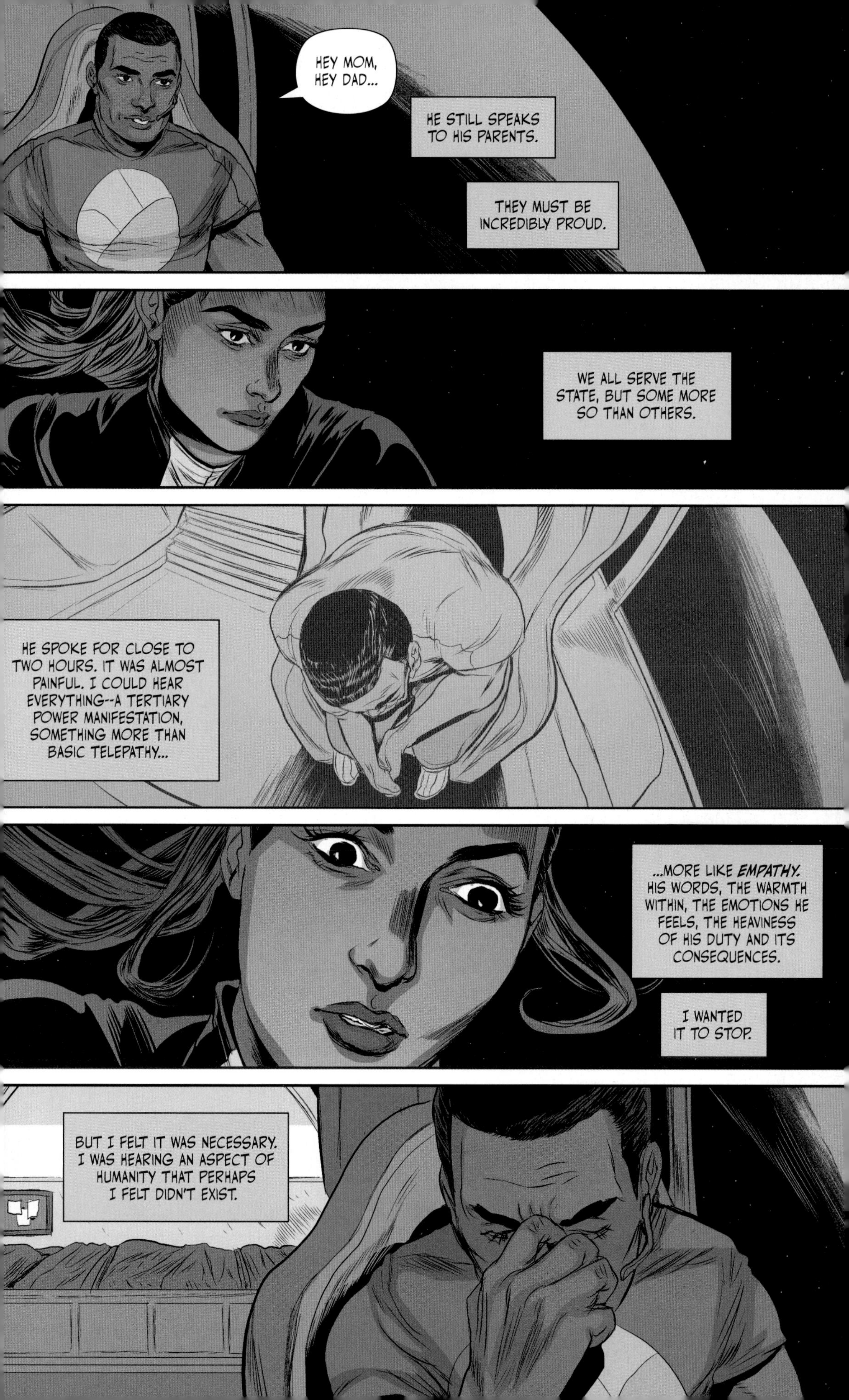
HEY MOM,
HEY DAD...
HE STILL SPEAKS TO HIS PARENTS.
THEY MUST BE INCREDIBLY PROUD.
WE ALL SERVE THE STATE, BUT SOME MORE SO THAN OTHERS.
HE SPOKE FOR CLOSE TO TWO HOURS. IT WAS ALMOST PAINFUL. I COULD HEAR EVERYTHING--A TERTIARY POWER MANIFESTATION, SOMETHING MORE THAN BASIC TELEPATHY...
...MORE LIKE *EMPATHY.* HIS WORDS, THE WARMTH WITHIN, THE EMOTIONS HE FEELS, THE HEAVINESS OF HIS DUTY AND ITS CONSEQUENCES.
I WANTED IT TO STOP.
BUT I FELT IT WAS NECESSARY. I WAS HEARING AN ASPECT OF HUMANITY THAT PERHAPS I FELT DIDN'T EXIST.

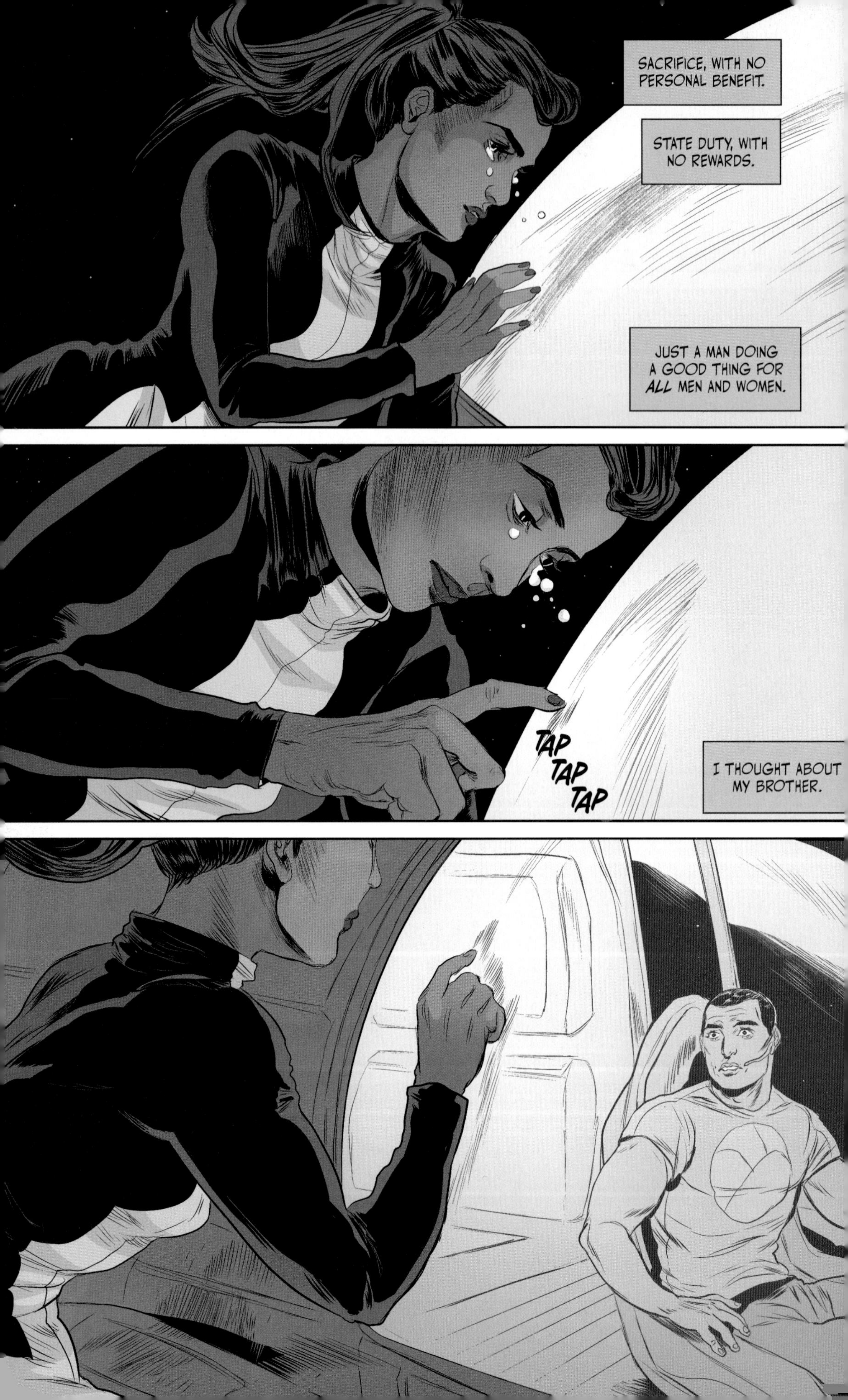
SACRIFICE, WITH NO PERSONAL BENEFIT.
STATE DUTY, WITH NO REWARDS.
JUST A MAN DOING A GOOD THING FOR ALL MEN AND WOMEN.
TAP TAP TAP
I THOUGHT ABOUT MY BROTHER.

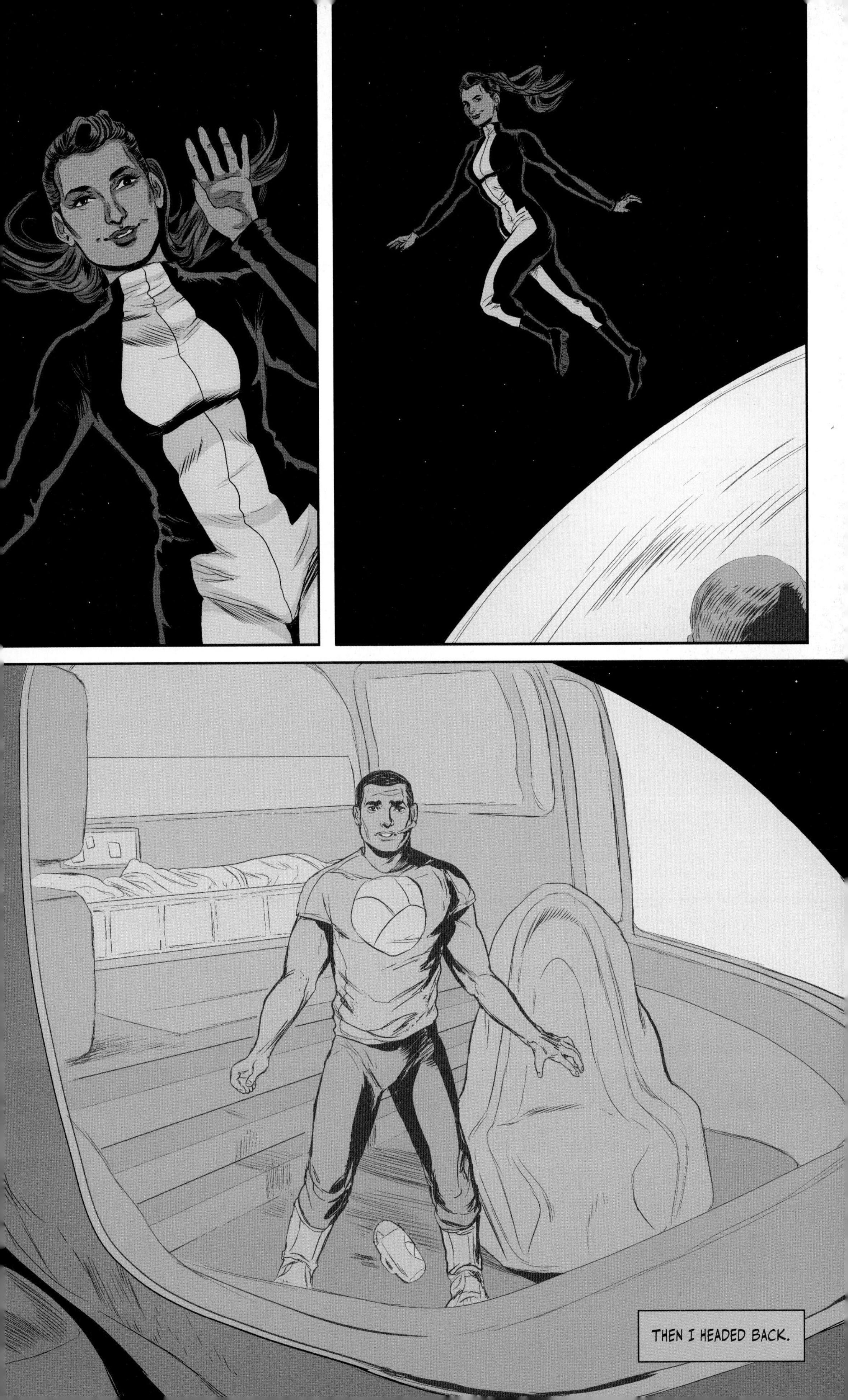
THEN I HEADED BACK.

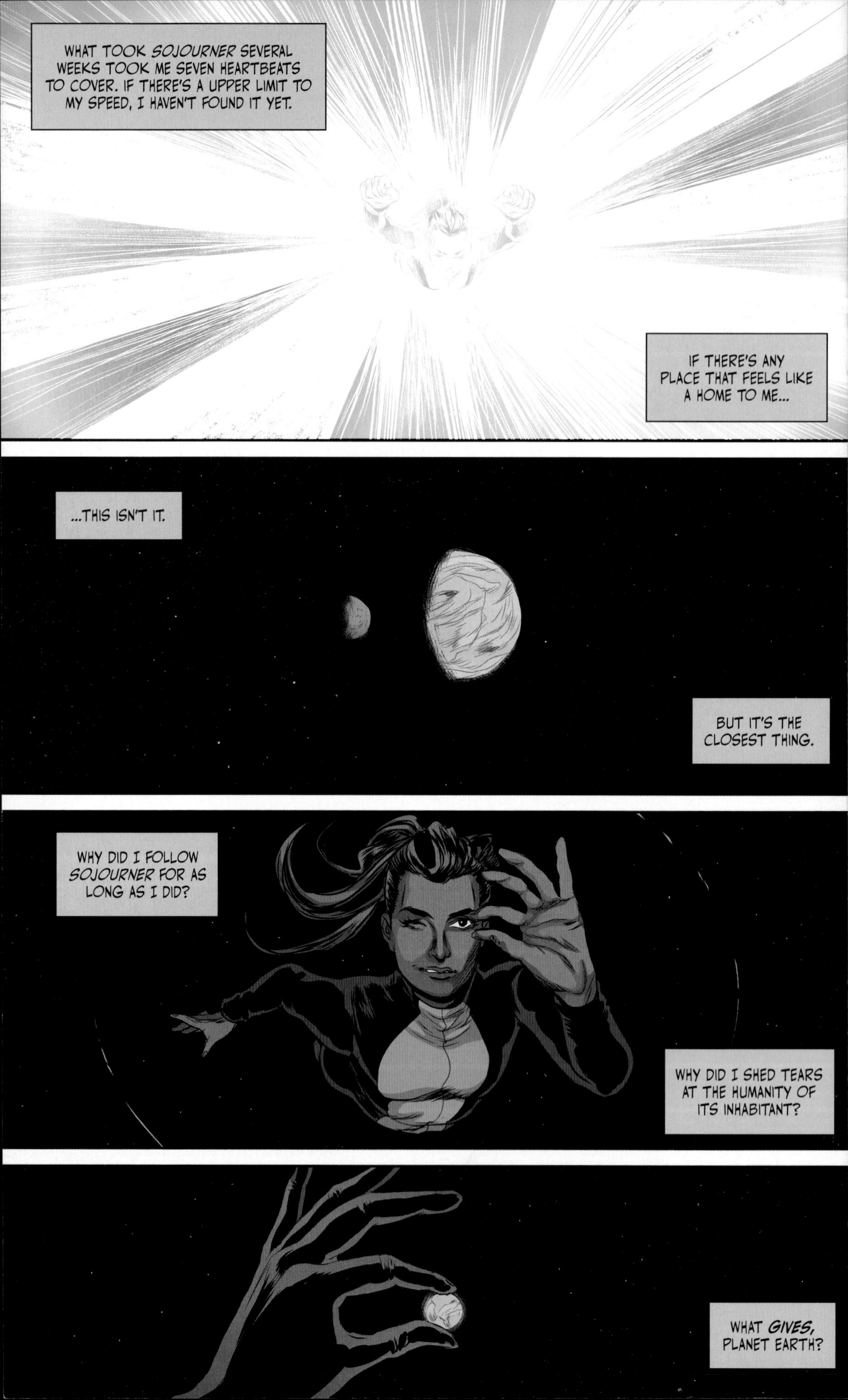
WHAT TOOK *SOJOURNER* SEVERAL WEEKS TOOK ME SEVEN HEARTBEATS TO COVER. IF THERE'S A UPPER LIMIT TO MY SPEED, I HAVEN'T FOUND IT YET.
IF THERE'S ANY PLACE THAT FEELS LIKE A HOME TO ME...
...THIS ISN'T IT.
BUT IT'S THE CLOSEST THING.
WHY DID I FOLLOW *SOJOURNER* FOR AS LONG AS I DID?
WHY DID I SHED TEARS AT THE HUMANITY OF ITS INHABITANT?
WHAT *GIVES*, PLANET EARTH?

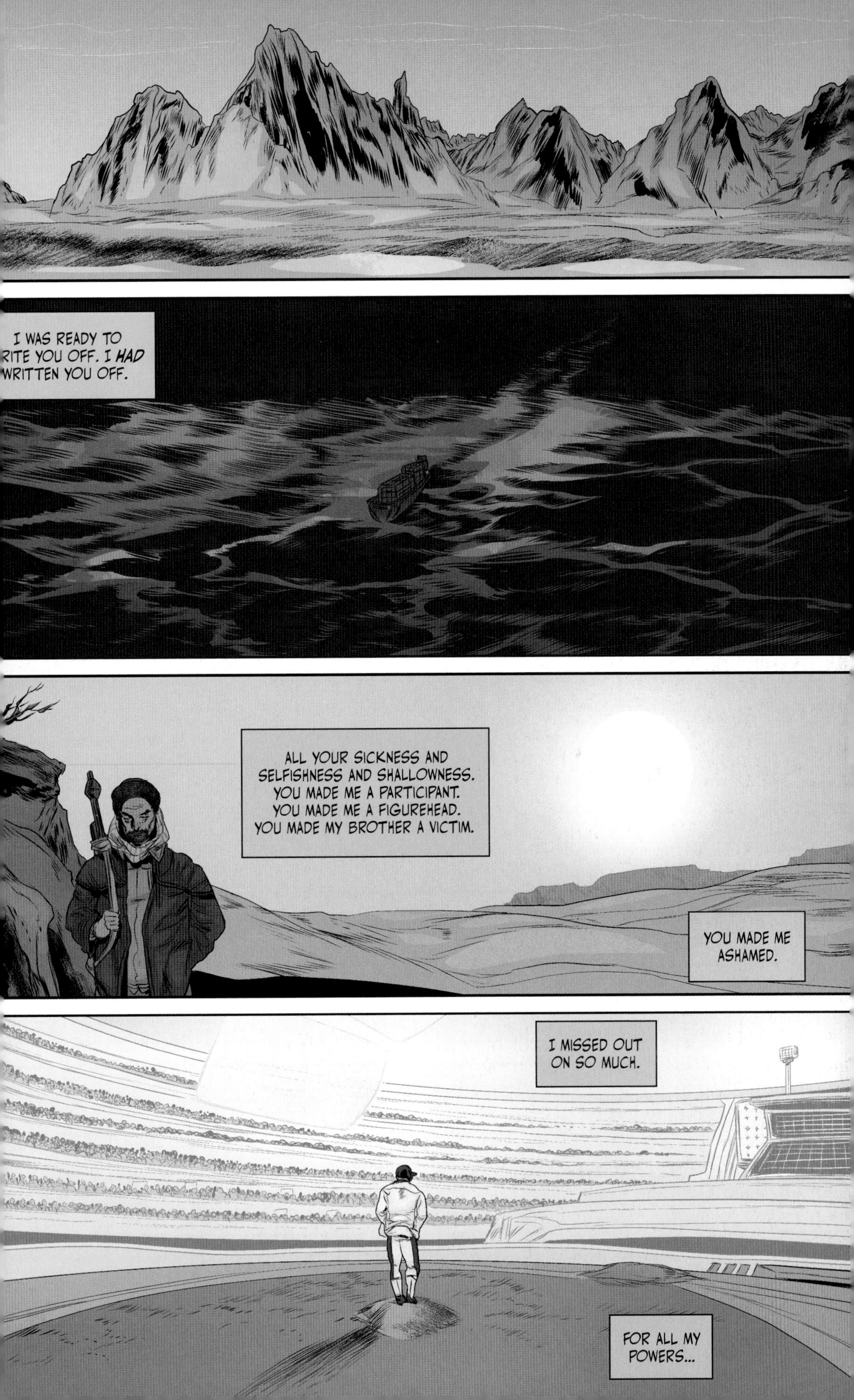
I WAS READY TO
RITE YOU OFF. I *HAD*
WRITTEN YOU OFF.
ALL YOUR SICKNESS AND
SELFISHNESS AND SHALLOWNESS.
YOU MADE ME A PARTICIPANT.
YOU MADE ME A FIGUREHEAD.
YOU MADE MY BROTHER A VICTIM.
YOU MADE ME
ASHAMED.
I MISSED OUT
ON SO MUCH.
FOR ALL MY
POWERS...

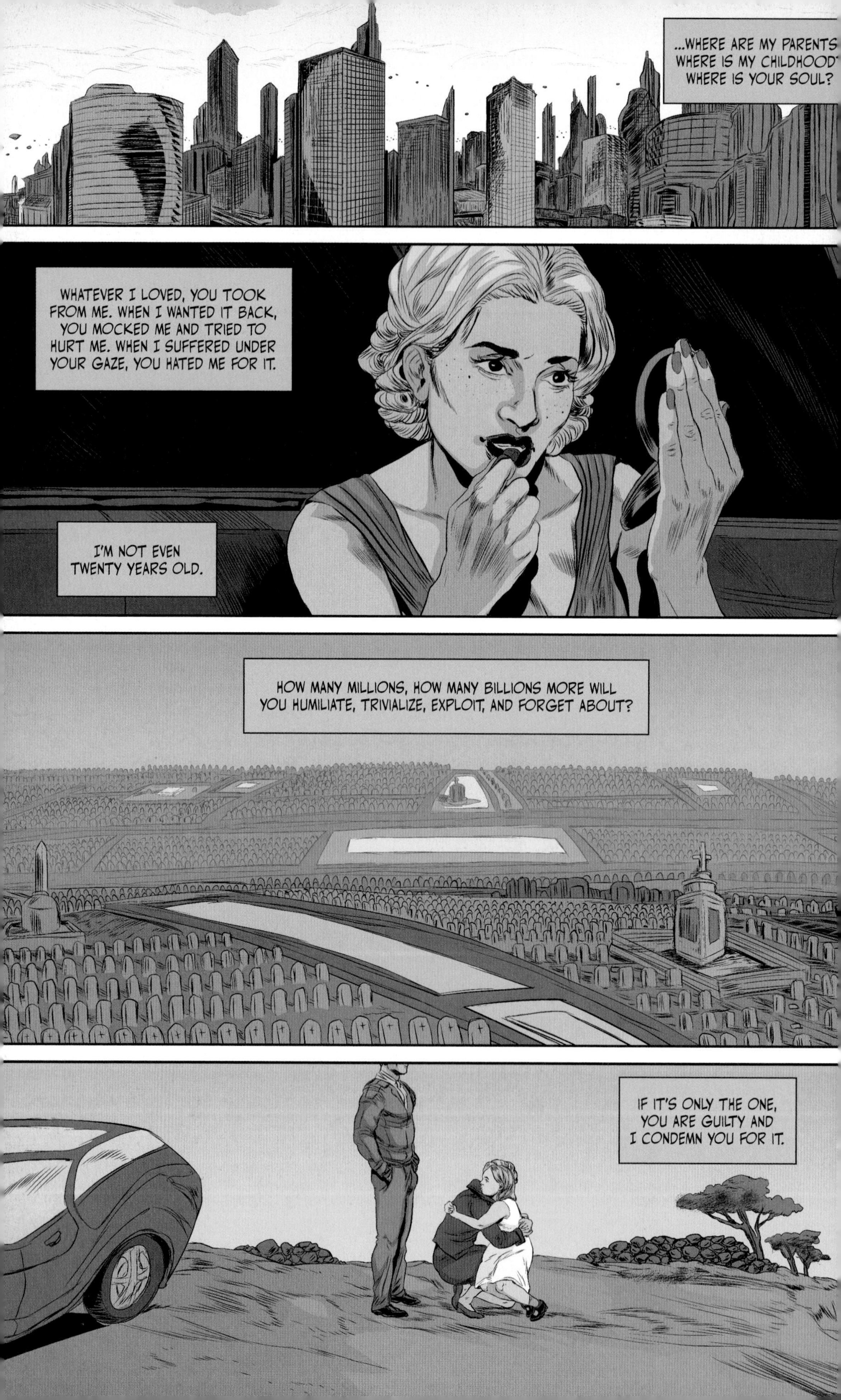
...WHERE ARE MY PARENTS? WHERE IS MY CHILDHOOD? WHERE IS YOUR SOUL?
WHATEVER I LOVED, YOU TOOK FROM ME. WHEN I WANTED IT BACK, YOU MOCKED ME AND TRIED TO HURT ME. WHEN I SUFFERED UNDER YOUR GAZE, YOU HATED ME FOR IT.
I'M NOT EVEN TWENTY YEARS OLD.
HOW MANY MILLIONS, HOW MANY BILLIONS MORE WILL YOU HUMILIATE, TRIVIALIZE, EXPLOIT, AND FORGET ABOUT?
IF IT'S ONLY THE ONE, YOU ARE GUILTY AND I CONDEMN YOU FOR IT.

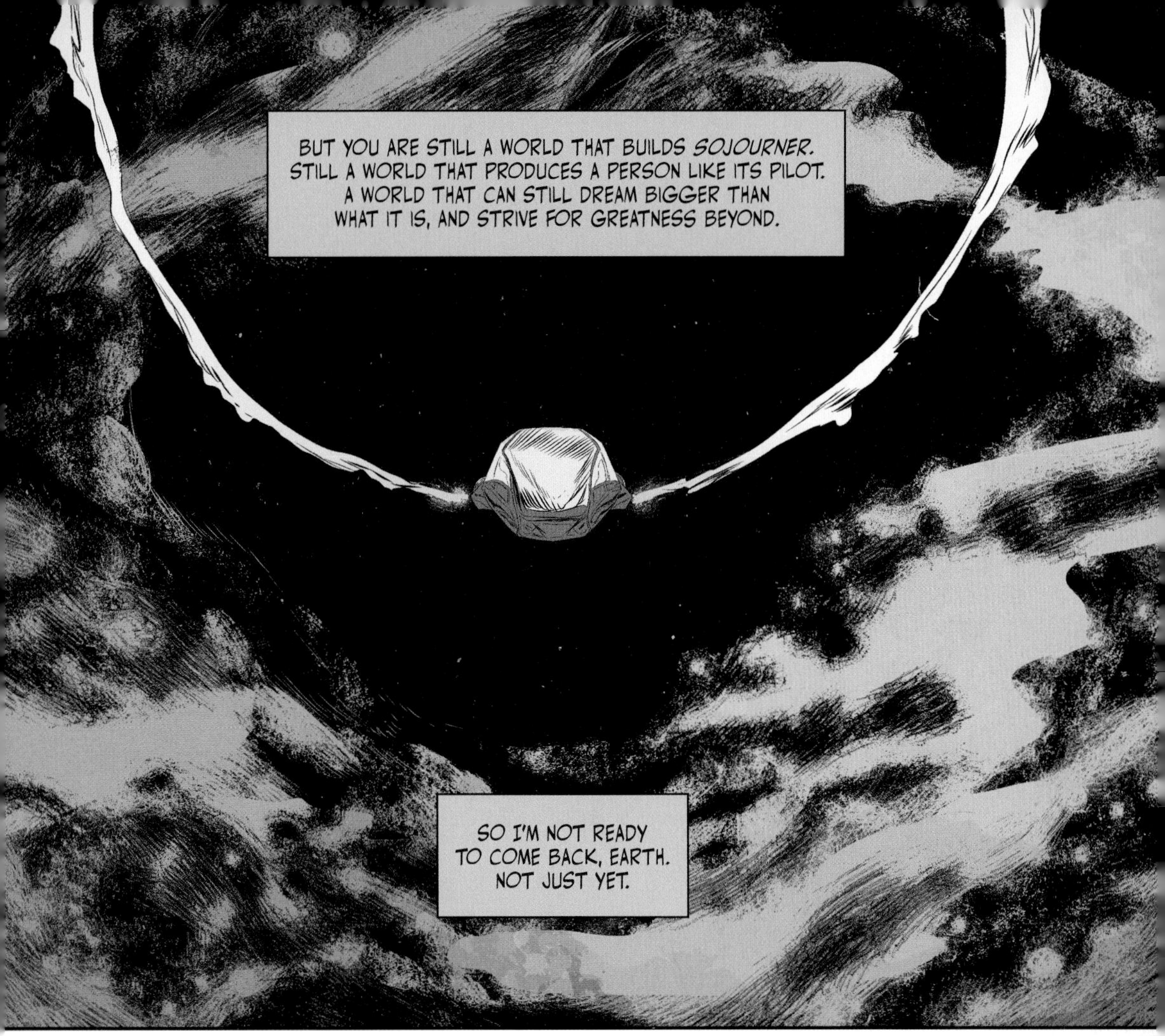
BUT YOU ARE STILL A WORLD THAT BUILDS *SOJOURNER*. STILL A WORLD THAT PRODUCES A PERSON LIKE ITS PILOT. A WORLD THAT CAN STILL DREAM BIGGER THAN WHAT IT IS, AND STRIVE FOR GREATNESS BEYOND.
SO I'M NOT READY TO COME BACK, EARTH. NOT JUST YET.

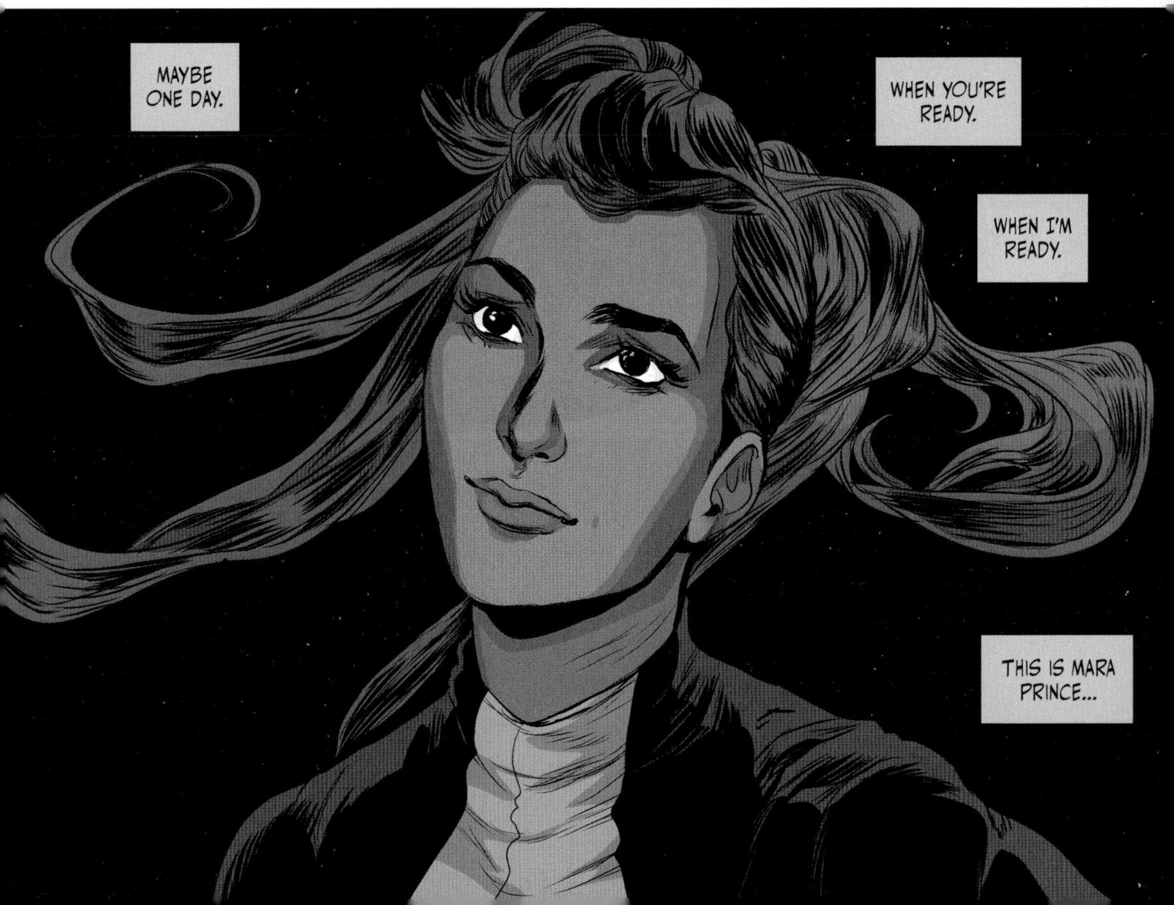
MAYBE ONE DAY.
WHEN YOU'RE READY.
WHEN I'M READY.
THIS IS MARA PRINCE...

...BROADCASTING
LIVE.

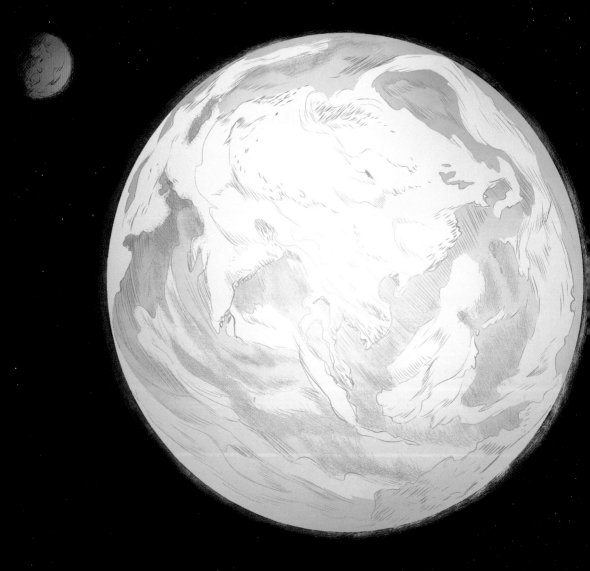

AND I'M OUT.

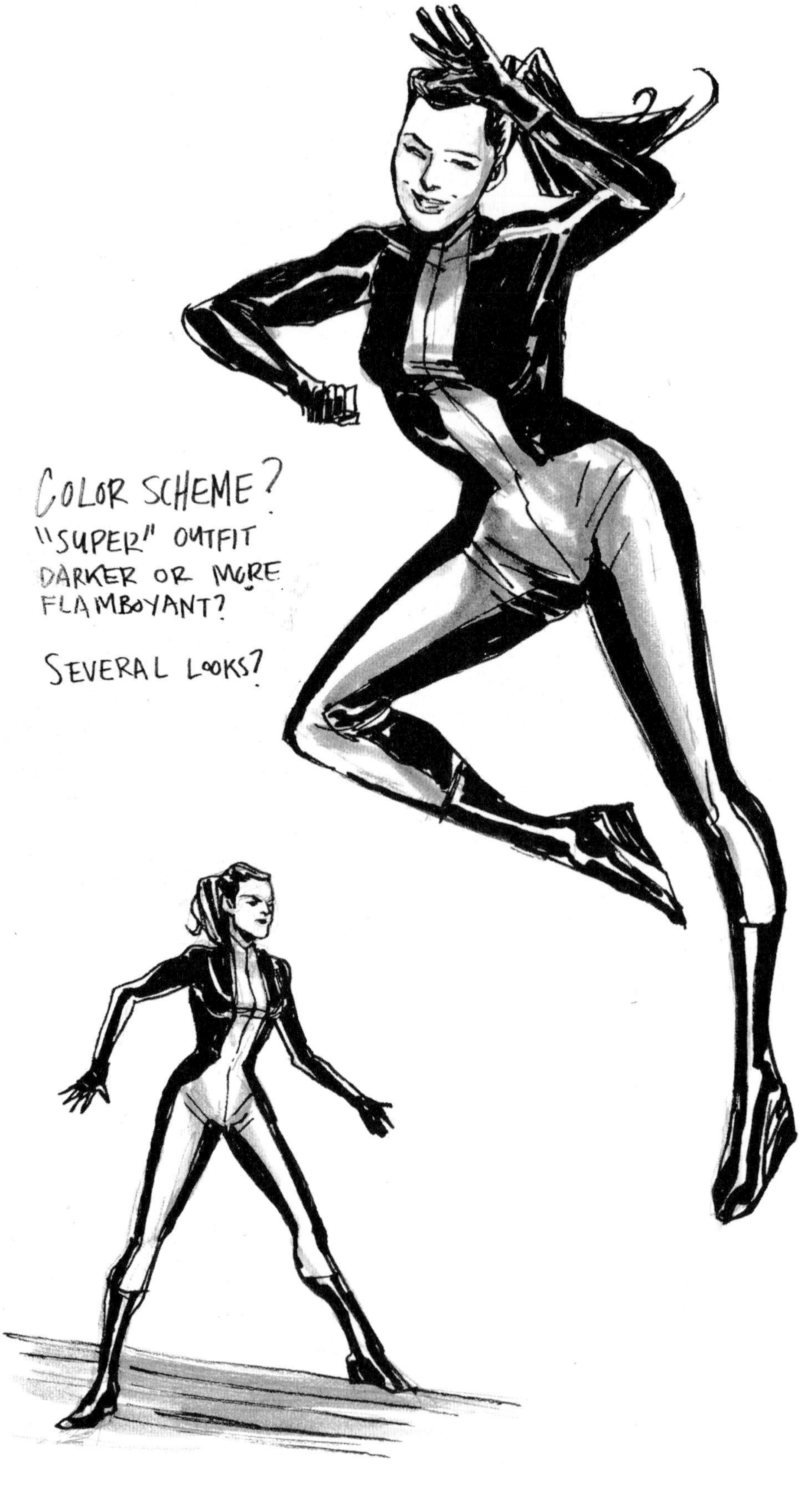
COLOR SCHEME?
"SUPER" OUTFIT
DARKER OR MORE
FLAMBOYANT?
SEVERAL LOOKS?

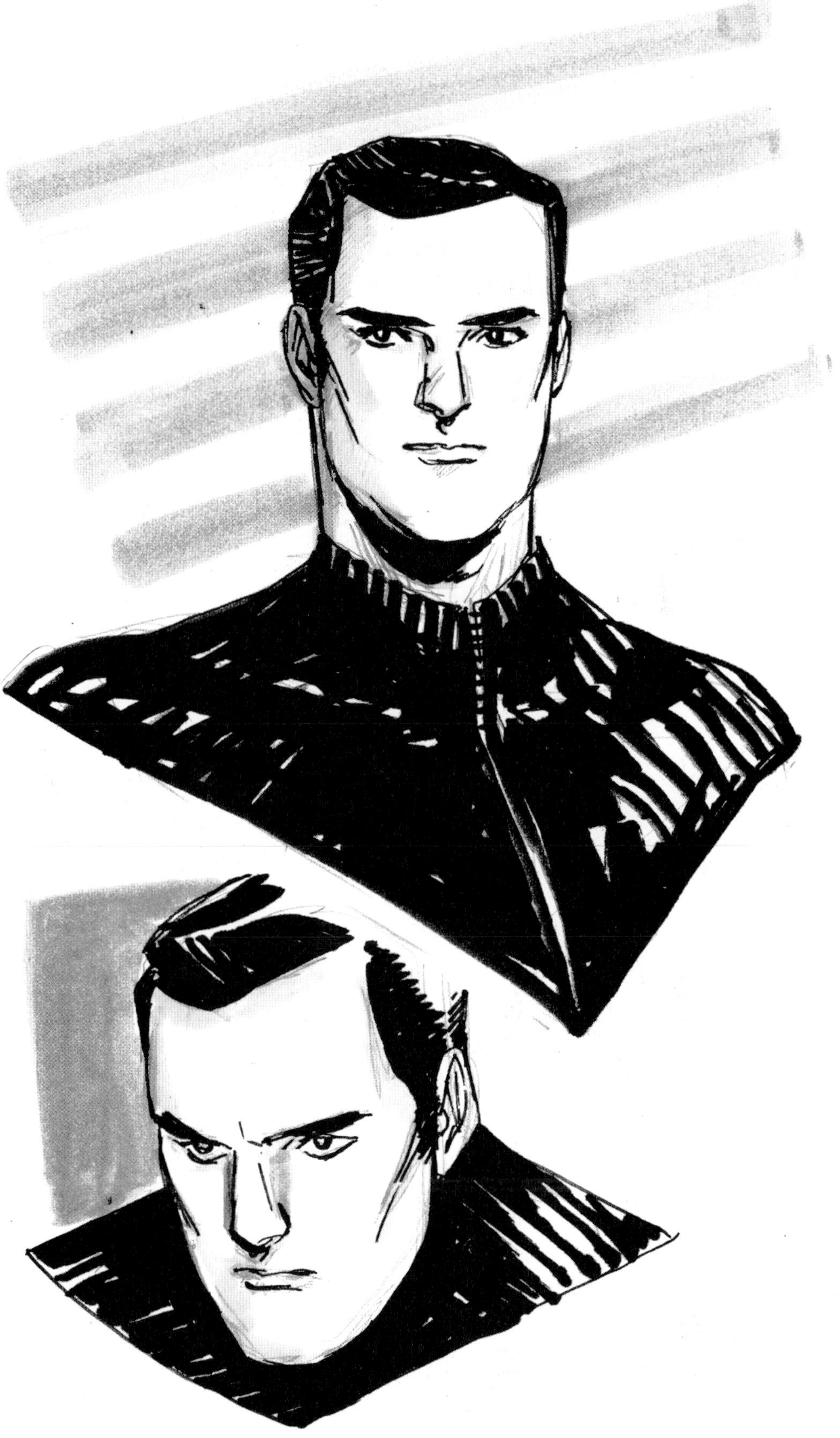

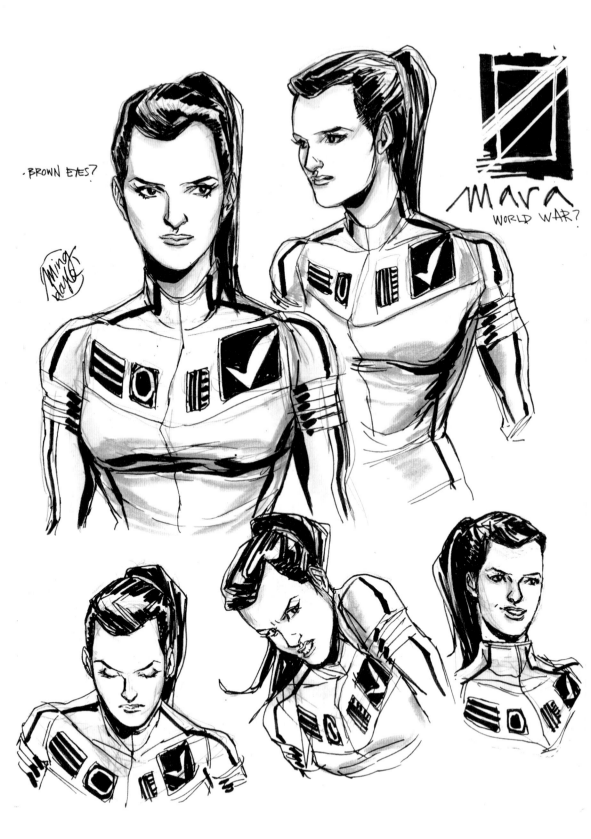

· BROWN EYES?

MARA
WORLD WAR?

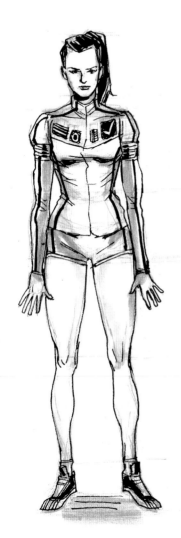

TYPE/PLACEMENT/
AMOUNT OF ADS?
COLORS?

VOLLEYBALL
UNIFORM

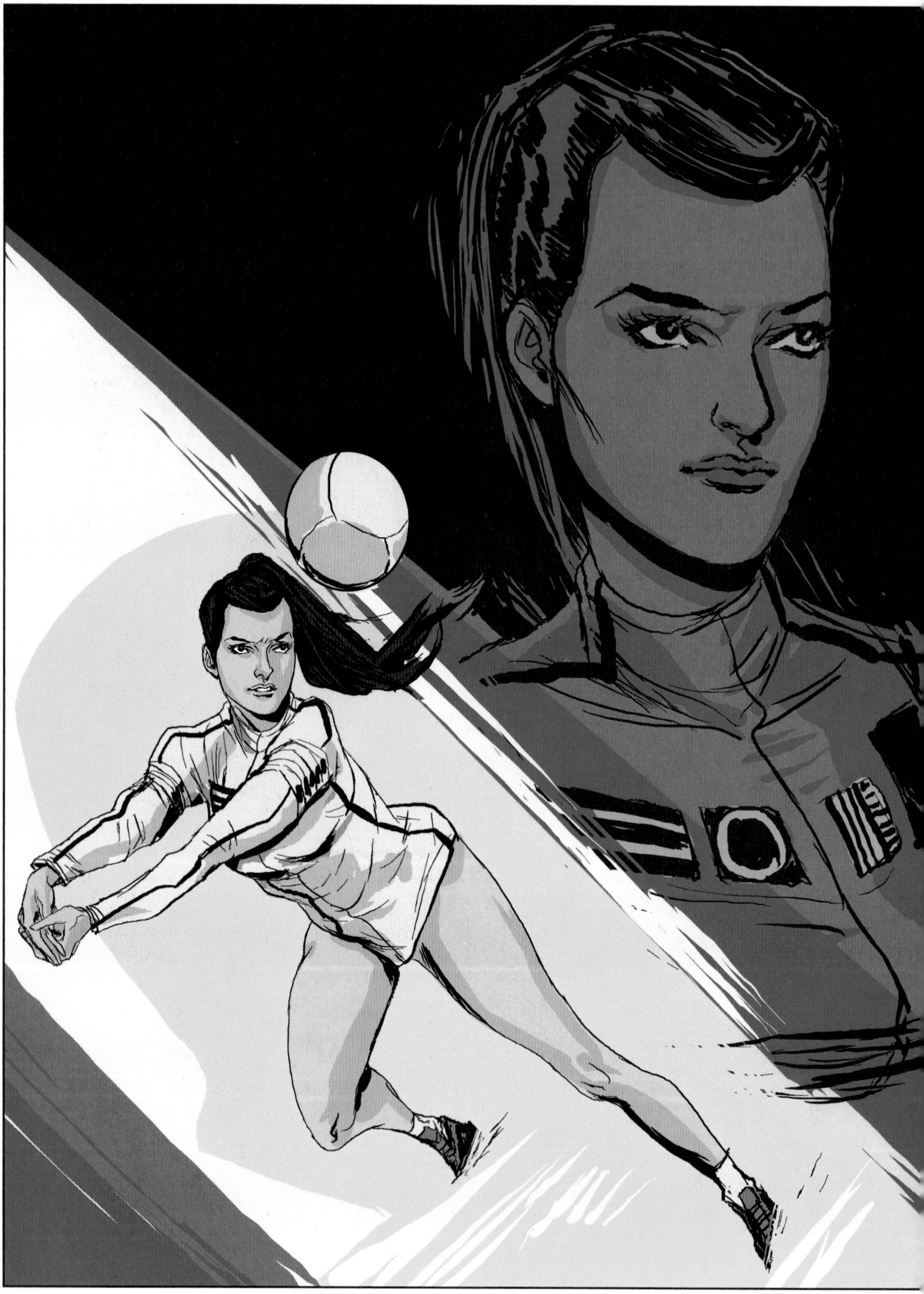

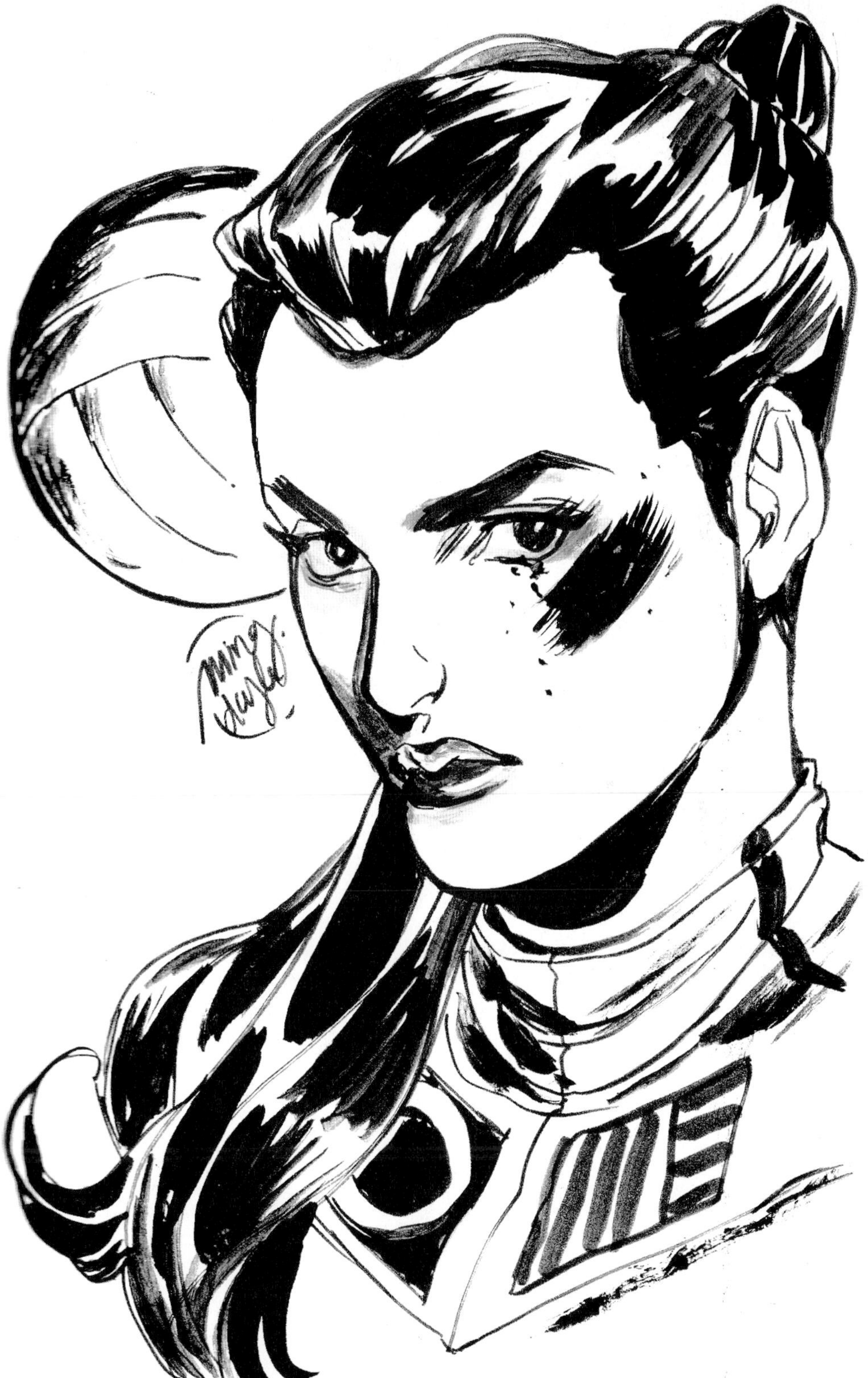

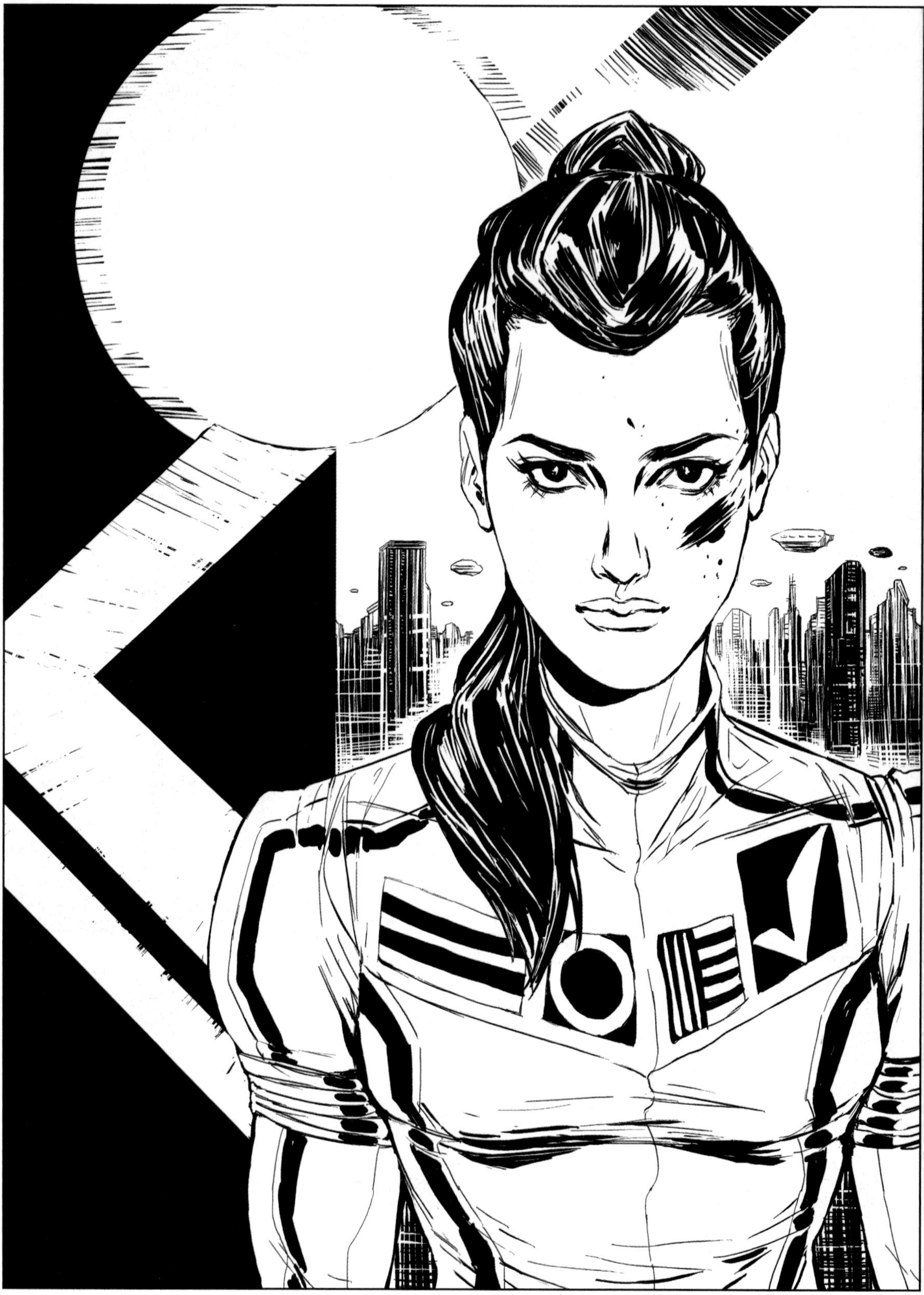

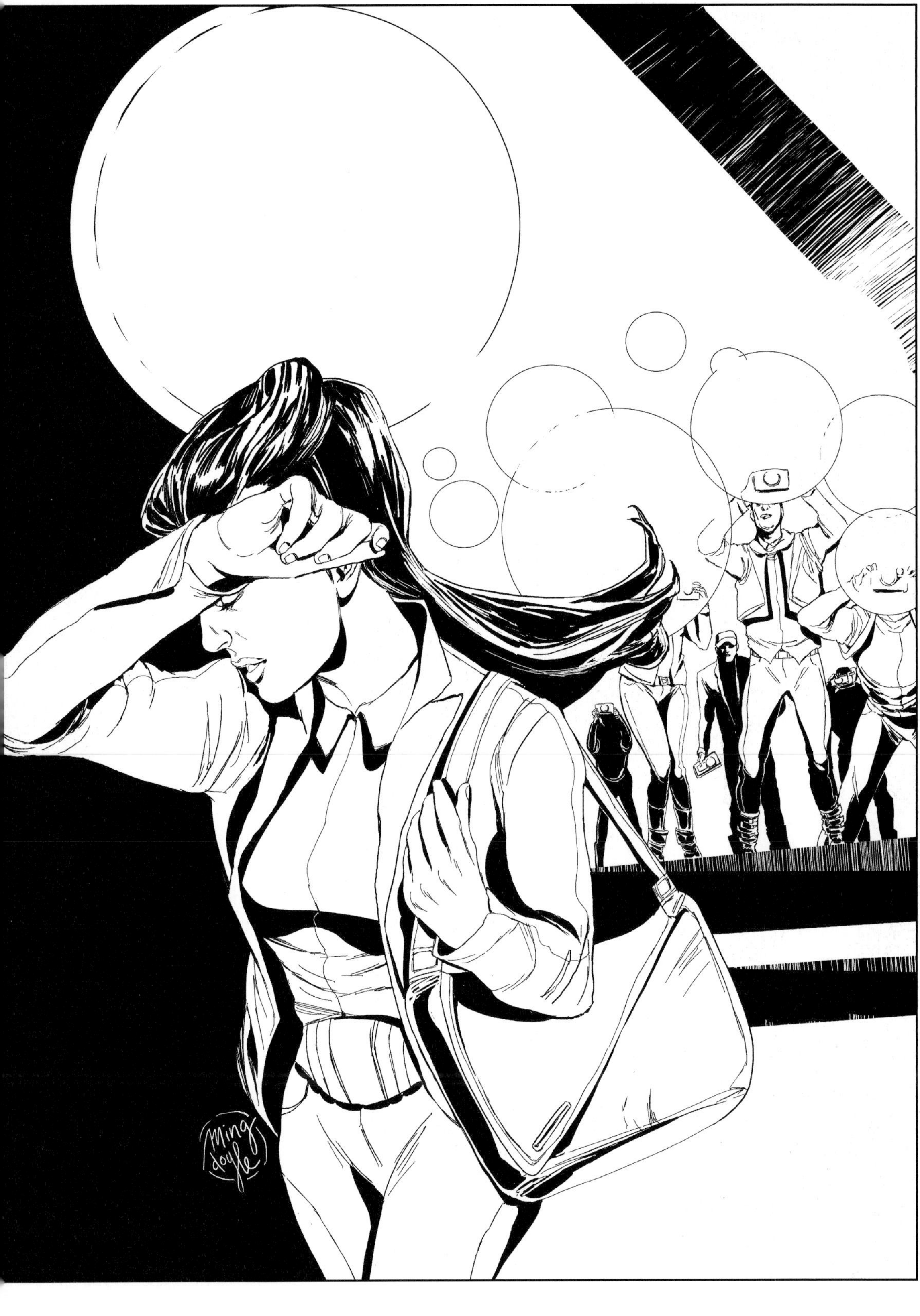
ming doyle

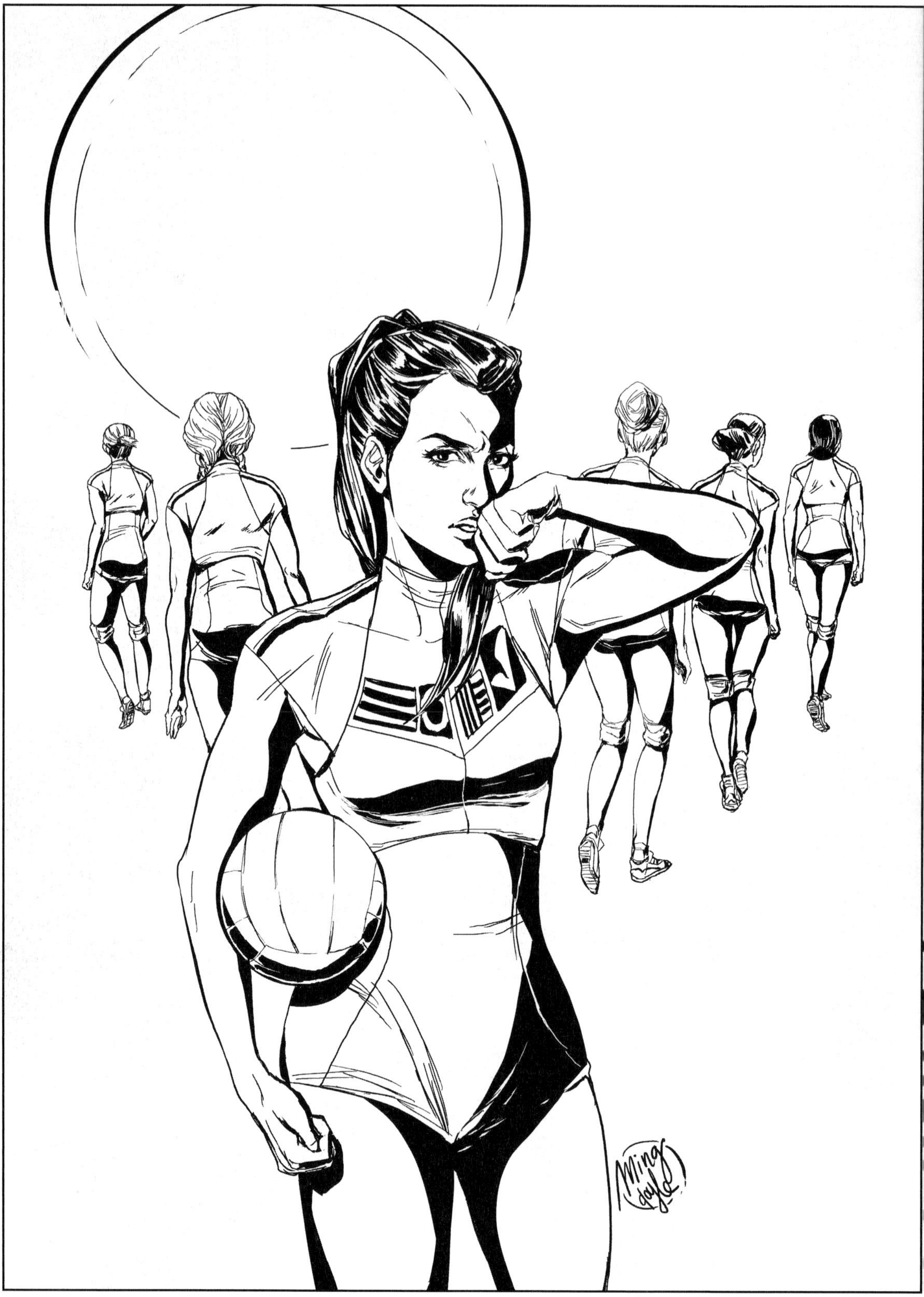
Ming doyle

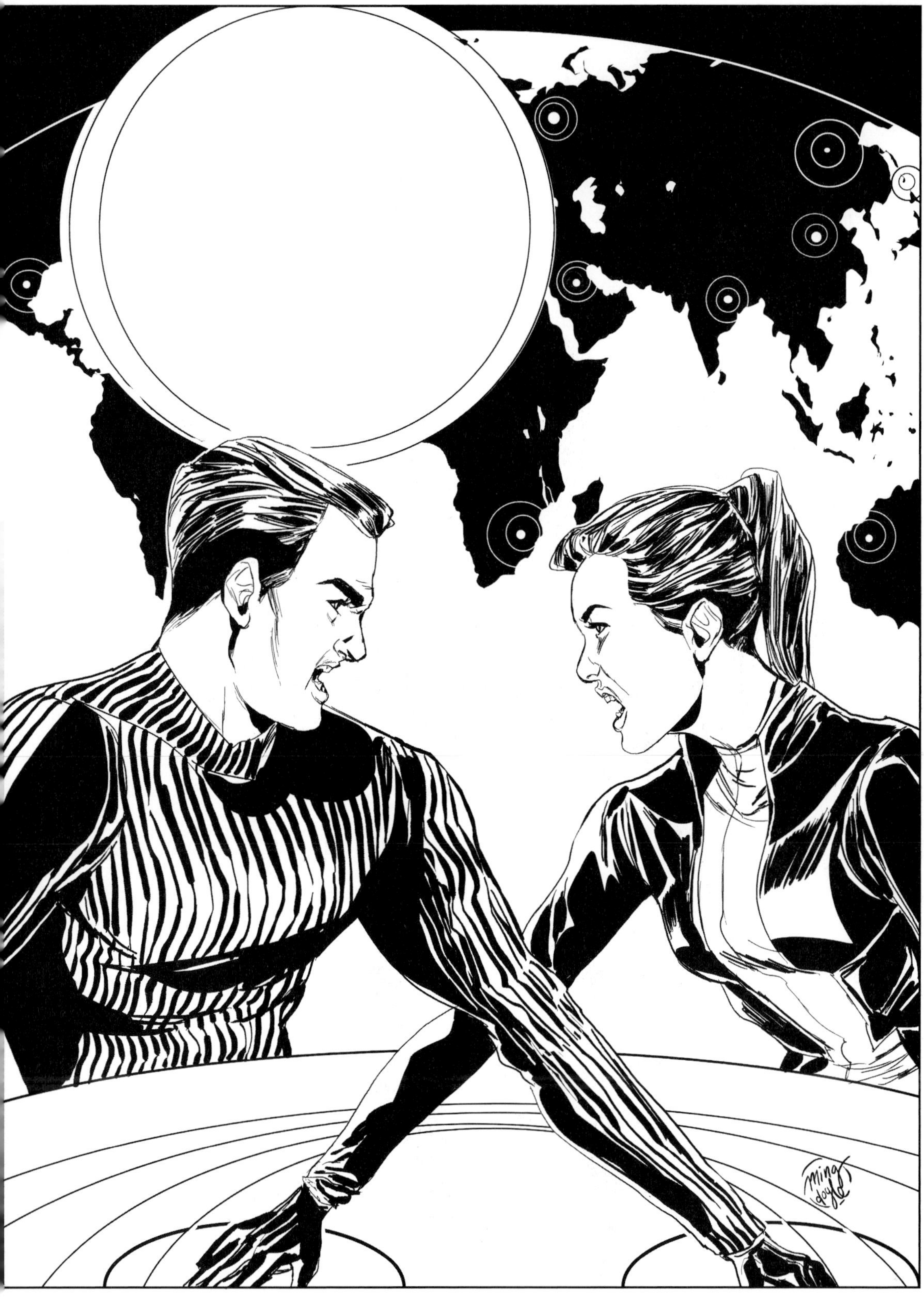
ming doyle

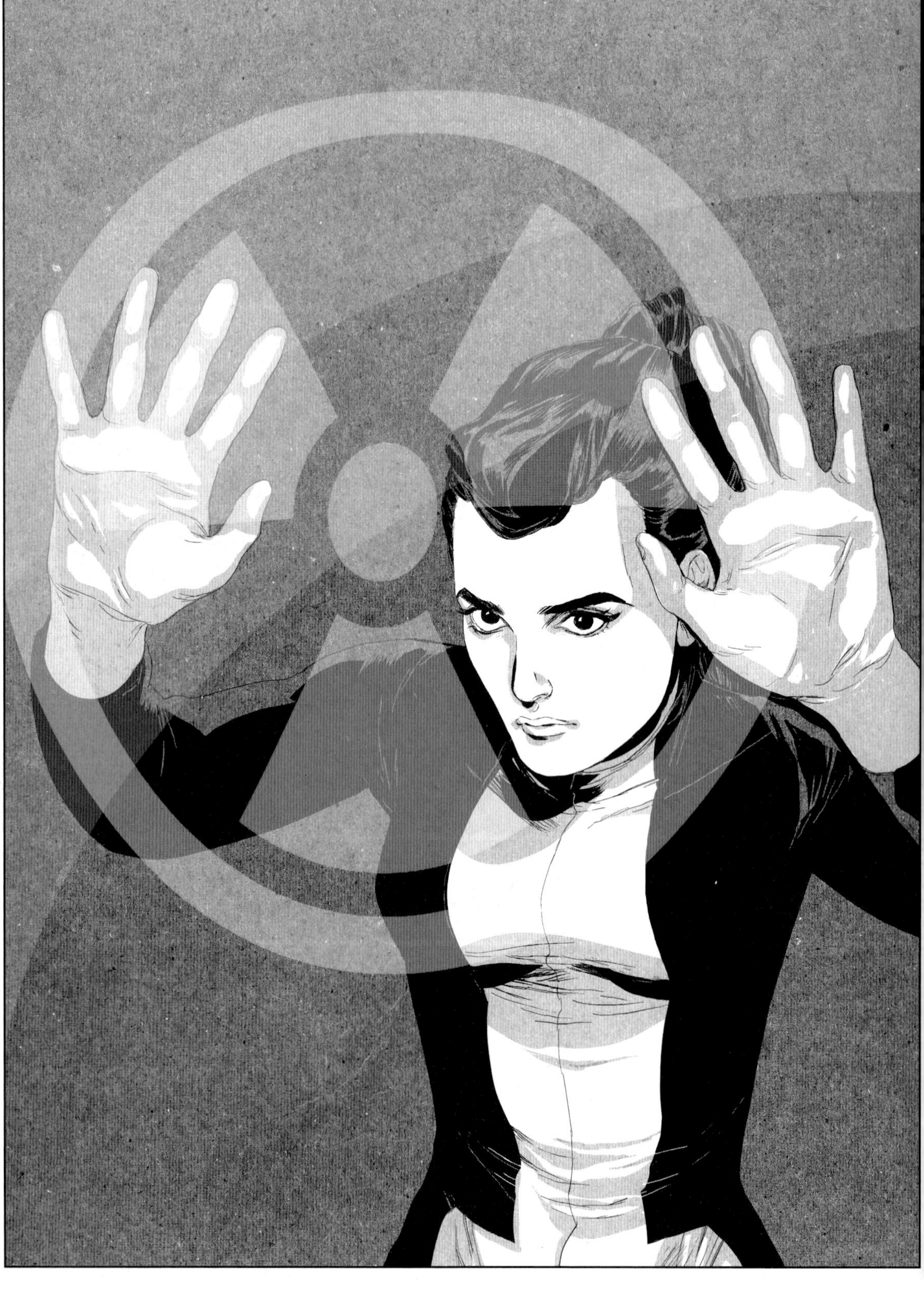

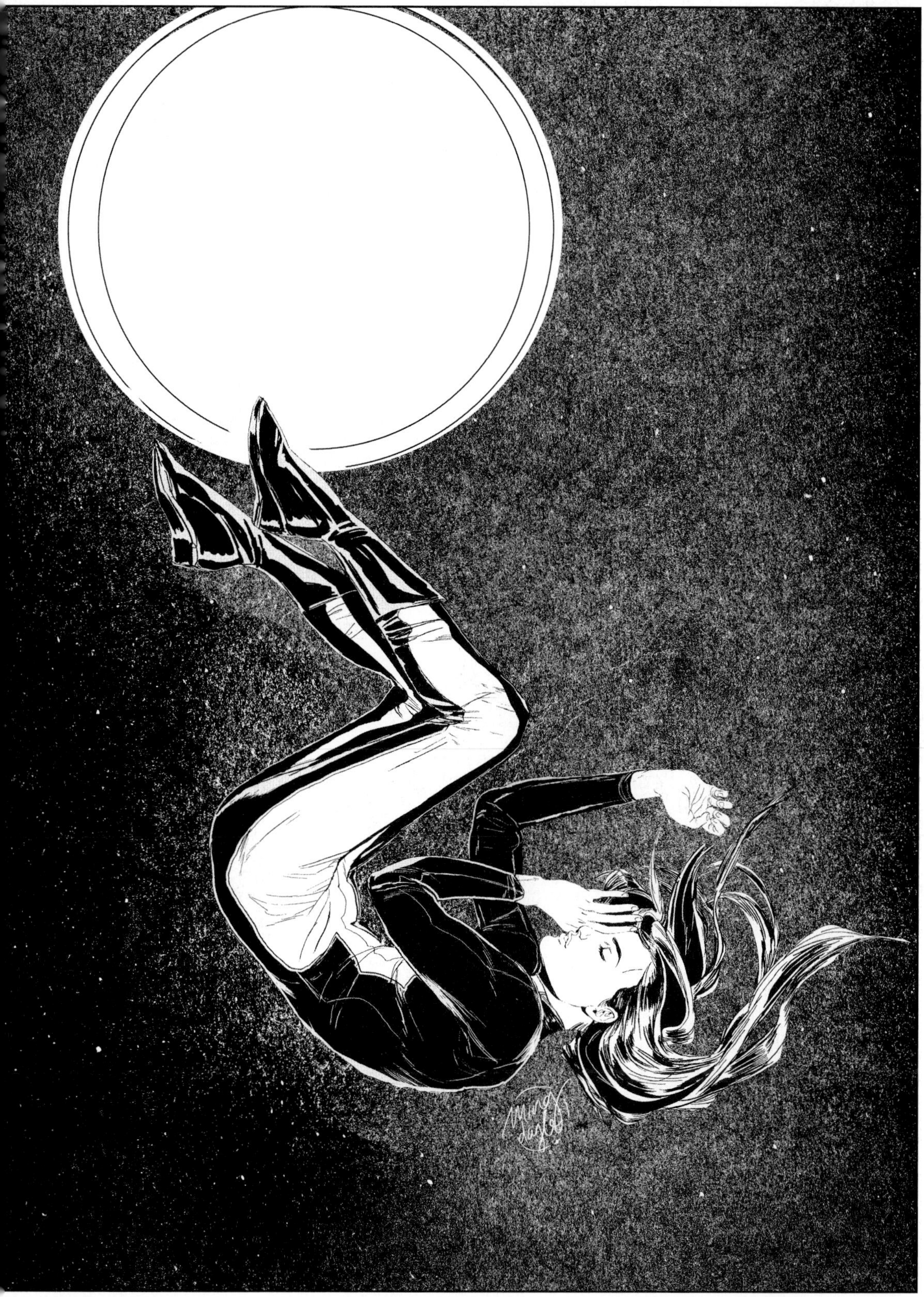

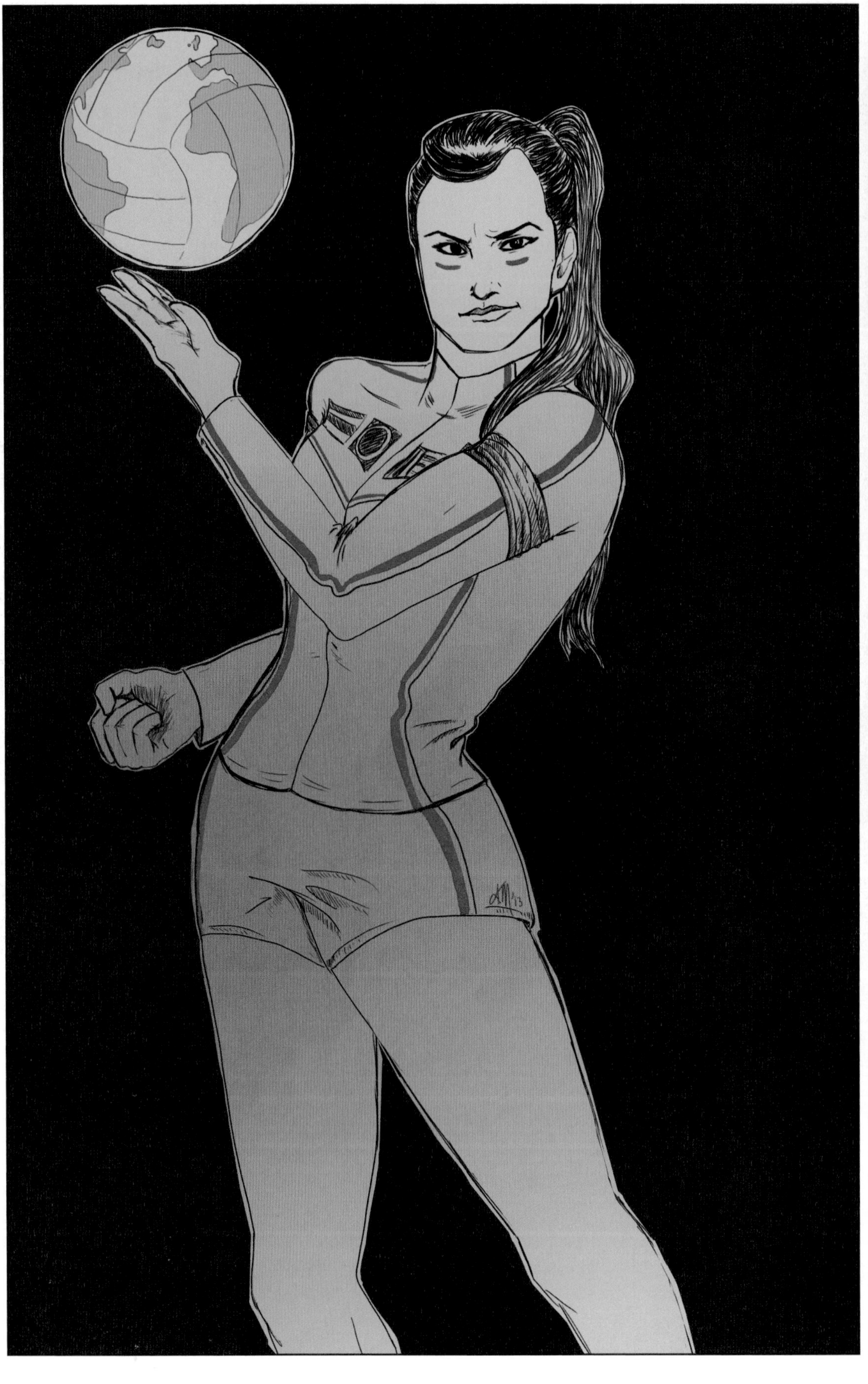

Art by Alyssa Maynard www.*alyssamaynard*.com

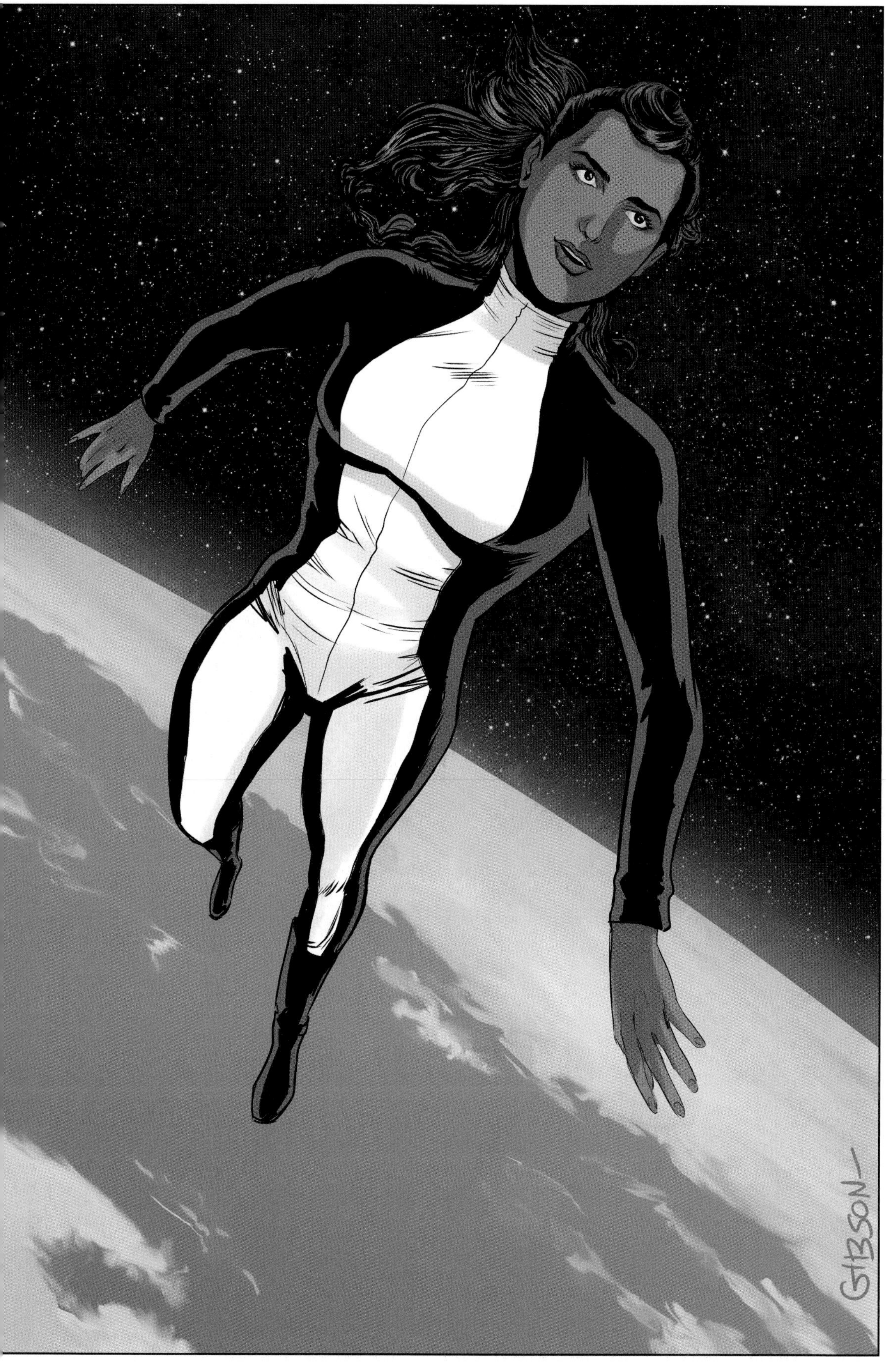
GIBSON

Art by Jordan Gibson *jordangibson.tumblr.com*

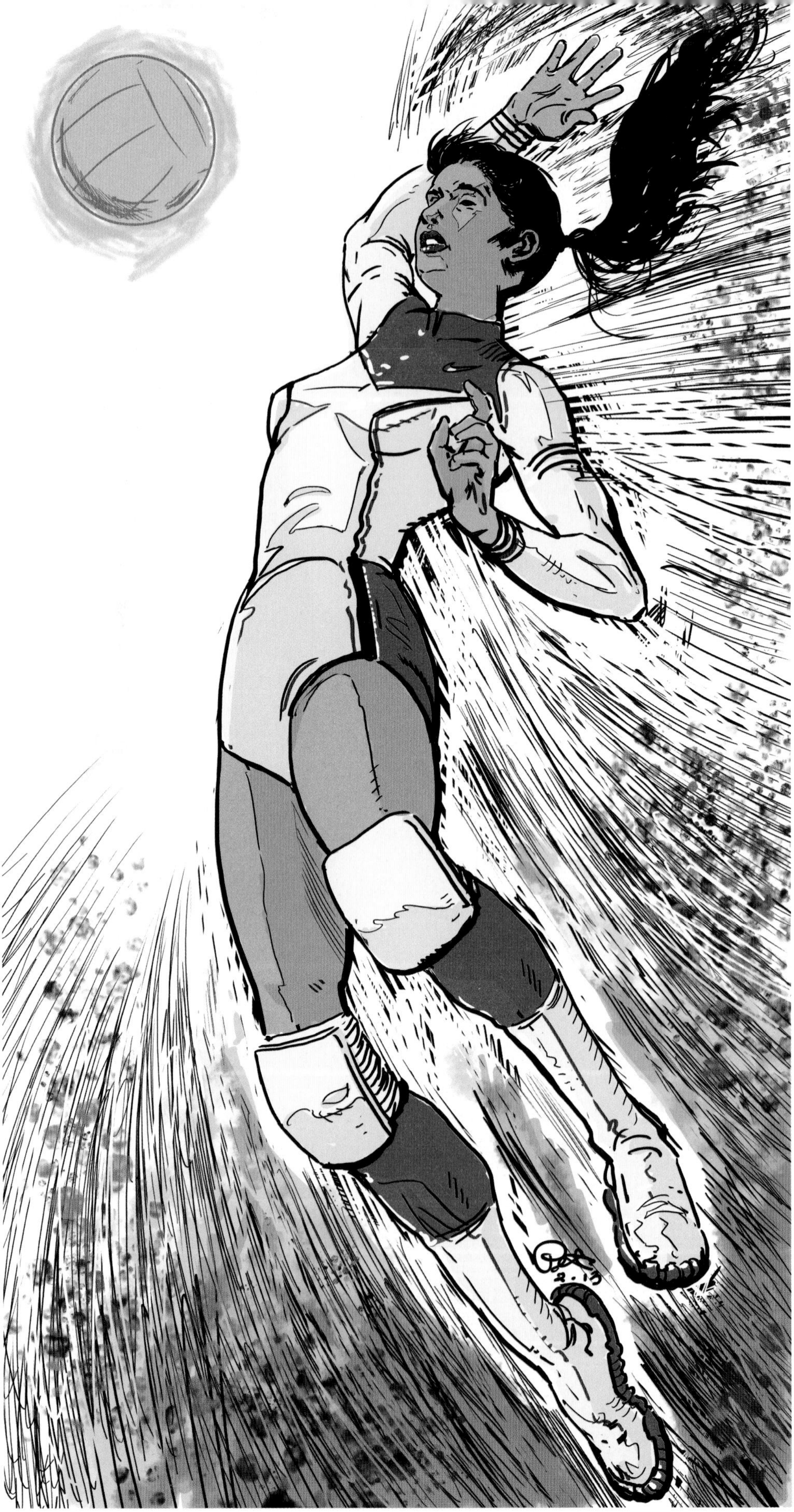

Art by Peter Krause   *www.peterkrauseillustration.com*

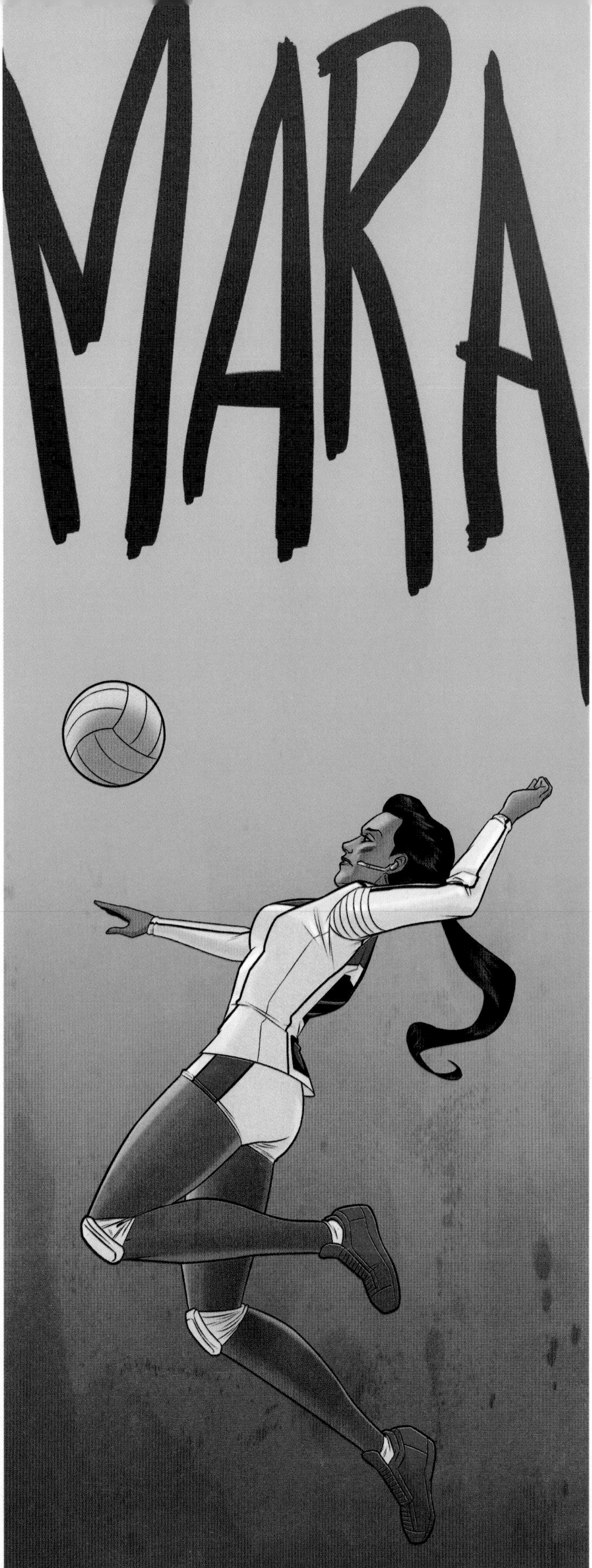
MARA

Art by Yasmin Liang *www.yazmeanie.com*

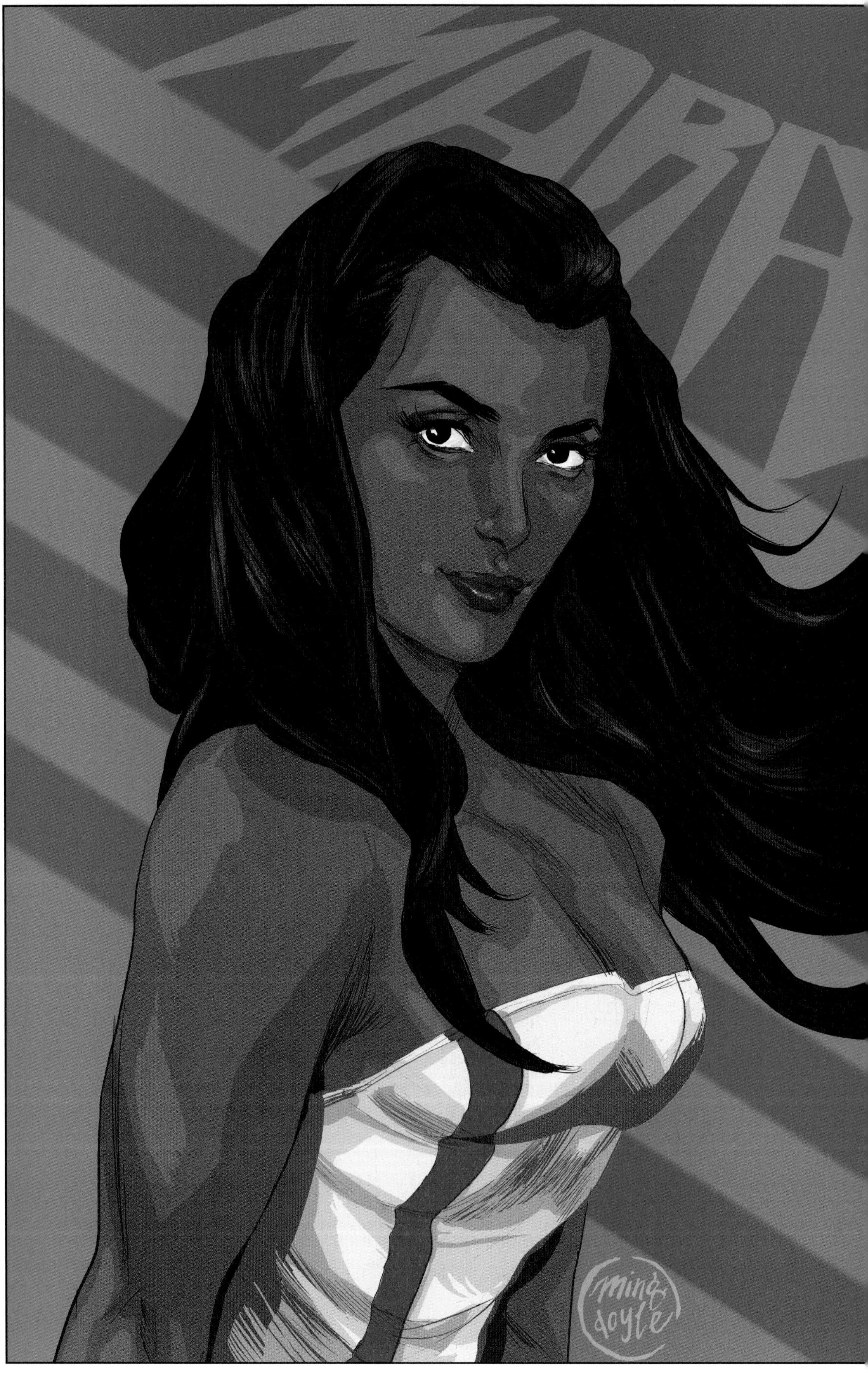
ming doyle

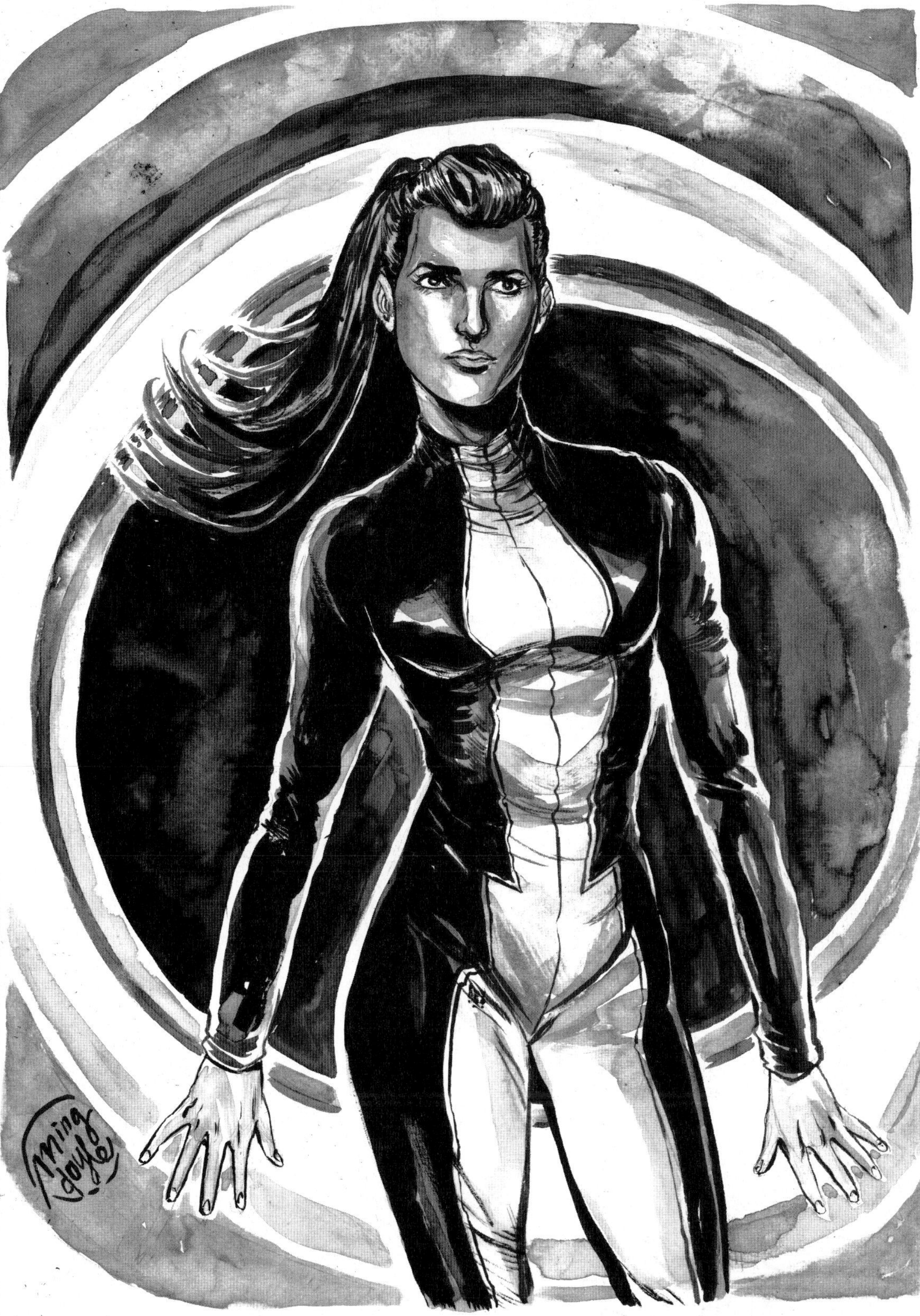
ming doyle

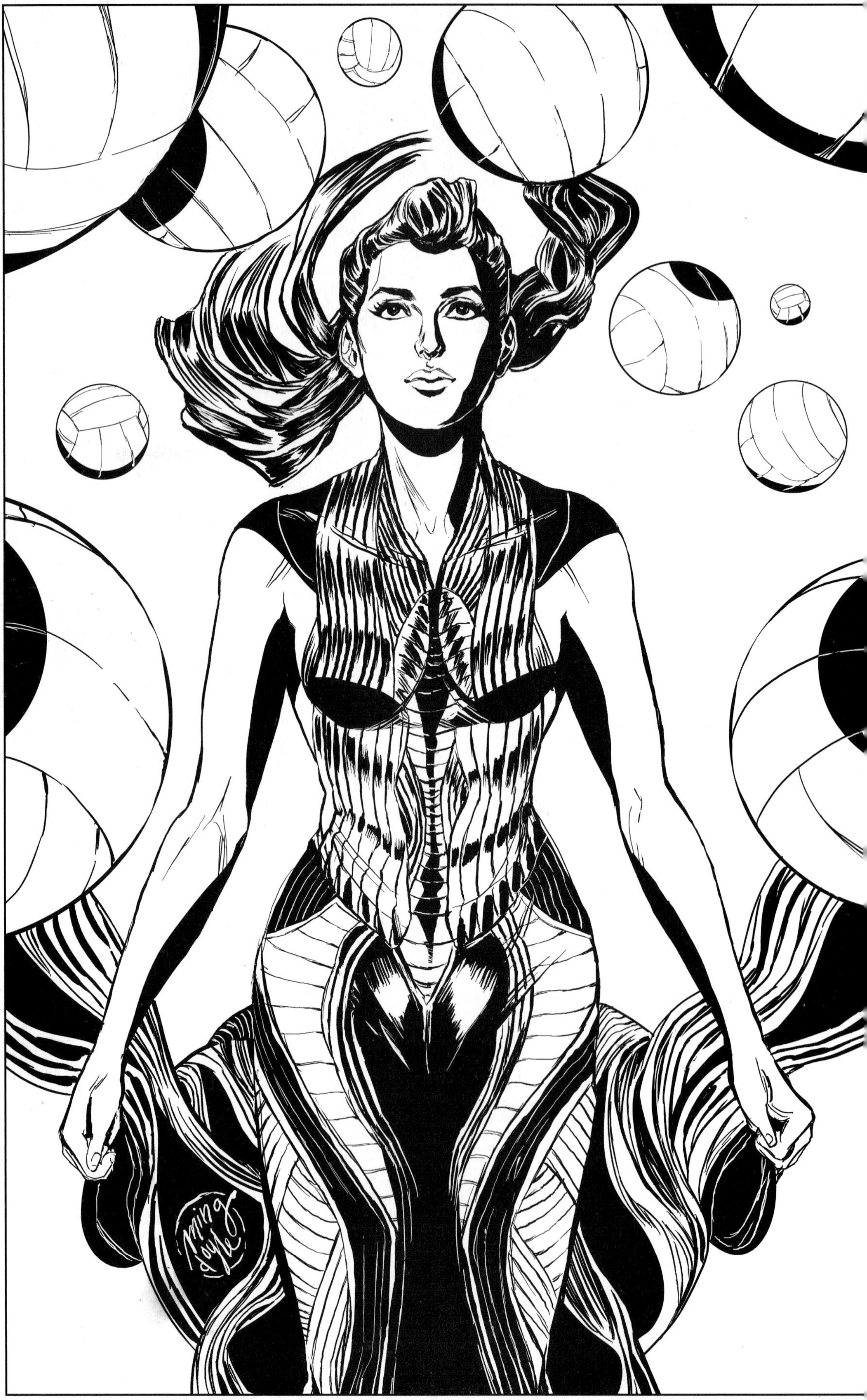